ACTION-RESEARCH IN COMMUNITY DEVELOPMENT

RAY LEES
Head of Social Studies,
Polytechnic of Central London

and

GEORGE SMITH
Department of Social and Administrative Studies,
University of Oxford

ROUTLEDGE DIRECT EDITIONS

ROUTLEDGE & KEGAN PAUL
London and Boston

First published in 1975
by Routledge & Kegan Paul Ltd
Broadway House, 68-74 Carter Lane,
London EC4V 5EL and
9 Park Street,
Boston, Mass. 02108, USA
Typed by Reba Lawless
Printed and bound in Great Britain
by Unwin Brothers Limited,
The Gresham Press, Old Woking, Surrey
A member of the Staples Printing Group
© Routledge & Kegan Paul Ltd 1975

ISBN 0 7100 8310 6

CONTENTS

v

INTRODUCTION

The papers brought together in this book reflect some of the experiences of people working in the central government-sponsored Community Development Project (CDP). Announced with a flourish in 1969 as part of Britain's 'Poverty Programme', CDP represented a new initiative in British social policy. It was described by the Home Office as 'a radical experiment in community development involving local and central government, voluntary agencies and the universities in a concerted search for better solutions to the problems of deprivation than we now possess . . . .' The commitment was open-ended, to action and research, and to the idea of 'experimental social administration' where new ideas would be field-tested in pilot areas.

But it took a long time to assemble the experiment, and its growth was far from smooth. Not until 1974 were all twelve local projects fully in operation, involving in total more than 100 action and research staff, with an overall budget, including money for action programmes, of about £¾ million a year. By then, however, the central team at the Home Office, originally a large group of administrators, researchers, consultants and advisers, had itself been reduced to a tiny handful, and the central research team, first redefined as 'research consultants', was phased out altogether in April 1974. In the meantime governments had changed, central departments been regrouped and local authorities reorganised first in the social services departments following Seebohm and subsequently in the April 1974 general reorganisation of local government. Each change has had its repercussions on CDP's organisation as it straddles central and local government, and meant a period of adjustment and change to the new situation.

The debate on poverty and its causes, too, has moved well beyond CDP's entry point in 1969, when the principal concern was with individual and family breakdown. The emphasis now is on wider questions of urban decline, and 'inequality' seen in terms of social structure rather than individual opportunity. And there have been a series of further experimental action and research projects launched by other government departments, notably the 'Inner Areas' scheme from the Department of the Environment, the 'Cycle of Deprivation' studies from the DHSS, the creation of the 'Urban Deprivation Unit'

vii

and the announcement in 1974 of 'Comprehensive Community Programmes' (CCPs) by the Home Office. These more recent initiatives inevitably drew attention away from CDP, particularly as their overall goals often look remarkably similar. Perhaps as a result, in June 1974 the Home Office announced a civil service 'management review' of CDP 'to examine the organisation, structure and method of operation of the Community Development Project and advise the Home Office of any changes that might improve its effectiveness.' The consultants' report was produced by the end of 1974; basically it argued for tighter central control of the CDP programme. While these recommendations were debated uncertainty grew about the future of the project. However, in March 1975 the Home Office announced that the major recommendations would not be taken up and the project was assured of continued existence in its present form for another two years. This assurance lasted less than two months, when uncertainty was revived by a further review and moratorium on new appointments, connected with the national economic crisis and the government's major review of expenditure. At the time of writing (July 1975), the position is unresolved and the future of CDP is still uncertain.

Throughout these changes teams at the local level had been through the difficult process of refining and redefining appropriate objectives and strategies for urban community development, testing these against the needs of their areas. This has led them a long way from the original conception of CDP as an experiment in social and community work.

A major outcome of this shift in emphasis was the production of the first inter-project report, published in 1974 - the result of collaboration between the twelve local projects. In a sense this marked a full circle in CDP's development - from at the start, a centrally directed experiment with the initiative coming from the central team at the Home Office, to a locally autonomous set of projects, collaborating at their own level to produce nationally relevant material. Since the inter-project report, a series of inter-project publications have been made available through the CDP Information and Intelligence Unit.

Papers in the first part of this collection chart the stages in this change. On the one hand an early Home Office paper outlines the administrative arrangements and sets out the original official expectations. On the other, Marjorie Mayo's paper provides an insight into the way this development worked in practice, tracing the rise and fall of the central apparatus - a cautionary tale for administrators and innovators alike; and one which raises basic questions about the possibility of 'in-house' reform. Joan Payne and Kleri Smith's paper provides hard data on the conditions in the twelve local areas, and underlines some of the major problems that forced local projects to broaden CDP's programme. Finally we include sections from the inter-project report, originally prepared for the Home Office by a working group drawn from local projects. This report was the first collective attempt to set out the framework within which projects wished to set their activities, and the analysis they had developed. It gives, too, an overview of the range of action programmes, and the very different styles of intervention to be found in the twelve project areas.

It is the intention of the second part to illustrate some of the

difficulties experienced in establishing local projects and in
making them fully operational. A 'suitable' local authority had to
agree to participate in the programme, a university or polytechnic
was needed to provide a research team, a management structure for
the project had to be created within the local authority, a geo-
graphical area for project activities selected and staff for action
and research teams recruited. It took varying lengths of time to
complete this process. Even after local authorities had accepted
projects, there was typically delay and lack of co-ordination in
assembling staff. David Corkey's paper shows how in one local project it took over two years to take all these initial steps. As the
director of a project, Corkey expresses his frustration at the
delay.

Making a project operational is not simply a matter of administrative arrangements. An important element must also be the perceptions and expectations of the project held by influential people.
The paper by Alex Mackay reports a study of the expectations of
councillors and officials in a local authority before the recruit-
ment of a full project team. Mackay discusses these in relation to
possible future project activities. This theme is taken up again in
the contribution by Ray Lees, but with particular emphasis on the
action research relationship and the possibility of differing expectations between these two groups within a project. This paper also
throws some light on the expectations of local people. Both these
discussions suggest that even when a project had been fully established, there was unlikely to be prior agreement between all interested parties about its purpose.

Part three of the book offers a range of case-studies, illustrat-
ing some of the work of local projects. Descriptions range from an
account of a tenants' campaign over housing improvements in a
Tynemouth estate, to a developing legal battle between residents and
a property company over housing freeholds in the Birmingham area;
from the progress of a locally run information centre in Coventry,
to an evaluation of a programme designed to increase the take-up of
welfare rights in Batley. Education was an important activity in
the early CDP projects, and Eric Midwinter argues strongly that it
should not be abandoned as projects move on in search of more
radical solutions, though the meaning of 'community education', as
Ray Lees shows, is capable of many different interpretations, even
by participants in the same educational project. National or
regional policies by aggregating characteristics frequently miss the
problems of particular areas or minority groups. CDP, with its
small area focus, is well placed to draw attention to their problems; Morag McGrath suggests some of the different priorities of
the immigrant population in Batley; finally the Glyncorrwg team
underline the problems facing an economically declining and isolated
mining area in South Wales.

Running through these contributions is the theme of participation
and collective effort to understand and tackle local problems, while
setting them in the framework of broader social and economic processes. The commitment is both to action and analysis, whether
through the insights of the social activist or through the skills of
the social scientist. Frequently the intention is to communicate
this learning experience to local people by involving them directly

in the programme, by 'informal adult education', meetings, leaflets, newsletters or community organisation.

The final section examines the role of community development and action-research in social change. Richard Batley and John Edwards, researching into the related Urban Programme, compare its approach and assumptions with the official expectations of CDP. Sam Bailie at the outset of the Oldham project presents a view of community development in the classical tradition - as a growth of personal capacities and awareness, while John Benington, project director in Coventry since 1970, traces the changing strategies of his project, as it came face to face, he would argue, with the essentially conflicting interests of different social groups or classes in society and the unequal distribution of power. Finally George Smith looks again at the idea of 'experimental social administration' in the light of CDP's history and experience.

These papers present sharply differing views on the potential of CDP, and offer no easy solutions to the problems that are raised. They reflect the diversity within CDP and the fundamental debate about objectives and strategy that continues to run through the programme, making it in turn an exciting and often frustrating experience for participants.

An important purpose of this book is to convey some elements of this debate to a wider audience. Local small-scale experiments clearly cannot solve the problems of deprivation, but by communicating their experiences, sharing the debate on poverty and inequality, and presenting possible solutions, they can help to bring these problems to the centre of public attention.

CDP is still in progress, and these papers represent the concerns of people who were, at the time of writing, still operating in the field - still 'inside the whale' in Orwell's classic phrase, but trying to peer out, and make sense of their surroundings. It may be argued that no one writing here is sufficiently distant to make a sound judgment on the events and activities they describe. But we are not seeking to present a definitive judgment on CDP. The very diversity of contributions is intended to guard against this, and to bring out the significance of different interpretations.

The programme has mobilised the skills of administrators, social activists and social scientists. Some have worked at national level, others in the local situation. All have been involved in an attempt to set up and test experiment and innovation and learn from that experience. This kind of endeavour is not easy. The following pages will show something of the way it has been tackled.

ACKNOWLEDGMENTS

The editors are very grateful to individual authors for preparing papers while under pressure from the day to day demands of their projects. No attempt has been made by the editors to mould a common approach; the views expressed are the responsibility of individual authors, not necessarily of their projects, local authorities, the Home Office or CDP as a whole. We are grateful to the Home Office for permission to include their paper on CDP, and to the projects for extracts from the inter-project report. The editors' task has been restricted to arranging and editing contributions, and here we are grateful for help from Helen Simpson. The complete book has been typed in its present form by Mrs Reba Lawless, who has been responsible for a speedy and efficient piece of work.

The preparation of this kind of book is very much a co-operative effort. Contributions typically emerge from a collective experience; individual authors gain from being part of a team, from discussion with colleagues, officials and local people. It is obviously not possible to list all who have contributed in this way; but it is important to record the process.

Ray Lees
George Smith

DETAILS OF CDP ORGANISATION

National

Function	Organisation
Central Team	Community Programmes Dept, Home Office
Research Consultant (previously Central Research Team)	Dept of Social Administration, Southampton University (phased out, April 1974)
Information and Intelligence Unit	Centre for Environmental Studies

Local

Local authority	Name of project area	Project area population (1971)	Research team affiliation
Coventry	Hillfields	16,500	Institute of Local Government Studies, Birmingham University
Liverpool	Vauxhall	14,100	Social Evaluation Unit, Oxford University
Southwark	Newington	13,600	South Bank Polytechnic
West Glamorgan	Glyncorrwg	8,600	Town Planning Dept, University of Wales Institute of Science and Technology
Newham	Canning Town	42,400	Social Evaluation Unit, Oxford University
Kirklees	Batley	42,000	Social Administration Dept, York University
Strath-clyde	Ferguslie Park, Paisley	12,300	Dept of Social and Economic Research, Glasgow University
Newcastle	Benwell	14,400	Dept of Sociology and Social Administration, University of Durham
Cumbria	Cleator Moor, Arlecdon/ Frizington	11,200	Social Administration Dept, York University
Birmingham	Saltley	13,900	Social Evaluation Unit, Oxford University
North Tyneside	Percy and Trinity	16,120	Dept of Behavioural Studies, Newcastle Polytechnic
Oldham	Clarksfield	25,300	Social Administration Dept, York University

Part one

THE NATIONAL COMMUNITY DEVELOPMENT PROJECT

Chapter 1

CDP: AN OFFICIAL VIEW
Home Office, 1971

PURPOSE

The CDP is a modest attempt at action research into the better
understanding and more comprehensive tackling of social needs, especially in local communities within the older urban areas, through
closer co-ordination of central and local official and unofficial
effort, informed and stimulated by citizen initiative and involvement. The concept of community development of this kind is not new;
but this is the first time that central and local government have
decided to make a joint venture into this field themselves.

In the past, official efforts to analyse and meet social needs in
the interlinked fields of employment, income security, housing,
general environmental planning, health provision, social work, education, leisure facilities, and so on, were largely compartmental-
ised. Nowadays, however, the number of compartments is gradually
diminishing (e.g. through developments like Seebohm); and their
degree of separation is also lessening (e.g. through improvements in
the techniques of planning and management). The CDP seeks to
identify and demonstrate, by reference to the problems of selected
small local communities, some practical ways of taking this trend
further, through consultation and action among the separate departments of central and local government and voluntary organisations
and the people of the local communities themselves. It attempts
this not by disrupting, supplanting or duplicating any of the work
of the existing agencies, but by trying to help them and the communities they serve to develop insights and channels of communication which can remain useful even after the project itself has come
to an end. In particular it aims to reinforce and not to damage
the spirit and efforts of elective local government.

Fuller communication and co-operation between citizens and the
providers of their services can of course be difficult to achieve,
and can themselves cause difficulties. Tact and patience and skill
have to be exercised by all concerned if the effort is not to
founder on resentful defensiveness or frustrated expectations. But
it is an essential part of the project that the people in the
localities where it operates should be given full and positive
opportunity to express their needs and views and aspirations

3

effectively - and that those seeking to co-operate with them should be receptive and sympathetic towards the ideas and even criticisms that can result. Local authorities taking part in the project do so on this understanding.

LOCAL ORGANISATION

Each of the twelve local authorities participating selects an appropriate locality within its area (usually from 5,000 to 15,000 population) in consultation with the Home Office. The aim is that the twelve localities should between them make up a fairly representative range of distinctive local urban communities with marked social needs.

1. Project teams

In each locality a small project team (normally a director and two assistants) is appointed by the local authority - by reference to personal suitability rather than to any preferred professional experience. The project director's staff grading will preferably be such as will facilitate contact with the local authority's own senior officials. The team will be most suitably located in a central department of the local authority, such as the town clerk's. It should come within the responsibility of a special project management committee of the council, drawn from chairmen or senior members of the council's main functional committees together with a Home Office advisory representative and (in a county area) a representative from the relevant county district. But the working operations should be through multi-disciplinary groups of officials (and often chief officers) from the local authority's various departments, in consultation with organisations and individuals from within the community itself.
These operations will have five main components.
    a. Assessment of needs in the locality selected, and especially of those that look like being unmet.
    b. Stimulation of local residents to participate in this assessment and to take some initiative and responsibility in what follows.
    c. Production, discussion and encouragement of practical ideas for meeting the needs wherever it is realistic to seek to do so, e.g. through adjustments in policies, methods or priorities, with special emphasis on the development of contact and co-operation at all levels between the various local authority departments and other resource-controlling agencies, and the local residents themselves.
    d. Promotion of a limited number of specific schemes designed both to plug immediate gaps in local social provision and to test new methods of achieving effective official/unofficial co-operation.
    e. Identification of needs and possible solutions which are beyond immediate local action but merit feeding back to wherever policy is formed.
    Local authority expenses in the employment of these project teams and in the carrying out of the schemes they promote attract a 75 per cent Exchequer grant.

2. Research teams

Supporting each project team is a research team employed by an
appropriate university or polytechnic. This will normally consist
of a research director and two or three staff. Its functions are
two-fold.
     a. Assistance to the project team in the assessment of the
locality's needs and of how they might best be met.
     b. Continuous monitoring and final evaluation of the project
team's work and its lessons, for feeding back to the local authority
itself and to other local and central interests.
     The costs of these research teams are fully reimbursed by the
Home Office to the universities or polytechnics concerned.

NATIONAL ORGANISATION

The project is co-ordinated nationally through a central team. This
is based in the Community Relations Department of the Home Office
(which is also responsible for the Urban Programme), and draws
membership and advice as required from other government departments
concerned and also from non-governmental bodies. One of its non-
governmental members directs a special research unit to assist the
local research teams in their work and to help draw the work together.

DURATION

The duration of the experiment in each locality will be governed
partly by the speed with which it can develop and the results that
emerge. In each case the project and research teams will probably
need a year or two to organise and get going, and about three years
after that to produce interesting results. So, broadly speaking,
the probable duration may be put at about five years. But in some
localities the experiment may have to be tapered off early because
of lack of success, and in others there may be a case for going on
longer.

Chapter 2

THE HISTORY AND EARLY DEVELOPMENT OF CDP

Marjorie Mayo

This chapter focuses on the early development of CDP - but first, it is important to place this development in a wider context. CDP did not emerge in a vacuum, but in a social, political and economic situation which had already given rise to other government attempts to attain similar goals - positive discrimination through Educational Priority Areas and the Urban Programme - greater co-ordination of welfare services through the post-Seebohm developments, or more participation following the Skeffington Report. Since CDP was launched, other Departments have continued to devise similar experiments, for example the Department of Environment's Six Towns study, or the Department of Employment's 'model offices' scheme.

Underlying these programmes, are two related but conflicting developments; first, the increasing pressure for state intervention in a promotional as well as a merely regulative role, in social as well as economic concerns; but second, the increasing public awareness of the contradictions and limitations of existing political and administrative institutions in responding to local needs and demands. As Miller and Rein concluded from the American experience: 'these fundamental flaws in the structure of government were exactly those with which community action was most concerned: over-centralisation, the lack of lateral communication between administrations, their indifference to the effectiveness of their work, and their irresponsiveness to the people they served. The faults were perceived as lying within institutions rather than the structure as a whole.'

The assumption, then, was that projects like CDP could both extend the range of intervention to new fields - and at the same time tackle some of the basic problems dogging existing forms of state intervention. Analysis of CDP's development both at project level, and in its central organisation should increase our understanding of how far this type of internal reform is administratively possible and at what point programmes are held up or ruled out - as certain changes are defined as 'out of bounds'.

CDP'S ORIGINS AND CONCEPTION

CDP arose from an alliance of different interests - a group of civil servants concerned for administrative reforms in the pre-Seebohm Report period, political necessity within a harassed Labour government, academics and social workers galvanised by transatlantic examples from the American 'War on Poverty', to name only the most influential. Not surprisingly each group had its own conception of the problems and of the most appropriate solutions, and not surprisingly the end product was not remarkable for its unity or clarity of intention.

The initial impetus for the creation of CDP came out of an interdepartmental Working Party formed in January 1968 and chaired by Derek Morrell, the 'charismatic' figure behind CDP's early stages. But an earlier strand had been discussions in the Home Office on changes in the law on children and young persons, during the spring of 1967. These proposals for more liberal forms of control for young offenders related to similar proposals for a more rational, more co-ordinated and more family and community based approach to individuals and families in trouble. The assumption here was both of a 'culture of poverty' - and of a cycle of poverty, beyond the control of the individual in question. But the analysis stopped firmly short of any fundamental questioning of the social structure within which these 'pockets' of poverty were thought to persist. The apparent paradox of the survival of poverty, deprivation and multi-problem families within a supposedly affluent Britain was seen, at least partly, 'as a technical and administrative problem'. In as far as it was not the result of unco-ordinated social services and other administrative imperfections, it was the result of faulty communication and attitude failures on the part of both the relevant authorities and of the poor, who lacked sufficient spirit of ambition and self-help to use the existing services constructively. For the majority, however, 'western social democracy has learned much about ways of making available . . . the benefits of science and technology.' 'General social and economic policies are narrowing the gap (between "haves" and "have nots") over a substantial proportion of the population' . . . although these policies had failed for the 'depressed minority' in question.

In other words, poverty and deprivation were conceptualised as the problems of a marginal group who had slipped through the net of welfare, whether through personal or cultural inadequacy or through the services' own lack of co-ordination or administrative weakness.

The solution to this problem was to be administrative reform coupled with an injection of the newly fashionable concept of 'community development' to stimulate self-help among the poor and deprived. This, in summary, was the working party's view on the role for CDP.

But a context had to be found to launch this initiative. One seemed ready-made in the forthcoming Seebohm Report, and development of the CDP proposals was speeded to coincide with the publication of this report. For a number of reasons it was felt likely that the major Seebohm proposals would be deferred; they involved extensive legislation, and a big increase in resources allocated to social work. Their implementation, too, was thought to depend upon local government reform and the Maud Committee was clearly a long way from producing its report. But the argument ran, ministers would wish to avoid adopting a wholly negative stance to the committee's work, and a pilot scheme of community development areas, involving neither legislation nor any sizeable claim on resources, might be a convenient form for the government's immediate response to the Seebohm recommendations.

In the event, the Seebohm Report's main recommendations were more speedily implemented than had been anticipated. But the CDP idea was taken up for other reasons; for the policy of 'positive discrimination' - to concentrate existing resources more effectively rather than deploy new resources - was increasingly vital for a government faced with permanent and worsening economic difficulties. It was a demonstration, too, of concern for 'the poor and needy' - a response to criticism that in other policy areas the government had singularly failed to help this sector. Following the decision over admission of the Kenyan Asians early in 1968, and Powell's speeches later in the same year, the policy of positive discrimination became inextricably bound up with the problem of race and the inner city. If immigration had to be restricted, there could at least be positive help for already established communities. Hence the rapidly created Urban Programme in 1968, and the linked CDP scheme, announced in 1969 - even if the pilot areas contained relatively few immigrants. The CDP idea had found a convenient vehicle.

The very diffusiveness of aims and objectives in early CDP documents, meant that the idea could gain support from different quarters and could potentially be lodged in several different programmes. It was flexible enough to be linked with an Urban Programme designed to tackle problems in immigrant areas, it could appeal to local authorities, often of different political complexion from central government, and fit in comfortably with the policies of the next administration when they took office in 1970.

The third major strand was the spread of ideas from the American Poverty Programme (together with the converse - the political lessons firmly drawn by the working party of civil servants who included in their brief a solemn list of warnings from US experience). Much of the early CDP terminology had a transatlantic flavour, 'community action', 'resident participation', 'cycle of poverty', 'down-town poverty'.

In the early days Dr A.H. Halsey, the first co-ordinator of research in CDP, was the most significant of these academics distilling and translating the American experience. He was a personal friend and influence on some of the civil servants involved, particularly of Morrell, whose own catholic and almost mystical ideas of 'community' might have otherwise reached less concrete form. Halsey's paper at the Anglo-American CDP conference at Ditchley Park in 1969 drew heavily on American theoretical literature and their experience in the field. (1)

This paper admitted some validity for the argument that the present social structure is biased against abolition of poverty and that there are 'massive vested interests in the status quo, amongst which is the apparatus of social administration itself'. The scope of the paper ranges far wider than that of the civil servants who had been concerned primarily with technical and administrative matters, rather than with questions of the social structure.

But although ranging wider than the administrative concept of the problem, Halsey's conceptualisation did not however seem to be fundamentally at variance with the basic CDP strategy. His con-clusions - that CDP promised 'a new style in politics and adminis-tration', based on rational enquiry by social scientists and trans-lated by the administrators into more rational social policy could certainly be related back to the technical and administrative con-cept of poverty and of its resolution. On the other hand, Halsey was also evidently ambiguous himself about the possibilities of CDP, for it was based on the assumption that an equal, just 'welfare' society could be attained through 'the existing political structure' - an assumption which he admitted 'may turn out to have been nothing more than a shibboleth of liberal society in decline.'

CDP IN OPERATION

CDP's central structure was designed then primarily to mount and sustain the technical and administrative reforms which were assumed to be the key to the problems of depressed minorities in the inner city. The non-political approach to the exercise was made explicit in the first Home Office papers:

CDPs involve no threat to existing channels for decision making, and for the allocation of resources. The object is not to dis-rupt or supplant the existing channels and not to set up some parallel organisation, but to enable each of the existing ser-vices to work more closely together, to see the problems whole, and so to make a more effective total contribution to the solu-tions of the problems of the area and the people in it, by taking decisions which reinforce, and are reinforced by, those taken by other relevant services. The need is for a new problem-solving machinery jointly operated by all the normal services. . . .

Locally this would take the form of an inter-service team, with a full time leader and two assistants working from a base in the area. Originally it was intended that they should be 'on loan' from relevant local authority departments without formal secondment, to-gether with further part-time staff from other statutory and volun-tary bodies. In this way each department involved would be in-fluenced via the advocacy of the loaned member of staff in favour of the strategy proposed for the CDP area. The loaned staff member would then be able to act, but 'only to the extent that his parent service was prepared to concede'.

Formal links between the inter-service team and the parent ser-vices would be provided by the local Steering Committee. This was despite all the warnings from American experience (e.g. Marris and Rein, 1972) about the problems of committee structures based on co-operation between widely differing agencies and interests with quite different goals and policies, and the obvious difficulties of agree-ing upon, let alone ever getting any joint programme into action.

The local structure was to relate to a similar structure at central government level: a central steering group. This was to include representatives from other relevant central government de-partments, the Scottish Office and Welsh Office together with local

authority representatives plus certain central staff such as the co-
ordinator and director of research. The central steering group was
to help a central working group establish and provide guidance for
the local projects and to consider 'recommendations to central
government/local government/voluntary organisations regarding the
organisation of social services in the light of the project's
success' and to make reports accordingly to the appropriate Ministers. The Ministers of all these departments were ultimately
responsible for CDP's progress and for the ways its findings were
put into effect.

Thus the original proposals for the structure of CDP were shaped
predominantly by the need to create a mechanism suitable to bring
about technical and administrative reform through existing channels
- and administrative channels at that. Still, the early papers also
included reference to a wider conception of the exercise, that
'elected members as well as officials would need to share this task'
(of serving on the local steering committee), although the political
element fitted uneasily with the central structure, and was not un-
reservedly welcomed. Even so, the early papers could be interpreted
in a way allowing a more 'political' approach; John Greve, for
example, writing on the aims of CDP in 1970, stated: 'We should
acknowledge that CDP is essentially a campaign. It is not a
politically neutral exercise in Social Administration, but quite
specifically concerned with innovations. It challenges the values
and distribution of resources that make up the status quo and is in
business to make changes.'

How closely this concept of CDP related to the intentions of the
founding fathers must remain an open question. What is clear is
that the original aims and consequent structure of CDP were
sufficiently diffuse and flexible to allow for considerable modification in operation. It will be argued subsequently that this
modification was inevitable; that the original proposals for the
structure of CDP were barely suited to the resolution of the purely
technical and administrative problems of the social services; and
that they were remarkably inadequate for the resolution of the wider
and more directly political problems of 'poverty' and the 'inner
city'.

FROM THE GOVERNMENT CDP TO THE HOME OFFICE CDP
TO AUTONOMOUS LOCAL PROJECTS

However strongly the foundations of CDP had been laid, the frequent
changes of key personnel could have been expected to produce some
kind of temporary disturbance. Being placed within the civil service, these temporary upheavals were to be expected every two or
three years when each of the administrators came up for transfer or
promotion. In the event, CDP has undergone even more than average
shifts of staff. In three years it has been under the charge of
four Assistant Under Secretaries, the Assistant Secretaryship has
also changed and there have been three different principals working
with the project.

The present set of administrators, then, are familiar with the
original conception and first years of CDP only via the written

word, and oral tradition. Similarly, with the departure of John
Greve, the research consultant in April 1974, none of the original
advisers from the early days of the project remains. There has been
a complete turnover of central personnel, though there is much
greater stability at local project level.

The structure of CDP has thus conspicuously lacked continuity,
even by civil service standards. Some of this was due to accident
or individual decisions. Some of it was also due to the political
changes of the summer of 1970 and their repercussions in the reorganisation of central government departments, particularly the
move of the Children's Department which contained CDP from the Home
Office to the DHSS, leaving CDP in the newly formed Home Office
Community Programmes Department.

Certainly as far as the professional advisers were concerned some
of this movement was also the result of tensions within the central
team about its own aims and objectives, which in turn related to
tensions springing from the demands which local teams were beginning
to make upon the centre.

Difficulties at the centre

Setting up the project as 'flexible', may have been the only
politically feasible way in which CDP could have been launched, the
only way of building a wide and powerful enough coalition to back
it. Inevitably, of course, CDP's development in action was made
proportionately more problematical by the very ambiguity which had
facilitated its creation in the first place. The to and fro of
personnel with different backgrounds and interests aggravated these
difficulties; time and energy were consumed at the centre in the
search for a consensus of goals and objectives, which could only be
achieved at the level of high-sounding generalisations; these had a
constant tendency to break down the nearer they came to operational
strategies.

Glimpses of these difficulties emerge from the central team meetings 1970-1. 'The central team appear not to be completely agreed
about the CDP objectives', as one of the participants summarised the
situation with a masterly understatement. And so not surprisingly
they continued to flounder around the problem of producing an
acceptable strategy. By March 1971 new personnel were attempting to
raise these issues in more professional terminology - for example,
a paper on Process in local CDP action: the place of working
groups, which focused on local management structures and the role of
working groups but also raised basic questions about the aims of CDP
and their operationalisation. A follow-up was the idea of developing a Critical Path, in several respects a more professional
managerial approach to producing a logical and efficient way through
the early planning phase of the local projects. It was not intended
to prescribe the actual course which each project should finally
take, but merely to indicate the most effective way of producing a
plan of action, whatever the action might be. In this sense the
Critical Path admitted the legitimacy of departing from the original
CDP model (in so far as that could, by this time, be construed from
the confusion surrounding the early papers). But the Critical Path

exercise did not re-examine or comment critically on CDP's original
aims: and this was partly responsible for it being labelled by
local teams as a retrograde attempt at control from the centre.
When it was presented to them in September 1970, it was hardly discussed in itself, argument instead focusing upon the original CDP
'model' and alternative models, and upon the (then highly strained)
relations between the local projects and the centre, and between the
action and research elements.

Since the Critical Path episode, the attempt to define goals and
to produce a co-ordinated action strategy centrally has been more or
less abandoned, despite individual ventures.

Regular central team meetings also broke down about this time.
This was partly the results of diversity of interests involved and
the consequent failure to agree on goals, strategies or tactics. It
also reflected the centre's limitations in a broader context, particularly its increasing difficulty in responding to pressure and
demands from local projects.

Pressure from the local teams

Early records give the impression that the newly appointed local
project directors expected the central team to have a clear picture
of the aims of CDP, and provide useful guidance in putting these
into practice. These expectations were consistently disappointed.
At one such meeting between directors and central team, 'the production of an agenda . . . did little to give shape and direction to
the proceedings which if anything were more repetitious than before,
and introspective to a degree which struck at least one participant
as verging on the neurotic.'

The result of these meetings held regularly at the centre in the
early phase was a build-up of frustrated expectations. Launched on
an uncertain course the project directors' attempts to find guidance
from the centre met with confusion about aims and strategies, and
their practical questions based on problems at local authority or
community level, received 'off the cuff' suggestions or judgments,
when in reality there was very little direct experience of these
conditions at the centre. Perhaps it was surprising that this
situation did not lead to more open tension earlier; this may be
partly explained by the newness and confusion of the local project
leaders themselves, their small number compared with the numbers of
administrators and professionals from the central team and their
obvious financial dependence on the continued good-will of the
centre (and it was not at all clear how far dissent could be
tolerated at that stage). Also the centre was still looked to for
support in two crucial aspects - influence with other government
departments and influence with their own local authorities.

The centre was faced from fairly early days with requests which
involved other government departments, for example issues like housing improvement grants. A proportion of these were 'lost' before
ever reaching the appropriate section of the relevant department,
either because they were ill-formulated for the administrative process and did not fit clearly into any existing channel, or perhaps
because some of them involved basic issues which one department

might be reluctant to raise with another. Even on predominantly administrative questions lateral communication to other departments through the centre was a frustrating experience for projects trying to get access to information or support for the problems of their area.

And in questions of policy, links with the other departments were even less effective, as soon as projects moved beyond their original brief on the personal social services. Government investment policy affecting job opportunities in several project areas can hardly be altered fundamentally without political support; basic criticism of social security procedure, such as the Wage Stop, or the co-habitation rule, are in reality even more obviously political questions, which will be changed not by inter-departmental 'memos' but by political campaigns. Without denying the considerable influence which civil servants can and do have in the shaping of policies, ultimately key economic decisions still depend on political factors; and where they appear not to, this may be simply because dominant interests are not opposed to the change.

As soon as the local CDP teams began to stray into these wider issues, the usefulness of the whole central structure was put into question. And the process was speeded up by the change of government and the loss of the original political 'sponsors' in June 1970. The formal central government machinery for implementing such changes, the central steering group came to an unproductive end around the same time; its third and final meeting was in July 1970.

LOCAL AUTHORITIES AND THE CENTRE: PROBLEMS IN THE PARTNERSHIP

The first four pilot projects were intended to be successful, to give the experiment a good start, and the most co-operative local authorities were initially sought. This may seem surprising in view of the characteristics of some of the final twelve (even allowing for later more objective attempts to choose areas on the basis of social indicators of deprivation). Once negotiations were opened up, there seems to have been a firm commitment on the part of the centre that these should end 'successfully', however many difficulties arose in the process. Part of this may have been the result of the inbuilt response among administrators to smooth over difficulties, and present a picture of apparent calm and order - to keep the 'ball rolling', wherever it leads, and hand over a going concern to one's successor. Perhaps it was also due to the vagueness of CDP as an experiment, and the lack of any clearly defined framework against which to weigh new developments, where there was little precedent to follow.

The result was often to waste valuable time on negotiations long after it was clear that they could not be successfully completed (for example the negotiations with Liverpool University which lasted a year and a half, during which the action team were at work without research support). Or after lengthy negotiation to reach a successful conclusion only by glossing over real difficulties, or making compromises which it would be anticipated would lead to trouble in the future, when these agreements were put to the test of practice.

In other words, in their anxiety to set up CDP projects, and gain support for the idea, the central negotiators were prone to gloss over real difficulties and make light of the challenge to be expected even from the originally limited conception of the exercise as one basically involving social service re-organisation.

Once local authorities had given their consent the project director had to cope as best he or she could with the consequent situation. In the early days, the project director was thought to have some levers of power beyond those of a regular local authority employee, through the link with central government. These links included more than just 75 per cent of the CDP fund behind the action budget, but also links through CDP's relationship with the Urban Programme (administered together from 1971). Offending CDP centrally might thus be expected to offend the source of Urban Aid benevolence - and vice versa. In practice the carrot proved quite unsuccessful in cases of real difficulty; and the only real stick, closing the local project down, has so far not been used; understandably since it could have been as counter-productive for the Home Office as for the local authority in question.

For example, by September 1970 there had been a public row in Southwark about CDP in front of the then Minister responsible for the Urban Programme - so much for the carrot - mainly because the research team had mentioned redevelopment as of possible relevance to the project. The Southwark situation clearly demonstrates the limitations of intervention by the central team in local authority affairs. It was partly that the centre ultimately lacked any effective reward or sanction and that they felt constrained to avoid any public controversy, particularly in their negotiations with local authorities in the delicate post-1970 election period. It was also partly perhaps a result of the very nature of the relationships which they were able to make with the local authority - which were essentially with the local administration, the town clerk or his deputy. The civil servants, by the very fact of being administrators, not politicians were never able to make effective intervention with the local politicians who were often the key actors, particularly when local controversy was aroused.

Meanwhile the CDP administrators tended in such difficult predicaments to search for formulae - guide-lines for action and decision-making in future, bureaucratic procedures to help them through such uncharted courses. In this case the formula-finding came to fruition at the Dorking conference in May 1972 with the decision that CDP local teams were primarily and in the first instance local authority employees. As such, in the last resort, they could not look to the centre to save them from the consequences of their actions. This was of course the other side of greater local autonomy (2) - the recognition that each team must succeed or fail on its own. This retreat by the centre was a tactical one - which can only be fully understood in relation to the other element in the pressure on the centre - the widening of aims and objectives by the local teams.

BROADER OBJECTIVES AT THE LOCAL LEVEL

Detailed accounts of developments at the local level are covered in
later chapters, but even without the detail it is obvious that there
have been major shifts in emphasis; CDP goals and strategies under-
went substantial alteration as teams came into contact with the
local situation. After even a few months experience from two projects, the central team in July 1970 was suggesting revision of the
original local team structure - partly because the secondment system
had never really been put into practice through lack of suitable
local talent and lack of suitable middle management grades locally
from which such talent could be drawn - but also because of shifts
in the major focus of the projects. Even in the first few months,
in Coventry and Liverpool, this had spread beyond the personal
social services into 'redevelopment, planning, clearing up demolition sites . . . ' which involved more departments and more interest
groups both locally, and centrally, though the implications of this
development on the central team were not fully recognised. Employment and transport were soon added to the list. As each new project
has begun to identify the key issues in its local area, more and
more major topics have been taken up, which severely stretch if not
actually break through the original CDP framework.
    In practice local projects could hardly have resisted some
broadening of goals if they were to win and preserve credibility in
their areas. A local authority in an area of industrial decline
does not need to be particularly far-sighted or radical to be concerned about the structural causes of the social problems with which
they have to cope through the social services or with the decline in
their income from rates, which means that they have fewer resources
for these growing needs. So a local CDP team in such an area trying
to work solely with and from the local authority, would still be
likely to become involved with these broader questions - industrial
decline, loss of job opportunities and reduction in the economically
active - for these directly affect the real interests of the local
authorities concerned. If the local team tried to fulfil the other
part of its brief and form meaningful relationships with local
community groups, the pressure might be expected to be correspondingly greater; to take an obvious example, the inhabitants of a
mining village where the last pits have recently closed could
scarcely have been expected to confine discussion of their needs to
the provision of playgroups or additions to the social services, and
say nothing of the basic problem of massive job loss and unemployment. Whatever they or their local authorities may or may not have
believed about Western Social Democracy's success in resolving the
basic economic and social problems for the majority of the population, in practice their own interests demanded wider examination
than the original CDP documents intended. It is these pressures,
rather than the influence of particular radical ideologies, that
have produced the shift in CDP's emphasis away from the resulting
social problems of personal and family breakdown, at least one stage
further back to their origin. The early CDP papers were sufficiently flexible to allow such a shift, without the necessity for a
major overhaul of basic assumptions; but in practice, the change
has badly strained the complex CDP machinery. This had been clear

for some time at the local level (some projects were initially located in the social services department) but was even more true at the centre which was quite unprepared for intervention on such broad and political questions. It was not in a position to provide the required technical advice very adequately either through links with other government departments, or through secondment of relevant experts to the central team. The panel of advisers at the centre remained concentrated on social and community work skills. Reorganisation after the 1970 election left CDP even more tied to one department, rather than part of some inter-departmental machinery administratively lodged in the Home Office. And thus its administrative or political weight was sharply reduced, at the very time when projects were expanding the range of their programmes, and more project teams were coming into action.

THE SOLUTION: 'DECENTRALISATION AND LOCAL AUTONOMY'

With the failure to agree centrally on objectives and strategies, the weakening of the centre's position following the political and administrative changes of 1970, the turnover and loss of staff from the central team, the problems of relating effectively to other government departments or local authorities, and the added pressures placed on central organisation by the ad hoc broadening of goals at the local level, it is hardly surprising that by 1972, the centre was faced with increasing dissatisfaction from local teams. By then, seven or eight project teams were in operation, though only one or two had as yet achieved full strength in both action and research. The central team, in contrast, was considerably smaller than at the start. The original model of a strong centre supporting local projects, drawing out the implications of their work and findings, and channelling them through to the relevant departments, was at least temporarily out of the running.

Tensions between centre and local projects were for a time resolved following a general conference in May 1972. In response to a nine point programme drawn up by local teams, a regular 'consultative council' was set up as a key focus for discussion, and as a body with some influence on strategy-making, though without a formal role in decision making. Being attended by all the teams as well as by the Home Office and the professional advisers, the consultative council by this time had a majority from the local teams rather than from the centre.

As the preceding analysis has attempted to demonstrate, this decentralisation had become a necessity, the only way out of an increasingly untenable position. The Dorking announcement came in fact as official recognition of the actual position in CDP.

CONCLUSION

Although the changes instituted or at least officially recognised in May 1972 had a history of causes and antecedents traceable back to the conception of CDP, and although some of their implications are still being worked out, the Dorking meeting may be taken as a convenient breaking point to mark a significant stage in the national development of the CDP.

Since Dorking, there have been attempts to revive aspects of the original central structure, notably an effort to revitalise inter-departmental links at central government level. On the other hand, recent attempts at co-ordination between action and research teams at the local level have started on quite a different footing. The autonomy of each individual team and the voluntary 'opting-in' basis of such co-operation has been built into these post-Dorking initiatives. Although one member of the central team (3) was seconded to help promote this inter-project co-operation, she was always clearly seen to be responsible to local teams.

Similar developments can be seen in inter-project research, and in the setting up of an information and intelligence unit - another of the Dorking proposals. The unit has now been set up, attached to the Centre for Environmental Studies, responsible to a steering committee, composed of representatives from the local projects, Home Office and CES.

But this move to decentralise responsibility leaves a major question against any overall monitoring and evaluation, despite the commitment of CDP to being a research as well as an action experiment. The history of the rise and fall of the central research unit would be another chapter in its own right. Briefly, the unit was set up in the autumn of 1971 to work with John Greve, who had been the national research director since the start of the project. The unit had the additional difficulty of having to work through local research teams based on separate universities and polytechnics, and never succeeded in breaking out beyond these limiting factors to establish an agreed role, either in supporting local teams or in establishing any systematic monitoring and evaluation of their efforts as a whole. The central research unit disappeared about the same time and for some similar reasons, as the original central team structure in the summer of 1972. The one surviving member was seconded to work with local projects, and John Greve's role was eventually redefined as that of 'research consultant' to the project as a whole.

In the future, then, co-ordination of both action and research strategies, and the national component of CDP will depend largely on the efforts of the local teams themselves. And in this they have given themselves a far more difficult task than the original central team, because of the much broader and more directly political scope of the issues and problems which they have decided to tackle. And they are further hampered by the problems of organising joint activities from widely scattered local areas, by means of infrequent meetings.

Understandably, this has already produced in some areas, an interest in the well-established mechanisms for political pressure - how to lobby MPs or use the national media for this end. But in taking up such traditional pressure group tactics for social reform (even if these are, at least in the short-run, realistic) CDP becomes much more comparable to any other pressure group. There would seem to be, implicit in the adoption of such methods a tacit recognition that the special built-in reform aspect of CDP has failed at least at the level of national political and administrative institutions.

The rise and fall of the central CDP apparatus, and its difficulties of relating to other government departments, to local
authorities and projects, particularly once local teams had begun to
broaden their objectives to more controversial and 'political'
issues, points up some of the underlying problems behind this type
of 'internal' reform.   It illustrates the basic tension between an
attempt at administrative innovation and the wider question of distribution and inequality with which it inevitably became involved
which cannot be settled merely by administrative and technical
changes.

NOTES

1 'Government against Poverty' paper given at the Ditchley conference and later published (Halsey, 1974).
2 Greater local autonomy for project teams had been formally
   announced shortly before this in a ministerial answer to a
   Parliamentary question from the member for Gravesend, 28 April
   1972.
3 The author, from the original central research team.

THE CONTEXT OF THE TWELVE PROJECT AREAS

Joan Payne and Kleri Smith

The twelve local areas where CDP teams have been set up were chosen
by a process of negotiation between the Home Office and local
authorities in which the relative problems of different districts
and considerations of political expediency were both relevant. Thus
it might be thought bad policy to locate the project in areas which
had been the target of other government programmes, like the Educational Priority Areas project, or where community groups were
already active. There was in any case inadequate data available to
permit a confident choice of areas on the basis of their measured
characteristics. The 1966 sample census was well out of date by
1971 or 1972, particularly in redevelopment areas or in districts
receiving large numbers of immigrants. Statistics kept by local
authorities vary considerably from one authority to another, and in
certain fields, particularly the provision of social services, reflect local authority practice more closely than they reflect actual
need. Crucial economic indicators, such as income levels and unemployment rates, tend not to be available for small areas. Beyond
all these problems there is the unanswerable question of what weight
should be given to the different aspects of deprivation. The Home
Office was therefore probably wise to avoid the pretence that areas
could be chosen for an experiment like CDP by their scores on a
quantifiable index of need.

Instead, an attempt was made to include several different types
of area showing a variety of problems. They range from isolated
villages in Glyncorrwg UD in Glamorgan and the remote parishes of
Cleator Moor and Arlecdon and Frizington in Cumberland which lost
their economic bases when the local mines closed, to the densely
populated districts of Saltley in Birmingham, Hillfields in Coventry
and Newington in Southwark, where newcomers to thriving regions can
find cheap housing. In between is a whole spectrum of communities:
Canning Town in Newham whose well unionised dockside labour force is
becoming redundant as shipbuilding and heavy industry moves out of
London; Vauxhall in Liverpool, also affected by the decline in the
docks, an area of walk-up and high rise council flats and large
scale dereliction; Benwell in Newcastle and Percy and Trinity in
Tynemouth, where the effects of the decline in the river industries
are aggravated by the general lack of investment in the North East,

and where certain council estates have the reputation of ghettoes.
Paisley is also in a special development area, but in Ferguslie Park
the problems of living on a heavily stigmatised estate overshadow
all others. The chief industry of the two textile towns of Oldham
and Batley, designated intermediate areas under the government's
regional programme, is also in decline: wage levels are low, and
residents are heavily dependent on neighbouring towns for
employment.

Data from the 1971 census has recently become available for
enumeration districts, small areas covering about 150 households -
two or three streets. By combining the data for all the enumeration
districts in each project area it was possible to obtain information
about the population within its boundaries which could be compared
with other CDP areas and with national figures. (1) By showing how
acute certain problems are in particular small areas, the data sets
the context against which programmes described later in this volume
have developed. But it also serves another function. · The inter-
project report of the national CDP stressed that

> problems of multi-deprivation have to be re-defined and re-
> interpreted in terms of structural constraints rather than
> psychological motivations, external rather than internal factors.
> The project teams are increasingly clear that the symptoms of
> disadvantage in their twelve areas cannot be explained adequately
> by any abnormal preponderance of individuals or families whose
> behaviour could be defined as 'pathological' (CDP, 1974: 8).

Some of the complex relationships between the industrial base of a
community, its housing market, and the social characteristics of its
population emerge from a study of the census data. The twelve areas
were not selected in order to demonstrate these relationships, and
there is no system in the variety of economic circumstances which
they represent. We cannot therefore formulate and test hypotheses
in any rigorous way. However, by combining the detailed knowledge
which project teams have acquired with census measures we are able
at least to illustrate some of the processes at work. (2)

The six villages of Glyncorrwg UD, the parishes of Cleator Moor
and Arlecdon and Frizington in Cumberland, and Batley in the West
Riding, where the whole town of 42,000 people is taken as the project area, offer a range of housing types of varying attractiveness,
within of course a wider regional housing market. However the remaining nine projects are situated in sectors of towns or cities
where the industrial trends affecting the wider area interact with
housing factors to determine the social classes, races and age
groups which congregate in that particular district. Despite this
interaction, Table 3.1 shows a broad correspondence between the
overall economic level of the community as indicated by whether any
special incentives are offered to industry under the government's
regional programme, and the economic strength of the population of
the CDP area. Thus in all the CDP's in special development areas
the proportion of the total population who are economically active
according to the census definition (i.e. in employment, unemployed,
or temporarily off work for other reasons) is lower than the
national average, while in all the areas receiving no assistance the
proportion is above the national average. Unemployment rates, rates
of migration into the local authority area, and the extent of

TABLE 3.1 Economic characteristics of CDP areas by development area status, compared with the whole of Great Britain

	% of the total population who are economically active	% of pop. aged 5+ who migrated into the LA area in the last 5 years	% of all in employment working outside the LA area	% of economically active males aged 15+ seeking work
Special development areas				
Cleator Moor and Arlecdon and Frizington (Cumberland)	44	6	31	10
Glyncorrwg (Glamorgan)	38	7	69	8
Ferguslie Park (Paisley)	39	5	31	22
Percy & Trinity (Tynemouth)	43	6	32	14
Benwell (Newcastle)	42	11	21	13
Development areas				
Vauxhall (Liverpool)*	52	2	17	17
Intermediate areas				
Clarksfield (Oldham)	49	9	28	5
Batley (West Riding)	46	17	48	5
No assistance				
Saltley (Birmingham)	49	17	5	7
Hillfields (Coventry)	48	18	13	7
Canning Town (Newham LB)	49	6	36	8
Newington (Southwark LB)	54	13	65	5
Great Britain	47	-**	-**	4

Sources: Census 1971 Small Area Statistics (Ward Library), 100% population, Table 5, and 10% sample, Tables 22 and 27; Census 1971 Great Britain, Economic Activity, part I (100%), London, HMSO 1973, Table 1.
* Liverpool is now in a special development area.
** Not published.

residents' dependence on employment outside the local authority area are also roughly related to development area status.

The elaboration of this relationship, and the study of deviations from it, show the importance of both industrial and housing factors. In three of the areas receiving no assistance - Saltley, Hillfields, and Newington - a substantial proportion of residents are recent migrants into the local authority area. These high migration rates reflect both the demand for labour in the three cities as a whole (also suggested by the small number of residents in Saltley and Hillfields working outside the local authority area) and the fact that in the particular districts where CDP is located there is housing which is cheap relative to the cost of housing in other districts, and which is equally accessible to newcomers to the city as to established residents. Table 3.2 shows household tenure in these areas. In both Saltley and Hillfields there are small terraced houses selling at low prices, plus a proportion of furnished rooms and flats. In Newington the available pool of housing consists of both furnished and unfurnished rooms in multi-occupied dwellings. One would not expect to find large numbers of recent migrants living in areas of these cities consisting mainly of council property; for if there is pressure on accommodation, new arrivals will almost certainly be kept out of council housing by waiting lists or residence requirements - Birmingham, for example, demands a residence qualification of five years.

Despite the apparent demand for labour in these three CDP areas, all had in 1971 unemployment rates above the national average - well above in the case of Saltley and Hillfields. Migrants to these areas tend in fact to take those jobs which are least desired by residents, those which offer the worst conditions and the worst pay, and are most vulnerable to redundancies. (3)

The majority of the newcomers to Saltley and Hillfields are immigrants from the 'New Commonwealth' (which excludes the white countries of Canada, Australia and New Zealand). Table 3.3 shows that 27 per cent of residents in Saltley were born in the New Commonwealth, including 19 per cent from Pakistan. Two-thirds of these entered Great Britain after 1960. 23 per cent of Hillfields residents are of New Commonwealth origin, 13 per cent from India, and three-quarters entered after 1960. In addition, 8 per cent of residents in each area were born in this country to parents who were both born in the New Commonwealth. Rather fewer Newington residents were born abroad, but there is still a variety of nationalities represented there. The clustering of immigrants from particular countries in certain parts of town is a product not only of the market forces which make it difficult to obtain housing elsewhere, but also of the advantages of mutual support derived from living close to relatives and friends from the same village. This is especially true where family ties in the old country are strong and the English language is strange. Thus most Pakistanis in Saltley come from the rural area of Mirpur, and in Batley also there is a colony of Muslim Indians from the state of Gujerat.

Inevitably, the coloured newcomers are not welcomed by many white residents, and the difficulties which people of different nationalities find in accepting each other's ways are not lessened by the fact that the newcomers are generally at a considerably earlier

TABLE 3.2 Household tenure and households in shared dwellings in Saltley (Birmingham), Hillfields (Coventry) and Newington (Southwark) CDP areas

	Owner-occupiers %	Council tenants %	Private unfurnished tenants %	Private furnished tenants %	Not stated %	Total %	In shared dwellings %
	% of private households						
Saltley	48	17	30	5	0	100	8
Hillfields	38	24	25	14	0	100	5
Newington	3	38	52	6	1	100	33

Source: Census 1971 Small Area Statistics (Ward Library), 100% households, Table 18. Note that in this and in subsequent tables percentages may not sum exactly to 100 because of rounding errors.

TABLE 3.3 Country of birth of residents in Saltley (Birmingham), Hillfields (Coventry) and Newington (Southwark)

	UK %	Irish Republic %	America* %	New Commonwealth			elsewhere and not stated %	Total %
				India %	Pakistan %	remainder %		
	% of residents born in							
Saltley	68	5	6	1	19	1	1	100
Hillfields	68	8	2	13	4	4	2	100
Newington	87	5	1	(0.2)	(0.3)	2	3	100

Source: Census 1971 Small Area Statistics (Ward Library), 100% population, Table 8.
* The majority being from the West Indies.

stage in the cycle of family formation than the bulk of the original residents. Immigrants naturally tend to be young and active, and of the original residents young couples starting families and those who can afford the move or who can get a council tenancy elsewhere often leave the district which they think is going downhill. The effect is seen dramatically in Figure 3.1. Virtually all of Saltley or Hillfields residents born in the New Commonwealth or born in this country to New Commonwealth parents are under 45 years of age, and there are very large numbers of children - particularly of very small children less than 5 years old. The remainder of the residents are considerably older not only than the immigrants but also than the population of Great Britain as a whole. Old white residents will be annoyed by coloured children playing in the streets, and the neighbours who would normally be able to do small services for them may not speak the same language - difficult conditions under which to achieve mutual sympathy.

Canning Town, in Newham, is rather different from the other three CDP areas not assisted under the regional programme. There the unemployment rate was 8 per cent in 1971 - twice the national average - and only 6 per cent of Canning Town residents had moved into the borough during the previous five years. With half of the households occupying council dwellings, this low rate of migration must be partly due to the obstacles to obtaining a council tenancy, but it also reflects the decline in recent years in the dockland industries on which Canning Town depends. Unlike Newington, Canning Town has poor transport connections with central London and is not attractive for workers there; nor do its residents have the skills required for office work. The report of Canning Town CDP, 'Industry and Employment in Canning Town' (1974), shows that many more jobs were lost during the late 1960s and early 1970s by the closure of dockland industries than were created by the light industry and warehousing replacing them, and that wage levels in the new jobs are lower. The CDP team argue that government regional policies ignore the problems of small pockets of decline within a context of regional growth.

In the population structure of Glyncorrwg UD we see the effects of a recent and dramatic loss of jobs caused by the pit closures of the late 1960s. The parishes of Cleator Moor and Arlecdon and Frizington have suffered from a long and gradual decline in iron ore mining starting as long ago as 1881, and though the population of Cleator Moor has now begun to rise again, that of Arlecdon and Frizington has continued to fall. In both areas there has been no alternative for many young people but to leave the villages to find work; turning back to Table 3.1 we see that many of those who remain are unemployed, and many more have to travel long distances to their jobs. While the Cumberland CDP area has reached a kind of stable depression, Glyncorrwg bears marks of a trauma. In Great Britain as a whole 46 per cent of the population are economically active. In Cumberland CDP the figure is 44 per cent - in Glyncorrwg 38 per cent. Table 3.4 shows the causes of this low level of activity in Glyncorrwg. 15.6 per cent of males aged 15 or more are retired although only 12.9 per cent have passed their 65th birthday, for at the time of the pit closures miners aged 55 or more were given special incentives to retire early. A further 4.6 per cent,

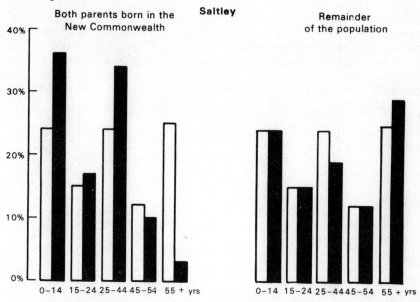

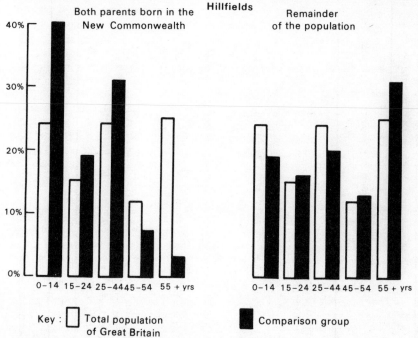

Key : ☐ Total population   ■ Comparison group
         of Great Britain

FIGURE 3.1   Age distribution of residents in the Saltley
(Birmingham) and Hillfields (Coventry) CDP areas with both parents
born in the New Commonwealth, compared with the age distribution of
the rest of the CDP area population and with the whole of Great
Britain
Sources: Census 1971 Small Area Statistics (Ward Library), 100%
population, Tables 3, 4, 6 and 7; Census 1971 Great Britain, Age,
Marital Condition and General Tables, London, HMSO 1974, Table 9.

TABLE 3.4 Economic activity of males aged 15 or more in CDP areas, compared with the whole of Great Britain

	Economically active			Economically inactive			Total
	In employment %	Seeking work %	Temporarily sick %	Retired %	Students %	Perm. sick and other %	%
Special development areas							
Cleator Moor and Arlecdon and Frizington (Cumberland)	73.1	8.2	1.7	11.3	2.3	3.4	100
Glyncorrwg (Glamorgan)	67.2	5.8	3.1	15.6	3.7	4.6	100
Ferguslie Park (Paisley)	63.0	18.8	3.7	9.5	1.5	3.5	100
Percy & Trinity (Tynemouth)	70.2	11.5	2.0	11.1	2.0	3.2	100
Benwell (Newcastle)	66.4	10.5	2.2	12.9	4.4	3.6	100
Development areas							
Vauxhall (Liverpool)	68.1	14.2	2.9	9.3	3.5	2.0	100
Intermediate areas							
Clarksfield (Oldham)	77.9	4.1	1.5	11.1	3.3	2.1	100
Batley (West Riding)	79.2	4.0	0.9	10.3	3.6	2.0	100
No assistance							
Saltley (Birmingham)	80.2	5.8	1.4	7.1	3.9	1.6	100
Hillfields (Coventry)	75.3	6.1	1.8	9.4	5.2	2.2	100
Canning Town (Newham LB)	76.5	6.4	2.1	10.3	2.5	2.2	100
Newington (Southwark LB)	81.8	4.4	1.0	7.8	3.4	1.6	100
Great Britain	77.0	3.4	1.0	11.6	4.9	2.0	100

Sources: Census 1971 Small Area Statistics (Ward Library), 100% population, Tables 6 and 7; Census 1971 Great Britain, Economic Activity, part I (100%), London, HMSO 1973, Table 1.

excluding students, are economically inactive for other reasons, and
the majority of these are likely to be permanently sick or disabled:
nearly five times more than the comparable estimate for Great
Britain. Loss of work through temporary sickness is also three
times higher in Glyncorrwg than in the rest of Great Britain. Thus
the unemployment rate recorded by the census - which, at 8 per cent
of economically active males, is already excessive - disguises the
true extent of the shortage of jobs there.

The undoubted fact of the migration of young people from these
areas would lead one to expect that the remaining population was
largely elderly. Figure 3.2 shows that, surprisingly, this is not
the case. The proportion of the population aged below 15 years is
larger in both Cumberland CDP and Glyncorrwg than in the rest of
Great Britain, and the proportion aged 60 or more is significantly
smaller. We can only speculate about the reasons for this, but both
are mining areas and life expectancies may be low. In the 1930s
conditions in Cleator Moor and Arlecdon and Frizington were particularly bad, and the people who suffered from malnutrition and
tuberculosis then may not have survived long enough to form a
generation of old age pensioners today. If the older generation is
dying and young adults are leaving, children are bound to form a
large proportion of the population.

Besides the two areas just described, three other CDP projects
are located in Special Development Areas: Ferguslie Park in
Paisley, Percy and Trinity in Tynemouth, and Benwell in Newcastle.

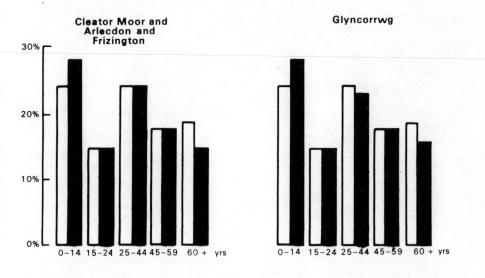

FIGURE 3.2 Age distribution of the population of the Cleator Moor
and Arlecdon and Frizington (Cumberland) and Glyncorrwg (Glamorgan)
CDP areas compared with the whole of Great Britain
Sources: As for Figure 3.1

In addition the Vauxhall project in Liverpool is in a designated
Development Area. The heavy engineering industries around which
Paisley was built have a diminishing need for labour, and the other
three areas are affected by the decline in dockside industries which
has also hit Newham. But although regional unemployment is high, in
these four small areas there are unemployment rates reminiscent of
the 1930s: 13 per cent in Benwell, 14 per cent in Percy and
Trinity, 17 per cent in Vauxhall and 22 per cent in Paisley. This
extreme concentration of men out of work within an area of high unemployment is a product of local authority policies in the management of council housing which tend to group families with economic
and social problems on the same estates, almost certainly the least
desirable ones. Sometimes this is done by the deliberate grading of
families by housing visitors; sometimes it is the result of un-
opposed market forces which mean that only those who are desperate
for housing will accept a tenancy there. Such estates typically
have low income levels, a rapid turnover of tenants, high ratios of
children to adults, and a stigma which attaches both to the estate
and to its residents.

This description applies to a substantial part of Percy ward in
the Percy and Trinity CDP area, to a small but extremely unpopular
estate in Benwell, (4) and to much of Ferguslie Park. Empty and
derelict dwellings are a feature of the latter, though there are
pockets within the area which have not been affected by the general
decline. Vauxhall shares several of the characteristics of these
three, but differs in that it is the traditional district in which
Irish catholics in Liverpool have settled, and so has an attraction
to people with family and community ties there. All four estates
consist largely of flats.

The age structure of the population of these estates, illustrated
in Figure 3.3, is seriously distorted. Compared with the general
population the estates in Ferguslie Park, Benwell, and Percy ward
have excessive numbers of children, and the figure for Percy ward
would certainly be increased if private dwellings could be excluded.
Correspondingly there is a deficiency of adults, especially of those
in the older age groups. As Byrne points out (1973), a high ratio
of children to adults is almost bound to create problems of noise
and vandalism, for the control exercised by adults in a more
balanced community cannot be provided. The population of Vauxhall
has an unusual age structure: there are very few of either young
children or young adults, but large numbers of teenagers and men and
women in middle age. This is the result of a corporation policy
starting around 1960 to reduce the population of the area by selective demolition of old terraced houses and walk-up flats. New
family units forming since that date have had difficulty in obtaining tenancies on the estate which were required for the displaced
households, and have been discouraged from moving to the new tower
blocks because of their unsuitability for children. The rise in the
proportion of teenagers in Vauxhall has meant that the policy has
had the unintended effect of increasing the already widespread
vandalism in the area.

Unemployment rates have already been described, but the estates
show several other symptoms of low household income. Sickness and
disability rates are high (see Table 3.4), and on the Paisley,

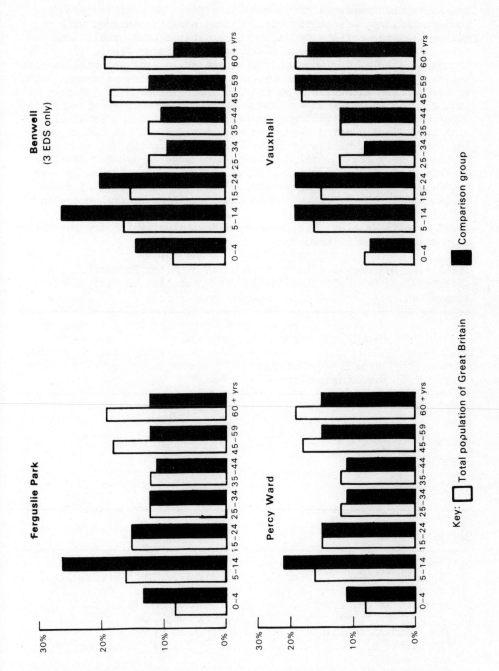

FIGURE 3.3 Age distribution of the population of Ferguslie Park (Paisley) and Vauxhall (Liverpool) CDP areas, and of Percy ward (Tynemouth) and three EDs in Benwell (Newcastle), compared with the total population of Great Britain
Sources: As for Figure 3.1

Tynemouth and Newcastle estates up to a fifth of families with dependent children are supported by a lone parent, compared with the national average of one in ten. These estates also have a high ratio of dependents to economically active persons (Table 3.1), though because of the unusual age structure in Vauxhall this is not the case there. On all four estates roughly a third of economically active men are labourers, and the proportion of council tenants owning a car ranges from a maximum of 12 per cent in Percy ward to 6 per cent and 2 per cent respectively in Vauxhall and Benwell.

A large family often means low resources, and it is not surprising that many households in these four areas contain six or more persons. Very few council dwellings are large enough for families of this size, with the result, shown in Table 3.5, of serious overcrowding. The level of overcrowding on these council estates exceeds that in any of the supposed slums awaiting redevelopment in the other CDP areas, and is two to three times greater than the level even in Saltley, Hillfields and Newington, which are receiving a constant influx of newcomers.

TABLE 3.5   Overcrowding in council housing in the Ferguslie Park (Paisley) and Vauxhall (Liverpool) CDP areas, and in Percy ward (Tynemouth) and three EDs in Benwell (Newcastle)

	% of all households in council dwellings	% of all households containing 6 or more persons*	% of households in council dwellings with 6 or more rooms**	% of households in council dwellings with over 1½ people per room
Ferguslie Park	97	22	2	14
Vauxhall	92	18	5	10
Percy ward	74	12	2	9
Benwell (3 EDs)	85	21	4	14
Great Britain	31	6	16	3

Sources: Census 1971 Small Area Statistics (Ward Library), 100% households, Tables 18, 19 and 21; Census 1971 Great Britain, Housing Summary Tables, London, HMSO 1974, Table 1; Census 1971 England and Wales, Housing, part IV, London, HMSO 1974, Table 11; Census 1971 Scotland, Housing Report, Edinburgh, HMSO 1975, Table 11.
* The standard tabulations for EDs published by OPCS do not give the number of households in council dwellings containing six or more persons.
** Excluding bathrooms, halls, etc., and kitchens less than six feet wide.

The last two CDP areas, the Clarksfield district of Oldham and the town of Batley in the West Riding, are both in intermediate

areas offering certain limited incentives to industry. Both towns
were built in the nineteenth century to supply the workforce for the
now shrinking textile industry, and though unemployment in 1971 was
not far above the national average, wages in the mills are low and
many sites are derelict. The decline in local industry has been
offset to some extent by the availability of employment in the surrounding district: 28 per cent of Clarksfield's labour force and
48 per cent of Batley's work outside the local authority area. However this does not solve the towns' fundamental problem, that their
financial resources are inadequate for the provision of services and
for the renewal of outworn public facilities.

   The syphoning off of a section of the workforce in both towns
into better paid jobs elsewhere created a labour shortage in the
textile firms despite the overall contraction of the industry. This
vacuum has been filled in recent years by New Commonwealth immigrants predominantly from India and Pakistan: these form 6 per cent
of the residents of Clarksfield and 5 per cent of the residents of
Batley. The vast majority of both groups entered Great Britain
after 1960, and have formed distinct cultural enclaves in districts
where old houses can be bought cheaply: thus three-quarters of the
New Commonwealth immigrants in Batley live in the town's East ward,
where they comprise 22 per cent of the population. Figure 3.4 shows
that the remaining white residents, like those in Hillfields and
Saltley, include disproportionately large numbers of old people and
relatively few in the age group 25 to 44.

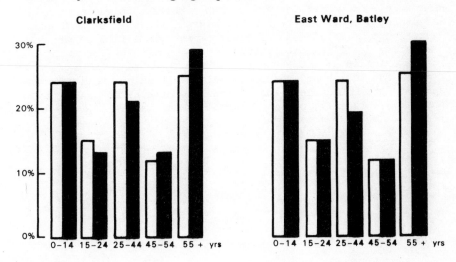

FIGURE 3.4 Age distribution of the population excluding residents
with both parents born in the New Commonwealth of the Clarksfield
(Oldham) CDP area and of East ward, Batley, compared with the total
population of Great Britain
Sources: As for Figure 3.1

   At first glance the twelve CDP areas present a rag-bag collection
of different kinds of problems. Too many children, overcrowding,
racial tension, or depopulation and too many who are old or sick -
both ends of every spectrum can be found. In the causes of the problems the diversity disappears: switches in industrial investment
seeking the greatest profits determine the growth or decline of
communities, even of places like Canning Town situated in a much
wider economic unit, and the power of different groups in the housing market, both private and public, determines who shall live where
and in what conditions. No amount of community development will
solve the problems unless these causes are tackled.

NOTES

1 The analysis was carried out by the Research Services Unit of
   Nuffield College, Oxford.
2 This chapter has drawn heavily on a variety of documents produced by the CDP teams, and on conversations with several team
   members.
3 Table 26 of the Census 1971 Small Area Statistics (Ward
   Library) gives a breakdown of the socio-economic group of heads
   of households who had migrated into the local authority area
   during the previous five years. However those figures cannot be
   used here, first because the information is given for a 10 per
   cent sample of households and so the numbers involved are small,
   and second because 22 per cent of migrant heads in Saltley and
   17 per cent in Hillfields were either not classified or had inadequately described occupations.
4 The description of the Newcastle estate is based on census
   figures for the three enumeration districts which broadly corre-
   spond to its boundaries, and of the Tynemouth estate on figures
   for Percy ward only, not on figures for the whole project areas.

Chapter 4

EXTRACTS FROM THE INTER-PROJECT REPORT

This report was the result of collaboration between the twelve local projects involved in the CDP programme. In summer 1973, the Home Secretary called for progress reports from the projects and in response individual reports were prepared. However local projects were anxious to emphasise that many issues they faced locally were not isolated problems, but symptoms of more basic underlying processes. Twelve separately prepared local reports could have missed these common themes, and it was decided to produce a general inter-project report. This was prepared by a working group drawn from the projects, using material from the local reports. The report was submitted to the Home Office in November 1973.

The following sections have been chosen to suggest something of the shared perspectives, but also to give an overview of the range of action programmes and the different styles of intervention found in the twelve project areas.

It is now four years since the Home Secretary announced in Parliament the launching of CDP as 'a neighbourhood-based experiment aimed at finding new ways of meeting the needs of people living in areas of high social deprivation'. The experiment was originally conceived and planned on a number of basic assumptions. It was assumed that problems of urban deprivation had their origins in the characteristics of local populations - in individual pathologies - and these could best be resolved by better field co-ordination of the personal social services, combined with the mobilisation of self-help and mutual aid in the community 'even among those who experience most difficulty in standing on their own feet'. To this end, CDPs were to be established in small areas of severe deprivation with local authority teams employed to identify needs; to promote greater co-ordination and accessibility of services at the field-level; to foster community involvement and to build a communication bridge between the people and local services. Research was to be located in local universities or polytechnics to provide data, advice and evaluation. In its formative stages CDP thus clearly followed perspectives on social problems dominant at the time; particular influences were the Seebohm Report and the growing emphasis on the development of professional social work, and from abroad the first wave of anti-poverty programmes in America and the idea of small-scale experimental projects.

The experiment has taken over three years to assemble, with the Home Office 'central team' in operation by mid 1969, the first of the 12 local projects (Liverpool and Coventry) getting off the ground in January 1970 and the last (Tynemouth, Oldham and Paisley) not beginning until October 1972. The experiment thus has had to contend with a very staggered start. Perhaps more seriously for local projects, most have had to wait a long time - sometimes more than a year - before research resources have become available. Even now research staff are still being recruited for some projects. Figure 4.1 shows the lengthy build-up and the ragged start to many projects.

A further important feature of this long setting-up period has been the change in the role of the Home Office. In April 1972, it was announced in Parliament that there would be less central control over both action and research and more encouragement of local initiative with support from the centre. This shift of responsibility and authority towards the field has been reflected in greater inter-project collaboration and initiative. The local projects now relate collectively to the Home Office through a regular Consultative Council; and the experiment now has the back-up of a central Information and Intelligence Unit.

	1969	1970	1971	1972	1973	1974
Home Office Team						
Southampton research						
Information and intelligence unit						
Coventry – Hillfields						
Liverpool – Vauxhall						
Southwark – Newington						
Glamorgan – Glyncorrwg						
Newham – Canning Town						
West Riding – Batley						
Newcastle – Benwell						
Cumberland – Cleator Moor						
Birmingham – Saltley						
Paisley – Ferguslie Park						
Tynemouth – Percy & Trinity						
Oldham – Clarksfield						

Key: ✱ Action director starts work
　　／／／ Joint action–research in operation
　　ᐯᐯᐯ Change of action director

Note: in Paisley and Southwark research got under way before action. Newcastle has had a researcher since October 1972 but a research team has yet to be appointed. Details for 1974 are provisional

FIGURE 4.1 Build up of the National Project, 1969-74

The Report then described in detail, characteristics of the twelve project areas, drawing out the underlying trends, particularly the processes of industrialisation and urbanisation which lay

behind the different forms of deprivation. These details have
already been covered in chapter 3 by Joan Payne and Kleri Smith.
Readers are also referred to the Inter-Project Report (CDP, 1974).

ACTION AND RESEARCH STRATEGIES

Confronted with this wider canvas of population movements, employment and housing changes, local teams have increasingly
questioned and moved away from the original 'social pathology'
assumptions of the experiment. They have begun to develop perspectives which better account for the unequal distribution of
both private and public goods and services, and provide explanation for the powerlessness of CDP populations to influence these
distributions.

But in addition they have to locate their own action and research programme in this developing framework. Inter-project
debate and discussion have increased awareness of this wider context, and the strategies of several later projects particularly
have been influenced by this approach. But in practice on the
ground there is great diversity. Programmes and strategies
attempted by each team reflect different assumptions and different opportunities for action in each area; and they reflect
too the different ideas of how social change is achieved. To
understand these differences, it is helpful to set out systematically possible strategies open to local teams, beginning by
distinguishing three main models of social change.

(i) Consensus models of social change are based on the
assumption that social problems are 'malfunctions' which can be
cured by adjustments and re-arrangements within the existing
operating systems. The problems are defined mainly in terms of
failures of co-ordination and communication, and the focus of
change is thus on management and administration and the non-
participant. The central tactic is debate.

(ii) Pluralist models of social change are based on the
assumption that social problems arise from 'imbalances' in the
democratic and bureaucratic systems. The problems are defined
mainly in terms of failures of participation and representation
of certain interests in the political process, and the focus of
change is thus on politicians, policy-makers and the disenfranchised. The central tactic is bargaining and negotiation.

(iii) Structural conflict models of social change are based on
the assumption that social problems arise from a fundamental conflict of interests between groups or classes in society. The
problems are defined mainly in terms of inequalities in the distribution of power and the focus of change is thus on the centres
of organised power (both private and public). The main tactic is
organisation and raising of levels of consciousness.

These are over simple definitions but they imply important
differences of emphasis. Given the possibility of developing
change at three main levels - national, local and grass-roots -
it is possible to distinguish nine different, though overlapping,
strategies (Figure 4.2). In using this diagram it is important
to point out that in practice individual CDP strategies will not

necessarily fall neatly into one category. The diagram is intended as a guide to sort out broad differences - not a strait-
jacket. In most projects there is a mixture of approaches, and
some degree of ambiguity and even contradiction in the strategies
being attempted.

Basic assumptions / Level	Consensus	Pluralism	Structural conflict
National	1 Social planning	4 National lobby	7 National pressure
Local	2 Organisational and service development	5 Local lobby	8 Local pressure
Grass-roots	3 'Traditional' community development	6 Community organisation	9 Community action

FIGURE 4.2 Models of social change and possible strategies on
three levels of operation

1. Social planning aims to bring about changes in policy by
planning as comprehensively as possible, taking into account the
physical, social and economic aspects of total situations. Problems are defined primarily as technical, rather than political,
and conflicts of interest are seen as reconcilable if they are
treated within a more total system. Commitment to the comprehensive social plan is sought first from senior professionals and
the role of the politician is seen as one of ratification for a
rational solution to an agreed problem.
2. Organisational development and service-delivery aim to
bring about changes in organisational practices, by managerial
and administrative re-arrangements. Better communication is
assumed to lead to closer co-ordination, and hence a more
efficient and relevant service. The overall goals of the organisation are not questioned, so much as the means of achieving
those goals. Organisational consultants are often employed to
propose, or legitimise, such re-arrangements.
3. 'Traditional' community development aims to bring about
changes in the functioning of individuals, groups, and 'communities' by facilitating their integration into more coherent
wholes. The 'community' is assumed to be homogenous in its needs
and where conflicts of interest are found, these are reconcilable
through better communication and inter-group relations. The process of community development is often seen as more important
than any product, that is development of community relationships
is seen as an end in itself, rather than primarily as a means of
solving common external problems. Nevertheless, new more comprehensive structures, like neighbourhood councils, are sought as a

means of representing the neighbourhood more effectively in relation to external decision-makers.

4. and 5. National and local lobbying. Strategies (4) and
(5) assume a state of competition and bargaining between different interest-groups within a plural system. They seek
changes, therefore, not first in the technical or bureaucratic
systems but in the political arena. The arenas for bargaining
over policies and the allocation of resources are assumed to be
those of the formal governmental process, so strategies are
pitched at politicians, councillors, parties and pressure groups.
Support is lobbied on the basis of reasoned evidence, and the expressed need of constituents.

6. Community organisation is probably the closest description
of much of the neighbourhood work going on currently in local
projects. The powerlessness of residents to control their own
life situations, or to influence the decisions which affect their
areas, is seen to be related partly to their lack of information,
access to relevant expertise and advocacy, and poor organisation.
Information centres, neighbourhood newspapers, legal and welfare
rights campaigns, financial and technical support for residents'
associations all aim to equip the residents of CDP areas with a
greater capacity to bargain for the protection of their interests. The provision of 'hard' information and 'hard' skills
seems to have helped resident groups to gain some points of
leverage to claim their rights under existing legislation and
policy, and to expose instances of poor quality service from
local agencies. However, much of this has been limited to very
here-and-now issues, and has been in reaction to agency programmes, rather than any real claiming of initiative for change.
The question is how far alliances can be formed between these
different action groups, and momentum kept up to sustain the
necessary long term processes of improvement and change.

7. 8. and 9. National pressure, local pressure, and community
action. These assume a longer term historical analysis, and aim
to relate selectively to the local community, forging links between its more active members and groups, and organised sections
of the working class. The intention is to sharpen local
consciousness of the underlying problems, and relate action and
pressure to the activities of the wider labour movement. The
question that remains is whether a clear enough awareness of the
underlying issues can be developed to stimulate a powerful movement for change from a local base.

ISSUES

The pilot phase of the experiment was characterised by local
diversity, and little comparative work. With the full complement
of projects there has been an increase in inter-project discussion, and this has encouraged the identification of critical
issues in common. In general, projects do not follow a 'comprehensive' or 'total' strategy - what in practice might easily
become a 'little bit of everything', but are searching for the
key issues.

Employment has become an issue of central importance, not merely because of the deteriorating economic conditions of many areas, but because it is clearly a key variable, with repercussions across the board.

Four of the projects are developing analyses of the wider dimensions of the employment problem. Glamorgan and Cleator Moor are focusing their attention on governmental policy (regional policy; the 'growth point' principle), whereas Newham and Newcastle are focusing on the private sector, particularly the effects of changes in a firm's investment upon the workforce and population of small areas. In the first case, the main emphasis is on a 'social planning' approach; the process has included data collection, a report by an economic consultant, and the development of a set of proposals for a more sensitive and flexible regional employment policy. These have been used to open up debate with the relevant government departments. The Glyncorrwg project is documenting the relative success and failure of this strategy and it will be important to compare their rather pessimistic experience so far with the alternative approach of Tynemouth, Newham and Newcastle. In these projects, data will be gathered on the investment patterns and operations of local firms. The differential effects of these trends will be analysed and discussed with local workplace contacts (trades council, shop-stewards committees). The aim is to provide discussion and organisation to look at the industrial issues of the neighbourhood as a whole and plan necessary action.

A further group of projects is focusing on support services for the unemployed. Cleator Moor, Glamorgan and Paisley are planning to survey the special needs and problems of the unemployed themselves, and Glamorgan particularly are working on the development of more relevant retraining programmes for those out of work. Coventry and Liverpool have focused on the support services for the young person making the transition from school life to work life.

Income and income maintenance. This issue is closely related to that of employment. Project areas generally have higher than average unemployment for their region and higher than average dependence upon state incomes and welfare benefits. In Ferguslie Park some 22 per cent of men were unemployed on the 1971 census figures (compared to 8 per cent for the Paisley Burgh).

In Coventry, the differential operations of social security have been approached via survey and research. This has revealed very limited knowledge of rights and an extensive range of unmet need, both among pensioners and other claimants. These findings are being presented to the appropriate departments and support gained from MPs, the national pressure groups (CPAG, Age Concern), and from local trades union organisation. But the question remains whether this type of approach which has been extensively tried by the poverty lobby for some years can achieve the necessary shifts in policy or practice. The Batley project is attempting to get change at the local level with a concerted programme to disseminate information on welfare rights and stimulate maximum take-up. Part of their strategy has been to place an 'expert' within a key agency. As the appointment of 'welfare

rights officers' to social service departments is gaining momentum, it will be important for CDP to examine this approach carefully and compare its effectiveness with other strategies which
aim not only to disseminate information, but to place hard knowledge and advocacy more directly in the hands of claimants themselves.

Rates are another issue with immediate relevance to income
levels, and the 1973 revaluation, shifting burden of this tax
away from industry and commerce on to the domestic ratepayer, has
highlighted the problem. Among domestic ratepayers the burden
has also shifted disproportionately on to council house tenants,
and in some areas on to the occupants of lower valued property.
This has hit many residents of the CDP areas hard. In Birmingham
for example, the increased rate contribution from the CDP area
easily outstrips the extra amount of money CDP brings in. The
two responses are action and analysis. In Birmingham, the
strategy has been to employ a worker to prepare collective
appeals with residents and in Coventry information on differential rate levels has been fed out to resident groups and to the
local Federation of Council Tenants, and to local councillors
where it was linked to another related issue - that of Fair Rents
set by the Rent Scrutiny Board.

Housing is perhaps the most complex issue faced by CDP teams.
Birmingham is tracing housing movement in the fluid situation of
a rapidly changing multi-racial area now under the shadow of a
renewal programme, and is looking closely at the micro-level of
movements within single streets. The Newham project is charting
how the different forms of investment in housing affect people's
chance of being housed. They aim to explore ways in which the
potential advantages of municipal housing can be more adequately
related to the interests of working class people. The Coventry
project is commissioning a research study of the wider interests
which appear to have influenced the allocation of land, and investment in renewal in the city since the war.

Most projects service groups concerned with redevelopment.
But there are two different approaches. Projects may take up a
housing issue, and encourage resident group development as a way
of solving that particular problem; or they may see the process
of involving people in collective action over housing problems as
a means of promoting a wider understanding of the political
system, and a catalyst for their engagement in more basic
political activity. The experience of the pilot projects with
redevelopment schemes underlines some of the reasons for this
shift in objectives.

The pilot projects began by dealing with redevelopment problems primarily in terms of management and administration. Concerted attempts were made by both Southwark and Coventry to press
for a more total approach, more coherent control and more sensitive co-ordination of the whole operation - a better flow of information about rights and about the timetable of clearance;
more efficient boarding-up of empty property to stop the chain of
dereliction; more participation and choice in the whole question
of the future of the area; more forward planning of general improvement areas, and the declaration of whole districts to

guarantee their security and arrest blight. Their cases were argued on the basis both of local evidence, and comparable experience from other authorities. The central Home Office team added their weight and dialogue was established with senior officials in local, regional and central government.

This approach followed the original Home Office model of change through dialogue - better communication leading to better co-ordination. However, neither team found these approaches effective in bringing about even relatively simple and inexpensive changes of practice. This experience underlined the crucial political interests at stake in urban renewal, it was not merely a question of technical adjustment. Later projects are involved in more sophisticated and long term attempts to tackle renewal problems from a similar standpoint. Birmingham, for example, proposes to set up an environmental team in the period before the renewal programme begins to operate, to work with local authority departments and yet be in a position to respond to residents' priorities. And Oldham is encouraging the formation of representative resident associations to process problems of renewal.

Following this pilot phase experience several projects have placed much greater emphasis on the second aim of using housing issues to develop wider awareness. Several projects are servicing groups of residents on local redevelopment issues with technical expertise from planners and public health inspectors acting as consultants to the local group. Although this intervention is on a very narrow front (involving small groups of streets at a time) experience suggests that through this combination of advocacy and community organisation, residents can bargain more powerfully for investment in their area, and in the process they can develop a much clearer awareness of the wider factors governing and constraining their housing opportunities.

Education. In the first pilot projects education was a major field of expenditure. Education was seen as an important link in the distribution of opportunities, and one open to change. Emphasis on education fitted with the early assumptions of the CDP experiment, and the Educational Priority Area programmes, but several later projects have avoided involvement in conventional education completely, or have experimented with education away from a school base. The central question is whether and in what form educational change can promote wider changes, and the ensuing debate has called into question several of the assumptions underlying the initial importance given to education.

Educational activities in CDP fall into three main types:

(a) Conventional educational development: improving and extending existing facilities, introduction of new equipment, development of pre-school provision, more teaching resources.

(b) 'Community education': particularly developing home-school links, the need for a curriculum relevant to inner-city areas, and the idea of the 'community school'. The aim is to change relationships between school and community and develop 'constructive discontent' which will encourage a critical stance among children towards their environment.

(c) Emphasis on work outside schools, on informal adult education, dealing with real life situations - problems of work, unemployment or rents with groups not already involved in the educational process. The aim is to stimulate knowledge and awareness, and encourage pressure for change among those directly affected.

Work in the first two categories will add to the experience of the EPA projects in developments of this type, though it will be important to collect more evidence on the wider and long term effects of 'community education'. At this stage EPA approaches seem to have had some success in 'loosening up' professional thinking and practice at the level of the local school, and in opening up the possibility of greater interaction on a day to day basis between pupils, teachers, parents and the local neighbourhood.

But it is work in adult education, informal sessions with resident groups and organisations which develop around concrete local issues, where CDP can make a distinctive contribution. The programmes developed in Liverpool have influenced the approaches to adult education adopted by other projects.

Cutting across these major issue areas, several projects are closely involved with a range of services for particular groups in their local population.

(a) The elderly: Coventry, Cleator Moor and Southwark are all involved with research into the needs of the elderly, though their emphases differ. The first is more concerned with the loss of status among the elderly and the possible reinforcement of this by existing welfare services which seem to set in motion a self-fulfilling prophecy of decline. The research aims to form a basis for proposals for radical changes in the structure of services for the elderly, with an emphasis on enhancing rather than undermining their status. The second is attempting ways of involving the elderly in developing plans to meet their needs. Southwark's approach contains both elements - examining the effectiveness of traditional services, and initiating new services where there is a clear need, for example an employment bureau for over 60s, a visiting service using local residents, and supporting self-help initiatives.

(b) Young people: Many of the projects, as part of their neighbourhood work or education programme, have become involved in supporting the development of services for young people. Cleator Moor and Southwark, however, are committed more substantially to developing a comprehensive and more relevant pattern of provision for young people in their leisure time. Both have appointed a play organiser to study the needs, set up pilot projects and recommend modification of existing services with an emphasis on the use of locally recruited workers and locally based management and control structures.

(c) Race relations: Birmingham and Batley are both conducting research into the needs of their immigrant (mainly Asian) populations. Both are concerned not only with the special ethnic aspects but with the fairness and adequacy of existing policies. Birmingham has taken up questions on the administration of the 'Pakistan Act' which affects many of the project residents, particularly the processing of applications and the problems of access to information. As part of its adult education programme

Coventry has established a network of language groups for Asian men and women. These meet in homes, temples, schools and in one case on the factory floor, and aim to equip the immigrant with basic skills in communication.

Interwoven with these major single issues of employment, income-maintenance, housing and education and particular groups serviced by the project are a set of organisational arrangements and developments, ways of increasing the co-ordination of local services, by promoting neighbourhood work, of increasing local participation and control, and of making local authority structures more responsive to the needs of CDP areas. Many of these developments overlap, and there are as usual quite distinct approaches being tried out by different projects.

Neighbourhood work, information and advice: CDP is a neighbourhood based experiment and all projects have rooted their work in this way. A very similar range of activities characterises the projects:

(i)   shop front information centres, either shared with the project offices or as independent resident controlled centres;

(ii) work with community groups offering information, advice, technical expertise (e.g. legal, welfare and housing rights), grants and hardware (duplicating facilities, video t.v. equipment);

(iii) project news-sheets disseminating information and data, or community newspapers run by local residents with support from CDP.

Despite these common activities, there are underlying differences. A major distinction is the degree of selectivity over the issues taken up. One extreme would be to respond to any issue brought forward, and the other to define in advance the problems to be handled. Projects are spread out between these extremes, most trying to balance and relate their own views on key issues with resident priorities. In several projects the move has been to strengthen information centres with the 'hard' skills of lawyers or planners, or through these centres attach such skills to resident groups. The assumption here is that resident controlled information centres, backed by these skills may be a more potent instrument in crisis situations, like eviction, than similar workers inside the local authority or schemes to co-ordinate local services.

Service delivery: A major concern of the original CDP objectives was to promote greater integration of services at the local level. Though this has become less central an objective in several projects, in others it remains a major element. Liverpool has developed an extensive Community Services Centre which brings together several local authority services into a common building, and seeks to integrate their activities and policies for the area. The scheme is linked to a resident run information centre, and related to other changes in the local authority. Paisley is developing a similar centre.

Both these developments in multi-service centres, and information and advice centres in fields as diverse as housing, consumer affairs, career guidance and employment bureaux are increasingly being turned to as solutions to the problems of disadvantaged areas. Within CDP there is both a chance to assess the workings of these two approaches individually, and in a comparative way, where they appear to play overlapping roles.

Neighbourhood democracy: With its heavy investment in neighbourhood work, stimulating and sustaining resident organisations, it is inevitable that CDP should be drawn into experiment and debate over schemes such as neighbourhood councils. Several projects are moving ahead to formalise the federation of resident groups that have grown up around the project, into embryo community councils. Others like Coventry have found that umbrella organisations of this kind are more likely to succeed as providers of general services (secretarial, banking, administration of grants, salaries to staff) than as a representative forum or as a campaigning body on behalf of the neighbourhood. Again CDP should be in a position to compare these different approaches.

Local authority: Change at the local level, neighbourhood work, participation and local control have to be seen in relation to the role of the local authority. CDP projects are in a position, if they choose, to work at both the local community, and the local authority level. But over and above the way particular services operate, is the role of the local authority in distributing goods and services within the area, the way it resolves policy and conflicts of interest and how it is geared to variations in local need. Liverpool is examining the framework of managerial processes within local authorities and in particular the trend towards more centralised and 'rationalised' planning, the corporate management structure and its responsiveness to pressures for participation. Paisley is exploring where power and influence lie in local political decision making in Paisley. Coventry is investigating the wider structure of interests which have influenced the allocation of resources (particularly land and housing) locally.

A further major issue which a number of projects have been exploring concerns the finance which is available to local authorities tackling disadvantage. Local authorities with CDP areas are increasingly constrained by the problems of decreasing resources with which to provide services where there is growing demand.

Though these wider questions may seem some distance from pilot community development projects, they are clearly basic to the local authorities' ability to respond substantially to the problem of CDP areas. Projects plan to examine in more detail suggested variations in the Rate Support Grant formula, and ideas like that of 'Old Town Development Corporations' for their possible effects on small disadvantaged areas.

The Report concluded by listing topics where the national CDP programme could be expected to produce findings and suggestions for policy change. These included aspects of regional policy, the problems of industrial change and its effect on small run-down areas, housing policy - particularly the way improvement programmes operate at the local level - income maintenance and the problems of selective policies, the results of developing local information services and community organisation, education - particularly of an informal kind with adults - as well as the more general questions of local participation and control.

The proposition that the residents of small declining neighbourhoods are powerless to intervene in the processes that shape
their lives is central to the CDP prescription. It is possible
to distinguish two different approaches in the way that local
teams have faced this issue. The first has been to work at ways
in which the local area can be connected up to the agencies that
serve it. At an initial level groups are encouraged to form in
the neighbourhood and to make explicit their demands. Developments of this approach have led to the appointment of advocates
to work with such groups and to the setting up of local institutions, a community forum or neighbourhood council to create a
semi-permanent framework, drawing together the interests in the
neighbourhood and representing them to the authorities. The
second approach depends more on reinforcing, often selectively,
the existing structures of the neighbourhood - tenants' associations, local councillors, social clubs, and trades union organisations enabling the organisations themselves to develop procedures to deal with the stresses in the neighbourhood and to form
connections with similar groups, in their own ways.

In presenting this inter-project report on the CDP experiment,
and setting out some of the possible outcomes, we run the risk of
appearing to reduce the problems to separate elements, and miss-
ing the crucial inter-connections. The problems of the twelve
CDP areas are not reducible to problems of employment, housing,
income and education. They are not isolated pockets suffering an
unfortunate combination of circumstances. They are a central
part of the dynamics of the urban system and as such represent
those who have lost out in the competition for jobs, housing and
educational opportunity.

In the same way that problems are inter-related, programmes to
solve them have to be complex and far reaching. The problems in
these areas are not going to be solved by marginal rearrangements
to take account of their special minority needs. From its small
area base, CDP can map the points at which private and public
policies are having negative and unequal effects. We can also
aim to explore strategies for developing local awareness of these
points, and for raising them to greater public attention. But
the major response must come from central and local government
with substantial changes in policy and allocation of resources.

Part two

ESTABLISHING LOCAL PROJECTS

Chapter 5

EARLY STAGES IN NORTH TYNESIDE CDP

David Corkey

INTRODUCTION

The Tynemouth CDP (now North Tyneside) was established in October 1972 with the appointment of a project director. This followed discussions over a period of some fifteen months between council officials and the Home Office. The decision to put forward Tynemouth as a possible area for a project was taken after the Home Office central research team had examined the 1966 census data for a number of towns in the northern region. The selection of Tynemouth completed the choosing of twelve project areas. Since October 1972, the main activities of the Tynemouth project team, which was finally recruited by February 1973, has been familiarisation with the project area, the assimilation of vast quantities of information coming from the local authority and the Home Office, the development of a wider perspective of the issues and problems presented to it, and the implementation of some initial action strategy. During this twelve month period there has been no research team.

STAGES IN SETTING UP THE PROJECT

The initial events leading to the establishing of the project in Tynemouth were as follows:
1 An examination by the Home Office central research team of the 1966 census data on a borough wide and ward basis;
2 the selection by the Home Office of three wards within Tynemouth as a possible area;
3 a letter of exploration of the idea to Tynemouth council in July 1971;
4 two meetings between council and Home Office officials in September and October 1971 to clarify the implications for the council, and seek agreement on the precise location for the project;
5 a formal invitation from the Home Office to the council in October 1971;
6 a report being tabled at the main council committee meeting in November 1971, and formal acceptance of the invitation in

council;
7   the announcement of Tynemouth's acceptance in Parliament on 2
     December 1971.

The research carried out by the Home Office prior to the
Tynemouth project area being selected was based mainly on social indices such as the percentage of children in the area under 5; the
percentage over 65; the levels of provision of household amenities;
income levels; and health and employment statistics. This led to
the initial choice of three wards, Percy, Trinity and Linskill, in
the borough of Tynemouth, but at the subsequent meetings with
council officials, the Home Office were convinced by them that it
was the Meadow Well Estate in Percy ward, which was the real problem
area. Any extension into the Trinity and Linskill wards would bring
one into areas where the problems were already being solved by slum
clearance and re-development programmes. To back this viewpoint,
the case loads of the social services department for the Meadow Well
area were produced. An uneasy compromise was reached whereby it was
agreed that Linskill ward be left out, since much of it had been
cleared, and that the exact boundaries of the project area should
not be determined until the project director was in post. In fact,
in the council minutes of November 1971 it was made explicit that
the area should comprise Percy and Trinity wards, and a part of
Chirton ward into which the 'problem area' of Meadow Well extended.

In January 1972 arrangements to establish the project committee
proceeded. Some confusion clearly emerged as to the relationship of
the steering committee, and the management committee. The council
thought it advisable to have a local committee comprising representatives of the local community, voluntary organisations and the ward
councillors. The Home Office view was that a project committee,
consisting of the chairmen of the principal committees, plus a co-
opted Home Office representative, should be established in the usual
way, and that the question of appointing a steering committee, if it
was to be taken up at all, should be decided only after the project
director was in post, and had been able to assess for himself the
needs of the locality. Despite this, a suggestion, which was fortunately not taken up, came forward to the council meeting in
January 1972 to establish this artificial piece of community involvement. The sole resolution of that meeting was that 'the Mayor,
together with the Chairmen of the Education, Finance, Health, Housing and Social Services Committees be appointed Community Development Project Sub-Committee of this Committee (General Purposes) to
consider and make recommendations to this committee on all matters
affecting the Community Development Project Scheme in The Borough of
Tynemouth.'

The next stage was the locating of the project within the local
authority. The Home Office recommended the principal officer's
grade for the project director's salary, range two, but between
them, the establishment officer and the social services director
agreed that this was too high. The reason being that 'the closest
parallels are likely to be drawn with the Social Services Department' and that setting the project director's salary higher than
that of the assistant director of social services or the principal
social worker 'could cause problems with existing staff', consequently, the council rejected the Home Office recommendation and

advertised with the salary grading at PO range one.

These events, the research based on the social indices, the selection of a 'problem area' and the opinions of council officials, the attempt to slot the project alongside a social work team, indicated the degree to which the setting up of the Tynemouth project was based on social pathology perspectives on the part of both the local authority and the Home Office. Fortunately, the lessons taken from other projects such as Coventry, and Glamorgan, along with the experience and perspectives of the action and research personnel, have enabled the project to develop not as an additional social work agency, but as an experiment, concerned to examine critically the factors which have led to the existence of powerlessness and poverty in the project area, and the ways in which public and private resources have been applied to produce the pattern of inbalance in the distribution of goods and services in the North Tyneside area as a whole.

INITIAL ACTION STRATEGIES

The action team began their work in February 1973 with a survey of community attitudes in the project area, and the production of a brief description of the services being applied to it. From this, and from resultant work with tenants in the area, two preliminary action strategies emerged (see Chapter 8, Working with Tenants).

1. Housing action in the North and South Meadow Well

This has involved a housing condition and tenants' wishes survey in the South Meadow Well, and the formation of a residents' working party to work on the issues and to negotiate with the council. In the North Meadow Well, the issues are repairs, rates and rent levels, and support is currently being given to local residents in establishing a 'Watch Dog Committee'.

2. Information in both Percy and Trinity wards

This has involved setting up an information centre in Percy ward, and an information shop in Trinity. These facilities are taking up immediate needs for hard information on welfare benefits, are providing a base for advocacy on behalf of those needs, and have enabled the development of collective pressure where a general issue has arisen.

RESEARCH

In September 1972, Newcastle University was approached by the Home Office with a view to inviting it to undertake the Tynemouth project's research programme, in addition to that of Newcastle CDP. After a preliminary discussion between Home Office and university officials, it emerged that neither the university, nor the two project directors were keen on this proposal. Consequently, at the suggestion of one of the university staff, an approach was made to Newcastle Polytechnic. Negotiations with the polytechnic went on for some eight months, possibly because as the polytechnic was a local authority based institution, there were more potential conflicts of interest. The head of the department of behavioural studies wished, therefore, to have some detailed terms of reference, defining the relationships between Tynemouth council, the action and research teams, and the polytechnic. To minimise potential conflicts, the proposal of a steering committee of all interested parties was raised. There was some disagreement about this, and also over the legal status of the terms of reference finally agreed. When agreement was reached in May 1973 it was found that a suitable research director could not be in post until January 1974.

Fortunately, however, the remaining research appointments were made in the late autumn and continual consultation regarding long term action and research strategies then developed very quickly. These will broadly include the following:

1   The production of a social history of North Tyneside to explain why areas like the CDP area have developed;
2   the construction of a deprivation index for North Tyneside, based on census enumeration districts;
3   a study of land ownership, and planning and development intentions;
4   a study of industrial ownership;
5   continuing to found, service and inform local organisations set up to do something about the problems;
6   continuing to provide information on social services, welfare benefits, welfare rights, and by assisting local groups in their take up of these.

It is envisaged that these action and research strategies will dovetail together, the research informing the action team, and policy formulation generally, and the action developing locally based projects around issues which call for short-term and also more substantial research. The long-term objectives of these strategies will be to re-assert political consciousness at the local level; to increase the capacity of the deprived to insist on an equitable distribution in the provision of employment, housing, social, educational, and other benefits; and to influence the policy and performance of governmental and non-governmental agencies in their deployment of these.

Chapter 6

EXPECTATIONS OF A LOCAL PROJECT

Alex Mackay

The national project has been described as an experiment to find new
ways of dealing with the problems of multiple deprivation. One of
its most novel features has been the establishment of three member
action teams whose job it is to seek out new approaches to reduce
the adverse circumstances confronting the disadvantaged and to place
these teams as integral parts of local authorities. Each team
occupies a unique position in local government as it neither
administers a particular service nor does it service (in the way in
which a town clerk's department does) other departments and this we
believe requires to be examined.

The action teams have been set up as parts of authorities which
can be held accountable for the disbursement of public funds but it
may be that this will have some unintended impact upon the work
which the team undertakes. Indeed, it seems inevitable that the
action team will be guided to some extent by the body which employs
it, and, according to some, this could be the major factor influencing the outcome of any change programme (Zald, 1969). In the past
in local government studies (Mackenzie, 1951: 345-56), heavy emphasis has been placed upon the extent of central government control
and this has meant that there has been a tendency to understate the
part which local authorities play as policy making structures in
their own right. However, in the CDP context councillors and major
officials occupy positions from which they could greatly influence
the actions of the project team.

One should anticipate, therefore, that these people may wield
sanctions and supply rewards which might well place constraints upon
what the project wishes to do and set for it opportunities to effect
change. While it seems to have been intended that CDP teams should
have a degree of freedom from the usual local authority committee
controls this may not work out in practice and they could be treated
much the same as any other local authority department. At present,
in Paisley, the council has drawn exclusively from its own membership a project committee which will oversee the work of the project,
advise the director and have a major say in the way funds allocated
to the CDP can be spent.

In early correspondence with the local authority central government stressed that success depended upon obtaining a commitment to

the CDP from chief officials. The team cannot demand of right the
support and co-operation of other departments and must rely upon receiving this through the goodwill of chief officials or through
negotiation and bargaining. This provides scope for them to exert
some pull over the CDP and there would seem to be good grounds for
believing that this will be in favour of maintaining the present
situation or changing it to the advantage of the bureaucracies which
administer services. Substantial changes invariably create increased costs for organisations (March and Simon, 1958: 173) and
have a disruptive potential which conflicts with their tendency to
promote stability as an organisational goal. These, and other
factors (Merton, 1952) tend to develop an outlook in officialdom
which does not readily accommodate innovation, and resistance to
changes initiated by the CDP should be expected.

It was conceived initially that local project teams should
attempt as part of their remit to effect changes in the provision of
services where these do not appear to be effective in reducing deprivation. As many of the services in the Paisley project area are
provided by the local authority it is very likely that the action
team will concentrate its attention upon the departments of the
authority which employs the project team. In terms of its osten-
sible purposes, therefore, it would seem reasonable to regard the
action team as a form of local political interest group acting with,
and for, a particular community, albeit that it operates within the
local government body itself. All interest groups face the problem
of securing access to decision makers and it could be that this en-
capsulation of the team in a local authority framework offers a good
opportunity for a low status community to gain effective access
(Truman, 1965: 264) to key figures in the Paisley Burgh.

As part of the process evaluation of the Paisley project we shall
be monitoring how the action team performs in trying to obtain results from local authority decision making favourable to the needs
of the Ferguslie Park community. Very often research on pressure
politics attempts to explain the actions of supposedly pressured
persons by concentrating on the groups themselves and not the people
who are the focus of attention. Indeed there is little said about
how or why the formal decision maker is influenced by the critical
characteristics of interest groups (Wahlke, Buchanan, Evlau and
Ferguson, 1960). By taking account of the pre-dispositions (Zisk,
Evlau and Prewitt, 1965: 618-46) which councillors and major
officials have about the CDP as partial determinants of their reaction towards it we hope to add to the explanatory (Weiss and Rein,
1969: 133-42) dimension of the evaluation.

For these reasons the research team determined to find out the
climate of thinking about the CDP among actors whom previous study
indicated are significant figures in the local authority structure.
Background information about the project has been supplied to councillors and chief officials by the Scottish Office which is responsible for the Scottish contribution to the national project. In
addition most had attended a meeting at which the aims of the project and means of achieving these had been explained. This prepara-
tory work conducted by central government was intended to secure the
Burgh's participation and to smooth the way for the introduction of
the action team into the authority. From informal but focused

interviews we tried to find out what these people had come to understand as the purposes of the project and how it would set about
trying to attain these ends. This would, in part, provide them with
a framework of expectations relating to CDP within which they would
determine their reactions to specific initiatives. However, we did
not think that prior to the possible injection of the CDP these
people had no views about the 'needs' and 'problems' which existed
in Ferguslie Park and we anticipated that their responses to the CDP
would be affected by these perceptions. At the time the interviews
were carried out no information had been provided to the residents
of Ferguslie Park about the intention to locate the project there
nor was the impending establishment of the project known to many
outside the top officials and councillors in the Burgh.

When the selected persons were interviewed we concentrated first
of all upon drawing out their impressions of pressing needs in the
area while deliberately refraining from specifying with whose problems we were concerned. This allowed respondents to set their own
priorities. The answers given can be divided into two categories;
first those which cover substantive problems related to the services
provided by the local authority and the other to personal deficiencies of those in the community who are most disadvantaged. With the
exception of the director of social work, chief officials perceived
as the most pressing need, situations which either adversely affected the working of their departments or, when dealt with, would improve the status of respective departments in the bureaucracy.

In the past few years there has been a steady exodus of tenants
from the housing estate which has resulted in the build up of a substantial number of empty houses which cannot be relet to suitable
tenants. This constitutes a major administrative problem for senior
housing department officials. According to them one of the most important jobs which the action team could perform would be to find
ways of encouraging residents to remain there and not, as at present, seek to obtain transfers to other council housing estates in
the Burgh. Beyond this it was hoped that the CDP could become involved in improving the anti-social behaviour of some tenants which
resulted in the area having a bad reputation. This coupled with up-
grading of the physical environment would make the estate a more
attractive place to live in and, hopefully, the letting of houses
would become as routine a matter as it is with other council houses
in the Burgh.

Those with responsibility for the maintenance of council houses
and the provision of parks and recreation areas shared the common
view that the greatest need was to lower the density of the housing
(which in effect means that empty blocks of houses should be demolished) and then to lay out the spaces provided as play or open
grass areas. It would be less expensive to remove empty houses than
to maintain empty and intact houses as they are constantly being
broken into and several set on fire. An extensive demolition programme would require movement of tenants in partially empty blocks;
CDP could be instrumental in facilitating the necessary removals.

There is a considerable amount of refuse and litter in back
yards, gardens and in the streets and those in charge of cleansing
services considered that residents should be encouraged to be more
careful with the disposal of rubbish. CDP could help to foster a

community spirit in the area and when residents began to take a pride in their home environment the cleanliness of the scheme would improve and the cleansing services would become more effective.

One must be hesitant about stressing the possible significance of such responses for the work which the CDP might undertake. Yet, at first sight one could hypothesise that the support or resistance shown in any one instance will depend on officials' views of the potential advantages, disadvantages or non-effect which there would be for the way in which their departments operate. The priority given to organisational interests provides striking confirmation of the view that 'a problem only exists for an organisation when it perceives some blockage of purposeful activity' (Gross, 1964: 558).

In the same category councillors were primarily concerned with the spiralling number of empty houses which would be regarded as a bad reflection on the housing policies which the council had pursued. As the same party has been in control of the council for many years (with a short interruption in the mid-1960s) and many of the present councillors have served on the council for some time this problem is a delicate political issue. Unless a halt is called to the outward movement, the patently unpalatable result could be the gradual demolition of substantial parts of the estate. The decision to participate in CDP and to concentrate its activities on Ferguslie Park can be seen as part of a rehabilitation programme which might stem the outflow. Other aspects of this are the building of a community centre and a substantial play area both of which might act as inducements to families to remain there. With the drift of tenants from Ferguslie Park to other estates an unfavourable reaction has emerged among tenants elsewhere and this has been communicated to local councillors representing these areas. Despite the existence of transfer rules which should ensure that only the tenants with the best housekeeping records are transferred there is some feeling that potentially disruptive tenants are being introduced into better areas.

According to the interviewees many families (this usually means the women in the households) failed to manage their income. This mismanagement resulted in families running into debts, especially rent arrears, and they were unable, because of extravagance, to provide basic family requirements. Many young people in the estate seemed to engage in senseless acts of destruction and this indicated to some extent at least, a lack of a proper upbringing. There is no doubt that unemployment among the male population is a serious problem and it was mentioned often but in many instances it was stated that this is not a good indicator of deprivation as quite a few in this situation remained so of their own volition. It was felt that there is a greater degree of social disharmony in this estate than in any other part of the town as evinced by the frequency and nature of disputes between neighbours and within families. This contributed significantly to the bad reputation which the estate had in the Burgh. Drunkenness and criminal activity generally are thought to be more prevalent here than elsewhere and also constitute significant social problems.

To overcome these problems what appears to be needed is to change the behaviour of some of the residents. The CDP should be an agency which, along with the social work department, should try to educate

the adult population generally to manage their affairs adequately
and become more self-reliant. An action priority should be to show
the women how to budget and to encourage them to develop the habits
of wise expenditure rather than waste their income. There was considerable support for the provision of either play groups or more
nursery school places as children from the area required an early
educational start. Apart from this work it was anticipated that the
action team should engage in setting up clubs, particularly for the
youth of the area as it was felt generally that at present there
were few facilities for the young. The lack of these leave the
youth to wander the streets aimlessly and they turn their energies
to destructive behaviour rather than engaging in sport and other
acceptable forms of recreation. Adults should also join in group
activities (the provision of a community centre would help) and
through greater interaction community spirit would develop. The results should be a reduction in neighbourhood disputes and in the
estate's unruly image.

One of the basic assumptions guiding the setting up of the
national project has been that people living in deprived communities
often require help to be aware of their entitlement to benefits and
services. They need assistance to negotiate the proper channels to
these services. Part of the failure to alleviate, if not remove,
deprivation is due to an inadequacy of communication from services
to clients. There was very little comment about this possible
aspect of the CDP's work from the officials although specific
groups, particularly the elderly, were cited as those to whom the
action team could direct its attention. On the other hand, it was
felt that there are many recipients of services who know the welfare
system very well and that, in consequence, it would be wasteful to
spend time providing information for them. On the whole, there was
little agreement with the assumption and there was some mention of
an over provision of social services. To admit the correctness of
the assumption could be taken to imply that the service providers
themselves did not take sufficient steps to keep the people informed
and were failing to discharge their responsibilities.

Councillors were generally much more favourably disposed to
accept the premise as being correct and produced several suggestions
as to how this could be implemented. The most popular was the introduction of a local newspaper, part of which could be used exclusively for this purpose. From their perspective this action
holds no political threat as there is no hint of policy failure. To
support efforts to maximise the uptake of benefits and use of services when entitlement is recognised would demonstrate the council's
desire to improve the situation of those living in a deprived community. The marked divergence of view between the councillors and
officials on this subject is, I think, due to the different positions which they occupy and the possible impact which adopting this
would have on the roles they perform.

The CDP also envisages that services might be less effective in
tackling deprivation because of sparse feedback from the population
it is intended to serve. The project therefore incorporates the
objective of increasing the community's capacity to assess its needs
and to articulate these to the appropriate formal decision makers.
With such improved communication it would be less likely that the

bureaucratic services would get out of phase with the requirements of the population.

Councillors and, to a much lesser extent, officials anticipate that CDP will operate as a communication link with the grass roots. This function seemed to be an important one to councillors as it could supply them with data about the situation on the ground independently of that provided by the departments themselves. Such knowledge could counterbalance that given by officials and so strengthen their position when dealing with bureaucrats. While the project team will be assured of having access to the formal decision makers on the council and can ensure that the needs of the community are presented to those in authority, there is no conception that the decision making process should be opened up to include the community directly. Except for two of their number, councillors did not favour CDP becoming involved with the formation of tenants' groups. Most saw such a development as a possible usurpation of their roles as representatives. However, this reluctance to encourage the CDP to engage in the setting up of local political groups has its origins in the existence in the recent past of a local tenants' association in the area which ousted three Labour councillors and replaced them with three of its members. It would seem that any such groups which do emerge will be unlikely to achieve readily the necessary legitimacy (Eckstein and Apter, 1963) in the eyes of councillors to gain participation in decision making.

While the elected members wish to see an increase in the flow of information about the needs from the community they expect this to be conducted in a manner which enhances their positions but does not introduce further political pressures from the community. Similarly, officials would seem to welcome feedback which is channelled through the organisation and seemed to think that this was how it would operate.

To provide the most effective service cover to those in need the CDP has stressed the desirability of bringing services more into touch with one another to plug gaps in welfare provision and eradicate duplication of services, both of which arose because services kept themselves distinct and communicated very little to one another. There was considerable support for this proposal from most chief officials who expressed a ready willingness to co-operate. Indeed it was hoped that, under the CDP guidance, regular meetings of chief officials could be arranged at which policy matters affecting more than one department could be dealt with to provide a more comprehensive service. To cover the range of services in which the CDP is interested would require the inclusion of central government and voluntary bodies but most officials thought only in terms of local authority services. From their replies it was apparent that officials who favoured more co-operation among themselves did so as a possible, although not highly rated, means of redressing the unequal distribution of authority in the bureaucracy. At present there are no such meetings and some officials regard this situation as favouring the pre-eminent position of one official with whom most had to negotiate and bargain for resources. This official saw no necessity for joint meetings as things went quite smoothly at present.

Councillors were less concerned with the need to increase co-

operation but there were instances in which this was very much
wanted. Along with housing department officials several councillors
thought that the Ministry of Social Security is failing to co-
operate with the local authority by refusing to make direct payment
of rent to the Housing Department from the benefits payable to
social security claimants. It is believed that because of this the
council has to initiate eviction action in many more cases than
would otherwise be necessary and that the outstanding amount of rent
arrears could be reduced significantly if the procedure they advocated was adopted.

The extent to which those interviewed endorsed the need for more
co-operation depended upon the benefits which they could see accruing to particular departments or to the authority as a whole and was
not directly concerned with improving the services supporting the
disadvantaged.

CONCLUSIONS

At this stage of the project's existence it would obviously be
premature to predict the course which Paisley CDP will take. However, at the outset there does appear to be a signal difference between the expectations held by councillors and chief officials of
the benefits which will emerge from participation in CDP and how it
should operate and the approach to tackling the problems of multiple
deprivation indicated in the background literature made available to
those involved in local CDPs.

The latter seems to approximate to a locality development model
(Cox, Rothman and Erlich, 1970) of purposive community change whereas the former is akin to a social planning orientation. Basically
locality development concentrates upon the promotion of self-help
schemes and the keynote of the strategy pursued is the involvement
of a broad section of the community into the determining and solving
of their own problems. The improvement of communication links
within the community and with the service agencies is a characteris-
tic tactic designed to achieve consensus among the interested
parties. This is anticipated as differences are thought to be re-
solvable through goodwill and negotiations as all are seeking the
same ends. The process through which change occurs is just as important in this model as the results obtained.

The focus in social planning is on the substantive social problems which those in authority perceive to exist. Members of the
community are seen as consumers only and it is probably assumed that
they lack the expertise to make worthwhile recommendations which
could improve their situations materially. Stress is placed upon
attaining particular goals and the best way of doing this is to acquire as much relevant information as possible and then make a
rational decision among possible options based on this data in the
established authority structures. Each approach indicates a different role for the community workers and represents divergent perspectives and attitudes towards the local power structure.

In practice strategies tend to be mixed and in the CDP, it is
probable that each of the twelve local projects will follow separate
courses. We would contend that this is in part due to the nature of

the many different problems which exist in the twelve areas and in part to the balance of forces at play in the various settings in which projects operate. On the basis of our initial work we would suggest that placing the CDP teams within local government bodies may, unless counteracted by effective pressures from the community, deflect the project from its original intention of drawing in the community to participate more directly in decision making, and instead mould it to the usual pattern of bureaucratic working.

Chapter 7

THE ACTION-RESEARCH RELATIONSHIP

Ray Lees

Once a project area has been selected, the procedure is for an action team to be appointed to the local authority's staff and a complementary research team formed from within a university or poly-technic. A fundamental feature of the CDP, therefore, is the effort to combine action, research and evaluation. It is assumed that an experimental approach, using social science methods of inquiry and evaluation as a built-in support for social action, constitutes a useful addition to more traditional ways of tackling problems of social welfare. Thus the CDP anticipates an intimate and productive working relationship between administrators, field-workers, research-oriented social scientists and local residents. However, it is not self-evident that this relationship can be easily achieved. It is the purpose of this chapter to suggest some of the possible difficulties for a research team working in such a complex situation. To focus on problems is not to denigrate the value of community development as an experimental project. The aim is to promote constructive discussion about the role of research in this area of social policy. This emphasis may also make a modest con-tribution to the wider debate on what should be the relationship be-tween social science and the formulation of public policy (Cherns, Sinclair and Jenkins, 1972).

The research component of each CDP has two main functions. The research group is intended to assist the action team in the assess-ment of the locality's needs and of how they may best be met. In addition it is concerned with the continuous monitoring and final evaluation of the project's work and recommendations, for feeding back to the local authority itself and to other local and central interests. This approach constitutes a new initiative in government policy in this country, but it bears close resemblance to many of the programmes sponsored by the United States Federal Government during the 1960s. The American experience has spawned a copious literature on approaches to the evaluation of action-research pro-jects (Homstein and Bunker, 1971; Zurcher and Bonjean, 1970) but little can be claimed in terms of hard transferrable knowledge. As one authority put it, 'despite the billions of dollars we have spent in such areas as manpower training, compensatory education, and welfare . . . we in fact know relatively little about the

effectiveness of many of the social action programmes that the
Government has initiated' (Evans, 1969).

If the American programmes can tell us little about how to ensure
successfully the community development process, certainly the
numerous writings are a useful starting point to consider the difficulties inherent in action-research in this field. It can be
argued that the American social, political and economic context is
so different from Britain that there is little to be gained from
this approach. American insights will, therefore, be discussed here
in relation to experience in the first phase of the local CDP based
in the West Riding of Yorkshire. The project is still at its early
stages, but a concerted effort has been made to examine and establish a relationship between the action and research teams. The experience may not be typical of other localities, but some of the
difficulties do seem to mirror the problems identified in American
action-research literature.

FORMULATING POLICY

One recurring theme that can be readily distinguished in these
writings is concerned with the weakness of policy recommendations
apparently based on social science. According to Moynihan (1969)
for example, social science failed in the policy-making surrounding
the American 'War on Poverty'. The failure occurred on two levels:
first, the social scientists advocated to the policy-makers a viewpoint for which the empirical evidence was 'fragmented, contradictory, incomplete'. Second, social scientists failed to take account
of the political implications of the policies they were advocating.
Leaving aside the controversy over whether these two failures did in
fact occur, Moynihan does raise the important question of what
should be the role of social science in the formulation of social
policy. His answer is that social scientists should be concerned
'not in the formulation of social policy, but in the measurement of
its results'.

According to the Home Office outline for the CDP, research
workers are expected at local level to contribute to the policy
making process. For example, during the first six months of the
West Riding project the action and research teams worked together to
produce a 'community profile', a description of the town intended to
help action teams determine their programme as well as to assist research teams in assessing its impact. One concern was to construct
relevant social indicators from existing sources of demographic,
economic and social data. A second was to gain an impression of the
felt needs of people in selected neighbourhoods. A third was to
look at decision-making within the town with particular reference to
local government, political parties and voluntary associations. For
the social scientist each of these endeavours involves problems of
selection, method and interpretation. Even after lengthy work, results are likely to be tentative and open to criticism. Six months'
research into an area, though placed in the wider context of such
specialist knowledge as already exists, cannot enable a social
scientist to say with certainty which of alternative strategies open
to community workers would be necessarily desirable or successful.

Moynihan's caution does seem to be appropriate.

This does not mean that the research worker has no role to play in the policy-making process for the project. One important task is to influence the formulation of the project's programme in such a way that it can be described and evaluated as rigorously as possible. Ideally, such an assessment would be based upon carefully designed and controlled research. Objectives would be stated so that an initiative could occur within the framework of the classic model of experimental design, in which before-after measures are made on a representative sample within the target area and on a comparable control sample of non-participants, preferably both randomly assigned. In looking at innovations occurring in a natural setting, it is always difficult to control factors in this way. This complexity of social behaviour is a problem facing all social scientists who try to study and explain processes of social change. American experience suggests that there are additional hazards facing the social scientist working within action-research projects in social policy - obstacles that occur because of the differing orientations of researchers, action workers and administrators (Caro, 1969).

For example, research requirements demand explicit statements of objectives and strategies, whereas action workers tend to find these difficult or even undesirable to commit themselves to. This is not only because the thinking of activists is not naturally in tune with matters of criteria, measures, control groups and the like. It is also because the researcher's commitment to rigorous procedures may run counter to the practitioner's need for flexibility and intuition in dealing with practical situations. A social action team is likely in their day-to-day work to be drawn into activities without explicit definitions of the aims they have in view. Even where they have a stated objective, the interaction of interests within a community and changing external circumstances may make modification necessary. This problem can be made more difficult by the professional beliefs of community workers. An influential view in this field claims that the community worker should not seek to persuade people to accept ideas of his own, but should aim at stimulating them to clarify and define their own needs for themselves and then to decide and plan what they themselves can do to improve their own situation. Two advantages are claimed for this 'non-directive' approach: first, people are much more likely to act on what they have freely decided to do than on what an agency has tried to persuade them to do; and second, through their participation in the process of thinking, deciding and planning they will incidently acquire more confidence and competence as people (Batten, 1967).

In deciding policy initiatives for the West Riding CDP, action workers have expressed considerable sympathy for this non-directive approach. There has been, therefore, some reluctance to lay down goals for the self-help groups that might emerge during the life of the project. The aim of promoting participation is in itself seen as a desirable goal and particular needs are seen as emerging as part of this process. The research problem in this situation is to define participation and to specify the variables relating to it. Participation will vary, for example, in its extensiveness, intensity, duration and purpose. There are also inherent difficulties

such as the tendency of groups to use their own means of social control, the willingness of people to participate, the role of professional competence and the relation between community groups and our
existing form of representative government. Such activities are not
readily susceptible to quantitative measures, hard data before-after
studies, or comparison with control groups, but this does not mean
they cannot be described, analysed and assessed by the social scientist. Political science already grapples with these kinds of
methodological problem. A community development programme will not
be tidy in its objectives or strategies. An important function of
research, therefore, must be to help understanding of why objectives
change and how community groups emerge, and to pinpoint some of the
advantages and limitations of the community development approach.

Not all initiatives need be open-ended in this way. Where the
research team participates in the formulation of objectives, it may
be possible to make part of a project's programme fit with a pre-
conceived research design. One aim of the West Riding project, for
example, is to discover how far a locally based campaign of education and publicity can increase the uptake of a wide range of selective welfare benefits. The action programme will include efforts to
improve the information giving of existing agencies by working to
increase the skills and knowledge of relevant staff and to mount an
advice and information campaign to improve public awareness of
available social benefits. From the research point of view this
initiative is compatible with a straightforward statistical analysis
of the take-up of the target benefits before, during and after the
campaign. A control can be introduced by doing an analysis for a
similar town that is not experiencing the programme. As well as
description and analysis of the methods used to encourage take-up
benefits, it should, therefore, be possible to measure part of the
effect of the campaign with quantitative data (see Chapter 11).

EVALUATING PROGRAMMES

However, a further obstacle to evaluative research identified in
American literature is the conflicting self-interest between the
role of project administration and that of objective evaluation.
The social scientist can find stimulation and professional advancement in describing the failure of initiatives in social policy, but
to action workers an admission of failure may be taken as disclosing
personal inadequacy. In this situation it does not take the perceptive project director long to become wary of hard, clear cut,
empirical investigations, for they are a two-edged sword - useful
when justifying the need for the project or when proving its success, but an embarrassment if disclosing failure. The less risky
course is to go for softer information that is more subject to
interpretation. The project leader is committed to his professional
work and wants information that will justify additional funds to
expand operations. The researcher, on the other hand, should be
concerned to examine the validity of these professional assumptions,
in relation to alternative approaches that could be initiated in
meeting social needs. This research neutrality poses a problem with
practitioners, who typically consider strong value commitment to

their projects important. The difficulty is likely to be exacerbated if the researcher approaches evaluation from the perspective
of a single academic discipline. Unless he has had work experience
in a similar kind of effort, he is unlikely to have much compre-
hension of or to develop sympathy for the practitioner's position.
In the same sense, it may be difficult for action workers with
limited academic experience in the social sciences to understand the
role of research.

In the West Riding CDP an effort has been made to prepare for and
thus reduce the effect of these inherent conflicts by discussion between research and action teams. Such exchanges have been helped by
a shared value commitment to the need for improving social policy
initiatives on behalf of underprivileged groups and a shared sympathy for the community development approach. Given this situation,
it would be easy for the research component to become subordinate to
the requirements of social action strategies. Research could become
totally concerned with looking at needs within the locality and with
contributing to decision-making on policy initiatives. The project
would then be conceived not so much as an experimental venture where
efforts were being made to evaluate alternative ways of meeting
needs, but rather as a concerted effort to demonstrate the value of
particular initiatives. The danger of this integrated approach is
that research could give way to advocacy, whereas in order to
achieve effective social policies nothing is more important than to
know whether or not community initiatives actually work. From this
point of view, it is important for action workers themselves to know
how their programmes are going so that known consequences can lead
to modification. Research should provide this feedback. To do this
effectively, the researcher must walk a tightrope between an
affiliation with the action project and the freedom to devise means
for evaluating their impact. If the exploratory nature of community
initiatives is acknowledged, evaluative research can in this way
contribute to the community development process and help to refine
community work skills.

This does seem to be one way to build a productive action-
research relationship within a local community development project,
but tensions and pressures are increased by the complex administrative structure in which a team has to operate. In the West Riding
CDP, for example, the project director and action workers are employed by the county council with finance largely provided by the
Home Office as part of a national experiment, whilst much of their
everyday work is directly concerned with the local borough council.
Thus the project team finds itself interacting with and partly responsible to public authorities at three distinct levels. The research workers become part of this process whilst remaining members
of a university department. As well as these formal links, the project is expected to work with individuals and groups within the
locality in order to help them gain more effective services and to
try to mobilise untapped resources of self-help and mutual aid. It
is unlikely that the varied people connected with the project in
this way will share the same assumptions and expectations about its
purpose. Thus problems about the role of research cannot be
entirely resolved simply within the context of the project staff.

It is an assumption of the CDP approach that social services can

be improved by community initiatives. This gives a brief for research to discover present inadequacies and for action to promote
participation in bringing about social improvement. Yet it is not
readily apparent that administrators of present services or elected
representatives will welcome these activities in all spheres. The
results of a questionnaire to senior officials in the West Riding,
relating to their expectations of the CDP, suggested that most
officials saw the project as bringing additional resources to help
solve already perceived social problems, but not to act as a catalyst to promote critical awareness of existing services. On the
other hand, the neighbourhood studies conducted by the project show
not only that local residents do have views on issues such as housing maintenance, public transport, shopping, play provision and the
environment, but also that they tend to be critical of and have
little faith in the ability of 'the authorities' to remedy these
problems. If one result of community work strategies is to stimulate people collectively to express these views and to work for improvements, then the scene is being set for the emergence of
pressure groups to promote change rather than self-help groups concerned only with complementing existing provision. Research plays
an important role in this critical appraisal of past and present
policies and its findings, whatever they are, will seldom be welcomed by all sides.

From this discussion it should now be clear that the lot of the
research worker in a CDP is likely to be a harassed and controversial one. Within the project he is attempting to evaluate as well
as contribute to an ongoing process over which he has little real
control. More widely, he is likely to expose to criticism the
activities of established administrators and other decision-makers,
at the same time as trying to improve the effectiveness of their
decision-making by personal contact. He is working with local residents as well as officials, though their views and wishes may be
in conflict. He is expected to feed back information quickly, yet
is an academic who is trying to produce results that can withstand
the methodological criticisms of his professional colleagues. Given
these difficulties and contradictions, why should social scientists
concern themselves with this kind of government sponsored action-
research? Some probably feel that they should not, for certainly
there has been difficulty attracting senior staff to this work.
Nevertheless, it does offer the opportunity both to study and to influence political and administrative process.

THE DECISION-MAKING PROCESS

Nowhere is this challenge more important than in the field of social
policy. An implicit assumption of the work done in university departments of social administration is that research findings will
help towards social improvement. Much notable work, like the
various poverty studies, is clearly geared to this end. Yet there
is no certain link between producing evidence of need and ensuring
effective political or administrative action to remedy a situation.
One of the critical tasks in social policy, therefore, remains the
effective communication of research findings to the policy-maker and

the discovery of ways and means to assure their absorption into
public decision-making. This does not mean that social scientists
should 'dictate' to policy-makers particular lines of action, but
rather that they should be sensitive to decision-making processes
in their efforts to influence policy formulation. The researcher
within a CDP has the possibility of developing this awareness. By
being a participant observer, he can gain a special perspective on
some of the key factors and limitations that control decision-
making. Being on the inside allows him a close if limited view of
the crucial power relations and circumstantial contexts that affect
critical decisions.

However, there are also certain obligations incumbent on the
social scientist who aspires to observe and influence decision-
making in this way. He must deal with questions that are relevant
to policy; he must produce findings that reach the policy-maker in
time; and he must set forth his findings in an easily understood
manner. On the other hand, it is necessary for the administrator
and the elected representatives to understand and sympathise with
the role of the social scientist. This may be particularly difficult for the cautious official to comprehend when it comes to
studying and writing about the decision-making process. Administrative acceptance of the utility of research may not include this perspective though it clearly is an important one for assessing CDPs.
As Marris and Rein (1967) concluded in the American context,

The whole process - the false starts, frustrations, adaptations,
the successive recasting of intentions, the detours and conflicts - needs to be comprehended. Only then can we understand
what has been achieved, and learn from experience. Research in
this sense is contemporary history. Even though no one ever
again will make exactly the same journey, to follow the adven-
tures of the Projects offers a general guide to the dangers and
discoveries of their field of action. From such a guide, anyone
may evaluate the experience according to his purpose.

Seen in this light, research in the Home Office CDP offers the
opportunity to build a collection of 'public administration cases'
analogous to the 'business cases' used in teaching at Harvard and
other business schools. This perspective would attempt to show how
the existence of a problem comes to be recognised and how individuals and groups decide what is to be done. It would fit very well
with the need to test the assumption that there should be more
citizen involvement, even on technical issues, before policies become fixed. If one aspiration is to improve the policy-making process, it is important to have on record how decisions are made: how
much information is necessary, who influences the outcome the most,
how disagreements are resolved, what procedures are used and in particular what is the effect of community initiatives on the way
choices are made. The interest should not be to expose to public
criticism particular individuals, but rather to identify the many
constraints which bear upon, and influence, political and administrative decision-making. This kind of case study material would
provide a useful addition to any specific policy recommendations
that might evolve from the CDP.

IN CONCLUSION

This chapter has discussed some of the constraints that are operating and opportunities available to research in the CDP context.
From the research point of view, perhaps what is most needed is a
judicious combination of the general case-history approach with
limited initiatives tied to experimental designs. What certainly
must be accommodated and should be openly acknowledged are the pressures generated by the political and administrative environment in
which this work occurs. It is simply not the case that elected representatives, administrators, project leaders, field-workers, local
residents and research-oriented social scientists will necessarily
see things in the same way. The kind of tension and difficulty considered here is not unique to the CDP. As research is increasingly
built into local administration, as is now happening in local
authority Social Services Departments, similar conflicts are likely
to emerge. The position of 'insider' should bring research opportunities - to identify unmet needs, to influence policy-making, to
evaluate policies and to describe the decision-making process.
Whether any of these can be taken will depend greatly on the role
that the research worker is able to establish and on his understanding of complex relationships.

Part three

ACTION IN THE LOCAL AREAS

Chapter 8

WORKING WITH TENANTS: TWO CASE STUDIES

John Foster

INTRODUCTION

1. Description of the area

Much of the Tynemouth CDP area comprises a large municipal housing estate, built in the inter-war period. These two case studies are an account of work carried out in two parts of this estate during 1973. This estate, known locally as the 'Ridges Estate', was planned and built between 1931 and 1939, and consists of almost 2,000 dwellings which have the unusual feature, although common in North Tyneside, of being designed not as self-contained houses but as flats. What appears to be a pair of 'semis' is in fact a block of four flats. This means that there is a much denser population than is apparent, with resulting overcrowding of shared paths and other common facilities.

The estate was built as a result of the Housing Act, 1930, for the provision of houses for the working class affected by slum clearance. People were moved from the river-side and inner-town area of North Shields, three-quarters of a mile away, to the new estate. At that time it was obviously a popular move; it could hardly fail to be when compared to the riverside slums known as 'the caves' from which people had moved. A local reporter who visited the estate when the first tenants moved in was full of praise for the new tenants. Talking to one of the tenants about the condition of her new home he reported '. . . what women would call "a picture"', on asking her where she had come from, he commented 'I could hardly credit my hearing when she mentioned one of the stair-ways which twist down the bankside into Clive Street. It is liter-ally a well of gloom and dirt' ('Shields News', 1934). But today, the estate reflects Kirby's point 'Although it was intended that most inter-war council dwellings should provide socially adequate accommodation for at least sixty years, it can be seen that they afford a standard of accommodation which is below that now official-ly deemed acceptable' (Kirby, 1971).

From the beginning, and increasingly since the early 1960s, the estate became more and more identified as a 'problem estate'. Sinfield found that 'for the rest of the people living in the

Borough, "the Ridges" symbolised a tough, dirty and disreputable world. Everyone knew what was meant by "of course they live in the Ridges"' (Sinfield, 1967). Part of this stigmatisation is a consequence of the type of area from which the original tenants were drawn. Even before the whole of the estate was completed there were protests from people at having their furniture de-infested by the council before they could move into their new homes. At the time the local press reported, 'There is considerable speculation as to how Tynemouth Corporation is going to deal with the knotty problems surrounding the transference of families from the slum clearance of North Shields to the re-housing estates. In particular, the problem of preventing the perhaps unwitting introduction of vermin to the new property has exercised the minds of the authorities, who realise that the matter is a delicate one' ('Shields News', 1933).

More recently the stigmatisation of the estate has been associated with its physical deterioration and neglected appearance; particular parts of the estate are used as a dumping ground for 'problem families'. Sinfield (1967), when describing the estate remarked that,

these houses were often in poor condition, with cracked and twisted metal windows that would not close properly. The responsibility of the bad state of the houses was disputed, the Council blaming the tenants and the tenants blaming the Council. It was widely believed that the housing department dumped different types of families in different areas - large families in this street, bad housekeepers and 'coloureds' in that, and pensioners here. This often seemed to be true, though whether by accident or design was not established.

Our experience to date concerning the concentration of 'problem families', especially in parts of the South Ridges would support Byrne's contention: 'residence in these areas is historically a consequence of a combination of social grading procedures and assessment of rent-paying capacity coupled with actual rental record, with a probable emphasis on the former' (Byrne, 1973).

2. Project strategy

The Tynemouth project developed an on-going strategy of work with groups of council tenants around the housing issue, by examining the condition of inter-war council housing stock in two areas of the project. We did this by an appraisal of the overall housing conditions and level of amenities in such stock on the estates and of the operation and processes of improvement schemes. This included an investigation into the construction by the local authority housing department through housing allocation policies of public housing ghettos.

Soon after the arrival of the project in North Shields, it became clear that the housing situation was, and still is, a major issue of concern for a large number of people living in the project area. The area was undergoing slum clearance, a council housing modernisation scheme and a general improvement area programme. A community attitudes survey carried out by the project into the reaction of tenants towards the provision of local services, the council's plans for the area and into the tenants' own preferences, indicated clear feelings of powerlessness and a lack of knowledge and information concerning the intentions of policy-making agencies. The project offices were from their opening used as an information centre. This meant we were able to establish contact with an increasing number of local people. We found that the most effective way of identifying the main issues in the area, was to talk to as many people as possible living there. It was in the shops, launderettes, clubs and pubs that issues were raised and information and ideas shared. These are the political meetings and exchanges that take place every day in working class areas.

CASE STUDY NO. 1: THE NORTH RIDGES

The project came on to the scene at a time when a large part of the Ridges Estate was undergoing an extensive programme of council modernisation. A change of name from the Ridges Estate to the Meadow-Well Estate took place in 1972 when the council decided that the modernisation programme was an opportunity to help change the image of the estate and give it a 'second chance'. Having taken the decision there was no stopping them, and they changed street names as well.

From an initial stock of 1,315 dwellings there would be on completion of the scheme, 1,087 dwellings, half of which would be self-contained houses. The programme began in March 1972, and the intention of the council was to have it completed by the original Department of Environment deadline of May 1973. The estate was divided into two contract areas, the major contractors being Taylor-Woodrow-Anglian Ltd, and Tarmac Construction Ltd.

Apart from a series of public meetings held after the start of the programme to explain what was happening, there was little attempt by either the council or the contractors to keep tenants informed of the progress of the scheme. Even though the vast majority of tenants welcomed the modernisation programme, the public meetings offered no more than a passing gesture in the way of 'participation'. They were told that the whole scheme would not take much longer than a year to complete, and were advised not to carry out any costly internal redecoration to their homes. But no sooner had the work started than the architects were informing the council that there would be delays unless a continuous supply of empty blocks of flats required by the contractors were made available. It was at this stage that the problem of decanting over 1,300 households into temporary accommodation became obvious.

There would have been fewer problems had the local authority maintained an adequate housing stock, but it then had a large housing waiting list as well as a slum clearance programme. This problem of a shortage of houses in which to temporarily decant tenants when their own homes were required by the contractors, became fundamentally important to the council's modernisation policy. The council had criticised tenants for not accepting alternative temporary accommodation offered, and indicated that this was a major contributing factor to the delays in the modernisation scheme. The crisis point was reached at a housing committee meeting held in

December 1972, when the town clerk was 'authorised to serve Notices to Quit in appropriate groups on all tenants . . . living in houses yet to be modernised so that as and when the houses are required, action should be taken forthwith to secure with the minimum of delay, the eviction of those tenants who refuse to accept the alternative accommodation offered.'

As the delays got longer the frustration and anger of the tenants increased. One group of tenants who were still waiting to have their homes modernised blocked off a road on the estate. This was being used by heavy wagons to dump and store materials used in work going on in another part of the estate. Tenants who made the journey into North Shields to call on the housing department for information, found that the officials were unable to give them the information they required. They were told that the delays were a result of some tenants refusing the temporary accommodation offered, and because of the difficulties the contractors had in obtaining materials and craftsmen. (1) The tenants' response to this was simple. None of this was their doing. Official explanations may have been true but they were still regarded as excuses. It was they who had to live with the dirt and upheaval. Basically, the tenants wanted to know when the work would be finished, when the contractors would start in particular streets, and where they would be temporarily rehoused. A year after the work began the housing officials themselves could only give very approximate answers to these questions.

When the project office opened on the estate the general view of the tenants was that the council had decided to play fair and had established a housing unit on the estate from which tenants could get the information they wanted. In fact the council had established a separate housing advice office on the estate, but tenants tended to regard the project as this, and largely ignored the official office. The optimism expressed about the project in this respect did not last long and it was soon clear to both ourselves and the tenants that apart from being more helpful than the local authority officials, and providing an individual advocacy service, we were not very effective in securing solutions to their problems. Contact was made with a number of tenants who came to the office. We discussed with them in detail the short-term effects of the modernisation scheme. Their individual problems over modernisation were common to a large number of other tenants on the estate. From this initial contact a regular group of eight tenants developed a commitment to organise themselves around this issue. That is, they realised that to secure from the council and the contractors the information and assurances they all wanted, they would have to organise. The group met with the project team several times in this period and clarified a number of points they wanted to discuss with the council. These included: the on-going problem over dates on which tenants would be temporarily rehoused; the basis for the decision about who was to be rehoused permanently outside the estate. This latter point arose because there would be 228 dwellings less after the modernisation had been completed, and many tenants wanted to leave the estate. What exactly was the council's policy regarding repairs to unmodernised properties, especially in relation to those tenants who would still be in their homes for some months?

There was also a demand for a rent reduction because of the conditions under which they were having to live. (2) This demand was
based on the lengthy delays that had held up the progress on the
modernisation programme, the consequent decline in the condition of
the estate and the accumulation of repairs in unmodernised properties that now needed attention. The tenants also wanted to discuss
the fact that the public health inspectors did not seem able to cope
with the number of requests concerning pest control, and, finally,
whether the contractors could re-route some of their heavy wagons
away from those parts of the estate where tenants were still living.
This group of tenants then went around the estate collating lists of
emergency repairs that tenants considered needed attention.

Early in August 1973, a meeting was organised by the group on the
estate which twenty-two tenants attended. The meeting took place in
the street, and there was a general exchange of views and experiences. This was much the same as the exchanges about the
modernisation that took place all the time on the estate between individuals and small groups, the difference being that this time it
was a public demonstration of solidarity. This format was repeated
the following week when forty tenants and their children came to the
project for a further meeting, where a team from the Audio-Visual
Unit, Education Technology Department at Newcastle Polytechnic made
a video-film of the discussion. The meeting was held in the open
again, and from it came the demand for a public meeting to discuss a
list of proposals outlined by a member of the tenants' group. Small
groups of three or four people were also organised and allocated
areas within the estate in which to collect signatures for a petition in favour of the public meeting. The video-film which was
shown as soon as the meeting ended aroused a great deal of interest
and amusement. It was necessary to play it back twice, the first
time for the tenants and the second time for their children. It was
agreed that the film would be shown at the public meeting.

At the beginning of September 1973, a letter and the petition
were sent to the council by the tenants' group, asking the members,
officials and contractors to meet them at a public meeting being
organised at the end of that month. During this period members of
the project were discussing and clarifying points concerning the
public meeting with the members of the tenants' group. With the resources of the project it was also possible for the group to draw on
practical assistance in the use of photocopying and duplicating
machines, typewriter and paper. Arrangements were made to hold the
meeting in a secondary school on the estate, and an agenda was circulated by the tenants' group to everyone living in unmodernised
properties. The fact that the tenants organised the meeting and
asked the council and contractors to attend was important. It
strengthened their own commitment, since it was well known in the
area that it was they who had organised the meeting. In some respects the meeting itself did not go as anticipated, although this
was related far more to our own expectations than those of the
tenants. It was our view that the meeting should be seen by those
living on the estate not only as an example of their own solidarity
on this issue, but as a means of challenging the power relationships
which are subtly or otherwise applied at meetings between tenants
and 'officials'. In this case it was necessary for the tenants to

assert their control over the meeting by both preparing and running
it themselves. We discussed with them how they might achieve this
at one level by arranging the seating in concentric circles, so that
the 'officials' had to sit in among the tenants and were not isolated from them. We advised the tenants' group to organise groups of
tenants who could if it was necessary support, challenge or question
the 'officials' and, to have them arrive early so that they could
take up strategic positions around the hall.

For reasons related more to their eagerness to have the meeting
than to their disagreement with our suggested approach, the meeting
did not take place in this fashion. A number of men from the
tenants' group went early to organise the seating, which they arranged in rows down the length of the hall. When members of the project arrived the hall was already full, with the councillors,
officials and architects sitting at the front.

The meeting was attended by almost 300 tenants who received information on the progress of the modernisation scheme which they had
been unsuccessful in obtaining by individual protest. They secured
confirmation on the policy over repairs, allowances and housing
allocation. As far as the project was concerned our general aim was
to raise the level of education and political consciousness in its
widest sense, and at the local level this was a question of working
with tenants to develop rank and file organisation. What we failed
to do effectively on this occasion was to relate not only the
tenants' own struggles with those of other groups of tenants in the
area, but to make clear the tactical advantages of particular forms
of action. These attitudes reflected our own feelings more than
those of the tenants, who at that time were more interested in
getting a mass turn-out for the meeting.

After the public meeting the tenants' group met and discussed how
they might utilise the tenants' enthusiasm. They decided to establish a street steward system so that a more accurate check on the
progress of the modernisation could be made, and to call themselves
the 'North Meadow-Well Watch Dog Committee'. We helped to draft a
leaflet which was distributed throughout the estate explaining the
reason for the street stewards and convening a meeting of those interested. This meeting was badly attended, with only ten people in
addition to the committee. We discussed the possible reasons for
the poor turn-out. It was clear that the major concern of the
majority of the tenants was knowing exactly what was happening over
the progress of the modernisation. It was apparent that the public
meeting had given them what they wanted to know.

The support for further action and active backing for the committee was now coming from one particular area of the estate, the
tenants of which had found out from the meeting that the contract in
their area had been suspended for six to eight months. It was these
tenants who for the first time realised that their area would be the
last one to be modernised.

At this point it became clear that a definite difference of interest was emerging between the tenants. Those who now knew that
their houses would be modernised in the coming months were primarily
interested in obtaining satisfactory temporary accommodation. For
those living in the area of the suspended contract any delay in the
programme meant a longer wait. This meant that tenants on other

parts of the estate who held out against the council for what they considered to be suitable temporary accommodation, even if it meant refusing two or three offers, were now causing unnecessary (as far as the other tenants were concerned) delays in the programme. This division was reflected in the committee, the majority of whom lived in the area of the suspended contract. We were unsuccessful in resolving this dispute. At one stage, the committee split into two groups representing the two sets of interests. The original committee went ahead with the idea of the street stewards but confined to their own area. One or two tenants in each street had the responsibility of seeing that every tenant needing repairs had them reported to the council and a check was kept to see that they were carried out.

By this time, late November 1973, we had less and less contact with the committee. The reason for this was the increased work in other parts of the project and a lack of clarity on our own part as to what else we could do.

Also by this time, the committee were dealing directly with the council and the other agencies involved. But the reduction of our contact with them took place at a time when disagreements between the majority and minority on the committee were increasing. If regular contact had been maintained the opportunity of working with the tenants to organise a strong rank and file street steward system might not have been lost. The Watch Dog Committee could see what was happening and on one occasion they discussed the role of the project in relation to their own work. Although we had worked with them in developing their organisation and had provided practical and general support, they did not want to become dependent on us. They have continued to meet and organise and recently asked us to discuss with them a series of proposals drafted for discussion with the ward councillors and the chairman of the housing committee. As for ourselves, the main problem was always one of developing a rank and file organisation of tenants that could effectively deal with a diminishing problem. As the modernisation proceeded, fewer and fewer tenants were directly affected by it. Although we were not entirely successful in the strategy we adopted, an increase in awareness and rank and file organisation was achieved.

There were alternative forms of action which we discussed but did not follow up. One was to develop a general organisational structure representing both the tenants living in modernised as well as the unmodernised property. This was discounted because of our own reluctance to develop a generalist community organisation as opposed to an issue-orientated action group. Alternatively, it might have been possible to organise around a general issue, like rent increases and the Housing Finance Act, and play down in the first instance the specific interests of the tenants affected by the modernisation programme. Although the question of the rent increases was discussed widely on the estate and the possibility of a rent strike was mentioned by a number of tenants, this did not develop momentum and in that situation opposition and organisation led by the project would not have been a legitimate form of action. (3)

CASE STUDY NO. 2:   THE SOUTH MEADOW-WELL

Our work with tenants on the South Meadow-Well Estate was very much
related to the issue of the council's modernisation programme in
progress on the North Meadow-Well Estate. A tenant from the estate
who had at one time been the secretary of a now defunct tenants'
association had been contacted by a number of tenants complaining
about the run-down condition of the estate and the council's policy
of using it as a dumping-ground for 'problem families'. He wanted
to know if there was a way we could offer support and suggested that
we call a meeting on the estate. We decided to test out the general
level of feeling on the estate. To do this we planned a series of
street meetings at which we would discuss with the tenants the problems. A leaflet was sent round to all the tenants outlining the
reasons for the meeting and giving the dates, times and place in
each of the streets where they would be held. On the day of each
meeting another leaflet was distributed in each of the streets. We
had already discussed this strategy with a number of tenants from
the estate when they came into the project office for information.
Before each meeting started we walked up and down the streets with
a loud-hailer asking people to come out to the meeting. The pattern
of the meetings was the same in each of the streets. By walking
into the estate with a loud-hailer we aroused their curiosity and at
first small groups gathered up and down the street watched by others
from their windows and front doors. As soon as we had got the
groups together other tenants came out and joined the meeting. We
had expected this initial reluctance to come out into the street and
while we were going up and down the street we were involved in a
number of good humoured exchanges about 'what the hell we were
trying to do', and 'we've heard it all before.' By the time the
meeting started there was on each occasion between thirty and fifty
tenants involved. At the start of the meetings the first thing the
tenants wanted to know was who we were and what we were doing there.
During the meetings they made it clear to us that there was a great
deal of anger on the estate at the lack of consideration of their
needs by the council. The single most important issue for the
majority of tenants was why the estate was not being modernised at
the same time as the North Meadow-Well. (4) Many tenants expressed
a healthy distrust of our ability to help, but after many tenants
had spoken about their own grievances and experiences with the
council, there was general agreement that an attempt at collective
action was worth considering. They knew that their individual protests to the council had not produced results. At these meetings we
suggested the idea of a survey and largely because the tenants
thought it might lead to something positive they agreed to it.
During a team meeting we had discussed the value of an action orientated survey as a means of developing an organisation and had decided that if this was supported by the tenants then we would suggest the formation of street based working groups. We also felt
that there might be some reluctance on the part of the tenants to
join a working group. When this was put at the end of the meetings
there was an immediate response from the tenants with people either
volunteering, being nominated or persuaded. The result of the
street meetings were the beginnings of five street working groups

each represented by between ten and thirteen tenants.

We met with each of the groups individually every week throughout July and early August 1973. As well as the majority demand for a modernisation programme we also discussed the question of the repair of fencing at the back of the gardens; the repair and clearance of blocked drains and pipes; the time it takes to get essential repairs done; the problems caused by not having covered stands for the dustbins; and, the resentment of some of the tenants that the estate was being used as a 'dumping ground' by the housing department. During these initial meetings we discussed how a housing conditions survey would enable them to work on the basis of hard information obtained from every household on the estate. A survey could also be organised to achieve the maximum involvement of the tenants and the feedback of its findings to the estate. The five working groups agreed to this approach and a draft questionnaire was compiled. From this a questionnaire designed to obtain information concerning the size of household, the nature of the housing conditions, and tenants' attitudes and preferences to suggested improvements was agreed.

After working on the questionnaire all the groups were keen to carry out the survey themselves. We arranged an explanatory programme on basic interviewing techniques, with the emphasis placed on a common approach to the questionnaire to ensure compatibility of findings. Before the interviewing a leaflet was sent to every tenant explaining what had been going on since the street meetings and the purpose of the survey. By this time there was more interest on the estate in what the street groups were doing since it was seen that something was actually happening. During the interviewing the questionnaire was a great topic of conversation in the local shops. Towards the end of July and throughout August 1973, a total of sixty-seven tenants from the estate carried out the interviewing. A proposal was discussed with the tenants to hold a public meeting towards the end of September 1973, to discuss the findings of the survey and in order to save time, it was agreed that we should have the information processed by computer. Originally, we had planned to do the coding with the tenants but this proved too slow and it was, therefore, agreed that we should also arrange to have the coding done.

On receiving the survey results a general meeting of all the working groups was convened so that together we could look at the results and determine the main points that had emerged. (5) Details were also finalised for the public meeting and it was agreed that a copy of the survey results should be circulated to every tenant on the estate.

The public meeting was held in the hall of a local school and ninety-seven tenants attended. The meeting started with a résumé by a member of the project of the history of the street groups, and this was followed by a discussion of the survey and its findings. A proposal from the floor that 'what they had to do was to get together as a group' was unanimously supported and a committee of fifteen tenants was elected with powers from the meeting to co-opt other tenants from the estate if it was necessary. After further discussion a general mandate came from the meeting for the working group to take the following points up with the council on the estate's behalf:

1 To start discussions with the council on the possibility of a
   modernisation scheme for the estate;
2 a scheme for improving the back and front gardens which incorporated new fences and gates;
3 a general clean-up of the estate;
4 discuss housing allocation with respect to those living in flats
   either too big or too small for their needs;
5 why when the borough is short of houses are flats allowed to
   stay empty;
6 the need to have inside toilets built for those tenants who
   still have outside toilets;
7 clarification regarding the council's repair procedure;
8 the need to have the dustbins enclosed to prevent them being
   continually knocked over;
9 the need for more garages;
10 the need for a general improvement in play facilities for the
   children on the estate; and,
11 to discuss with the post office the need for a sub-post office
   on the estate and the provision of more public telephones.

At the first meeting of the group they decided to call themselves
the South Meadow-Well Residents' Working Party and to co-opt five
more tenants on to the group. This meant that of the twenty tenants
on the working party, nine were tenants elected at the public meeting and not involved with the original street working groups. Most
of the tenants who had been actively involved in the street groups,
who were not on the elected working party, had already indicated at
the meeting of all the street groups held prior to the public meeting that they would be unable to commit themselves to a group that
would need to meet frequently. Most of them would be prepared to
give occasional practical assistance to the working party. We
therefore discussed with the working party how to maintain contact
with this group of tenants and with others living on the estate.
They agreed to start a residents' newsletter which would be circulated to every tenant whenever any information emerged from their
negotiations with the council and the post office, and to ask the
group of tenants who had been involved with the street groups to act
as distributors. They also considered our own suggestion that this
group of tenants, subject to the agreement of the rest of the
tenants on the estate should act as street stewards. We reasoned
that this would extend the rank and file basis of the working party.
The stewards could not only distribute the newsletter but maintain
discussion on the estate about the work and progress of the working
party and feed back information from the tenants. A member of the
working party who was also an active trade unionist proposed that if
they were to have a chairman and secretary these roles should be
rotated to prevent the possibility of a division emerging between
officers and the rest.
     Since the election of the working party they have obtained a
seeding grant from the project primarily to finance the production
of their newsletter and to buy letter-headed paper. At the present
time they still rely on the project for duplicating and photocopying
facilities. They met the ward councillors and received support for
their proposals, and they are now in the process of arranging meetings with the chairman of the housing committee and officials from

the post office. They meet at least every fortnight in the project
office and continue to invite us to their meetings. They are now
fully in control of their own organisation and in this respect our
own role has changed dramatically from that of organiser and initia-
tor, to one of provider of practical assistance and advice. We
maintain regular contact with them and they still discuss in great
detail with us their plans and the progress they are making. We
have also provided assistance with the organisation of a day school
on local government and committee organisation which they arranged
as part of their preparation for negotiating with the council.

The South Meadow-Well Residents' Working Party is still in its
early stages of organisation but they are already aware of the need
to maintain constant feedback of information to the tenants on the
estate and for rank and file control and support of their organisation. Our approach in working with them has been to encourage this
development and that of their own skills. We have also attempted to
relate the work they are doing and their own experiences to those of
other tenants in the area. To date this has been done around the
following issues: the effects of the Housing Finance Act, 1972, and
specifically the question of rent increases in relation to council
tenants; housing allocation procedures and their relationship to
the creation of ghetto areas; and, the problems of damp and con-
densation, for tenants on both sides of the Meadow-Well Estate.

NOTES

1 In the early 1970s it was soon evident that every local
   authority in Tyneside had taken advantage of the government's
   75 per cent grants available under the Housing Act, 1969. The
   amount of work available at the time contributed to the
   shortages of materials and the scarcity of craftsmen. At the
   same time, the local authority became increasingly dependent
   upon the contractors.
2 The council adopted a scheme of half rent for casual tenancies
   for tenants prepared to move to other unmodernised properties on
   the estate, when their own home was required by the contractors.
3 By legitimacy, we mean that this would not have been an effective strategy at this time, since on this occasion tenants did
   not feel as strongly about this issue as they did about the
   effects of the modernisation programme.
4 A minor repairs programme was carried out in the South Meadow-
   Well during 1963-4. The council decided that this prohibited
   its inclusion in the modernisation scheme started in 1972.
5 At the time of the survey there were 637 occupied flats on the
   estate out of a total housing stock of 651. Despite the fact
   that the survey took place at the height of the summer period
   when many people were away on holiday, 474 households (74 per
   cent) were interviewed. The general picture that emerged is
   that, on the whole, tenants are living at high density, in
   houses in poor state of repair.

Chapter 9

THE LEASEHOLD PROBLEM IN SALTLEY

Geoff Green

The Birmingham project is in Saltley - one of the vulnerable middle-ring districts squashed between prosperous suburbs and the re-developed inner core. Most houses were built modestly though solidly, towards the end of the last century and sold on 99-year leases. The landowner or freeholder retained the land and the houseowner or leaseholder rented it for a few pounds a year. Some leases have now expired, but the majority granted after 1875 will expire some time before the end of the century. When they do, the houses (as well as the land) revert back to the freeholder, and owner-occupiers become tenants. This system of land tenure is the core of a problem which had distressed many individual residents and contributed more generally to the area's deterioration. The first half of this article sets out the dimensions of the leasehold system and looks in depth at the problems it creates. The second half describes how the project has responded.

The problem was unexpected. Leasehold houses are concentrated in pockets up and down the country - in the West Midlands, London and South Wales especially - so those of us coming from elsewhere had no direct experience. Not much had been written about it either nationally or within Birmingham. We uncovered the facts slowly in our first six months as we analysed the area and identified people's priorities. We found many residents worried and frustrated because they couldn't buy their freeholds despite their legal right to do so. They were variously critical of the freeholders, of Birmingham corporation, and their solicitors, describing them respectively as obstructive, neglectful and inept. Hazily they recollected forming an association to sort things out, but they didn't know what had happened to it. Collective action had been suspended for individual negotiation, and this had proved unsuccessful.

Everybody has a clearer picture now - residents, councillors and ourselves. It was built up by following up what residents had to say, then feeding it back for their response. First, there was evidence from professional people helping or hindering leasehold transactions. Estate agents, solicitors, valuers and local government officials, all helped in piecing together an explanation of various difficulties - helped to isolate the sticking points in the procedure for buying freeholds or 'enfranchising'. Second, a 1 in 8

household survey carried out by the research team in June 1973 provided a statistical backcloth. Not only did it describe the dimensions of the leasehold problem, but it set it in a broader social
and economic context. Of the households in owner-occupation (53 per
cent of the total), 80 per cent were leaseholders and a further 5
per cent had bought the freehold after buying the house. The remaining length of leases in the CDP area is shown in Table 9.1.

TABLE 9.1   Length of remaining leases, 1973 figures

Length of remaining leases	%
10 years or less	1
11-15 years	4
16-20 years	17
21-5 years	26
26-30 years	28
31-5 years	7
More than 35 years	8
Don't know	8

N = 212 (100%)

Survey fieldwork carried out in June 1973.   Percentages rounded
up.

Most leases are now short enough for the difference between
leasehold and freehold to have a profound effect. Basically as the
lease gets shorter, the value of the property to the leaseholder de-
clines, and his tenure gets less like owner-occupation and more like
a private tenancy. As the lease runs out the leaseholder's stake in
the property (however much he has improved it) shrinks to nothing
and he actually becomes a tenant. At an individual level it means
insecurity for leaseholders who live in a declining asset, and additional frustration for those who want to buy their freeholds but
cannot. The knowledge that a freeholder can serve a dilapidation
order (requiring the owner-occupier to spend money to put his house
into a good state of repair) creates uncertainty. That the freeholder can apply for planning permission to redevelop the leaseholder's property creates uncertainty. Not knowing how the corporation will respond to these planning applications creates insecurity.
Not knowing when these actions by external agencies are going to
take place creates uncertainty. Not knowing the probable outcome of
these actions creates uncertainty. Not having any access to or control over this external decision-making leads to frustration. Overall it is a black future, so stable, relatively prosperous residents
move out seeking security elsewhere. And potential residents with a
similar outlook are dissuaded from moving in or effectively prevented because they can't obtain a mortgage: building societies are
reluctant to lend on leases shorter than forty years, and the corporation (the other major source of finance) requires by law a
mortgagor to finish payment ten years before the lease expires.
This effectively limits the mortgage repayment period and ups the
weekly outlay. Many prospective buyers consequently find it cheaper

on a month to month basis to afford a more expensive house in the
suburbs, where, though the capital sum is higher, repayment can be
spread over 20-30 years: and there are fewer legal complications.

Individual decisions like these add up to population movements
which make the local community less viable. The 'Push' factors
aren't so great that large numbers of houses remain vacant. Rather
the population changes its composition, becoming poorer and less
able to organise resistance to Saltley's decline. The established
white community loses its able, more prosperous members to the
suburbs, and is not renewed by sons and daughters settling in
Saltley as they used to do. Those who are left stranded here get
older. When they sell out or die, their houses are bought by
Pakistanis, primarily from the Mirpur district of Kashmir. The
immigrants are able to avoid mortgage problems, first by staying
with relatives and friends, and then by financial co-operation with
members of an extended family. These ties make Saltley attractive
to them, and in return they help Saltley by promoting a young,
economically active and well organised community. Unfortunately
these valuable attributes are not used to best advantage. Most
immigrants have difficulty understanding English and English institutions, which means they are no more articulate than the whites,
and just as powerless against those who repress or neglect the area.
Add to this divisions and often antagonism between immigrant and
white groups and it is easy to see why there has been so little
fight for Saltley's survival.

Of course there are many additional factors which combine to push
the area into decline - heavy traffic, dirt and noise from industry
are good examples. The full picture of cause and harmful effect is
complex and solutions difficult to find. This makes it the more
galling that the relatively clear cut leasehold sequence outlined -
land tenure leading to legal difficulties with economic and social
consequences - should in theory be broken but isn't. In principle
the 1967 Leasehold Reform Act gives leaseholders a legal right to
buy their freeholds so long as they fulfil a number of conditions,
which in Saltley boil down to a five year residential qualification.
These provisions should be enough. They are not. Clearly the
leasehold problem does not arise simply out of a system of land
tenure, but additionally because the Act is not working.

The housing survey underlines this failure. It shows a very low
rate of take-up of freeholds by owner-occupiers over the last seven
years. It could be as low as 0.7 per cent a year because only 5 per
cent of existing owner-occupiers bought their freeholds when they
were leaseholders. Or it could be a maximum of 2.7 per cent a year
if we add in to the calculation an additional 14 per cent who bought
their houses already freehold (because they could all have replaced
owner-occupiers who bought freeholds separately as leaseholders).
However this maximum rate is more likely to include many deals between landlords and freeholders where existing residents are not involved. Either the freeholder - often a big operator - buys in the
lease of a tenanted property, marries it with the freehold and when
the house becomes vacant, sells it freehold to a new owner-occupier
or in a similar, but inverted operation, where a landlord leaseholder buys in the freehold, marries it to his lease and, when the
house becomes vacant, sells it freehold to an owner-occupier. Such

deals are widespread. Consequently we would estimate the take-up of freeholds by owner-occupiers themselves is in the order of 1-2 per cent a year. Which is not to say they haven't tried. Nearly half want to buy their freeholds and another 17 per cent would like to under certain conditions. Indeed Table 9.2 shows 14 per cent have already tried and failed and another 12 per cent are trying now. The statistical picture is filled out by our experience with local resident groups, and our dealings with more than 200 individual leaseholders.

TABLE 9.2 Leaseholders' attitudes towards buying their freeholds

Position	%	Attempts to buy freehold	%
Trying to buy freehold at present	12	Trying now	12
Wishes to buy freehold	33	Never tried	70
Would like to buy freehold under certain conditions	17	Tried but failed	14
Does not wish to buy freehold	37	Was offered but refused	4

N = 212 (100%)

Note: Leaseholders make up 43 per cent of households in the Saltley area.

Why then is the Act not working, or more precisely, why are leaseholders failing to enfranchise under an Act specifically designed to help them? There are three groups of reasons which in practice are intertwined but which we might distinguish for the purposes of this analysis. First is the onus the Act places upon leaseholders to take the initiative, and the advantage, therefore, the freeholder has by just sitting tight. (Contrast this with the hypothetical alternative which automatically conveys the freehold to a leaseholder unless the freeholder takes action to prevent it.) The freeholder can use this favoured position to protect his interest, but often he crosses the boundary from reasonable defence into obstruction. We have evidence of large numbers of leaseholders' inquiries being ignored. We know of a number of freeholders who have responded with unreasonable conditions, saying for example, that the leaseholder must purchase neighbouring freehold interests along with his own. And finally, the most important onus of all, freeholders ask unreasonable prices for their freeholds, obliging the leaseholder to spend time and money going to the Lands Tribunal. I will return to cost later.
It would be misleading to suggest that all the problems of onus arise out of a freeholder's intransigence, because he is not the only person negotiating with the leaseholder. In Saltley there are usually two or more intermediary lessees who have to be bought out if the leaseholder is to secure the whole chain of interests. Each can be just as consciously obstructive as the freeholder, but their position in the chain creates additional onus problems. Their presence often masks the identity of the freeholder. Normally the leaseholder pays his ground rent to one of them, who takes his cut and passes it on to another, who takes another cut before passing

the residue to the freeholder. The leaseholder doesn't normally
worry about the freeholder's identity until he takes steps to enfranchise. Then he has to find out who owns what. The onus is on
him directly or indirectly through a solicitor, and the process of
discovery can be time consuming and expensive.

The leaseholder faces all these problems, primarily because the
Act forces him to take the initiative. They are grouped together
(and distinguished from others) because they would not occur if the
onus was on the freeholder to defend his rights. But they are not
totally explained in this way. These and other difficulties, which
fall under a second 'implementation' head, arise because of the way
the Act is put into effect. Usually residents go to solicitors to
carry out the transaction, and the traditional way solicitors go
about their task raises problems. They work on a one-off basis
which prevents them making much money from the deal. So they give
it a low priority; so low in some cases that it takes a client two
years even to get to the preliminary stage of finding the freeholder. Solicitors prefer to negotiate informally instead of re-
sorting to the formal procedures laid down in the Act. This spins
out the time it takes, often breaking the leaseholder's resolve to
see it through. A large number of disillusioned leaseholders have
come to the project to get their case resurrected, either not having
heard from their solicitors for months, so not knowing how far they
have got, or having made inquiries, finding they have made little
progress. There is in fact a dearth of the kind of positive advice
which sets out the full picture of possibilities, and puts the
leaseholder's position in context. In short, most solicitors are
inefficient, and most leaseholders are ill-informed with little control over the service they employ.

The first two groups of difficulties covered so far have focused
on the law, ignoring for the sake of clarity the third group - the
social and economic factors which shape the context of any deal.
Yet the leaseholder's economic strength not only determines whether
he can afford his freehold, but contributes independently to the
outcome of negotiations. The distinction is important. On the one
hand the leaseholder may anticipate negotiations with the freeholder running smoothly towards a fair settlement. In such a case
he weighs cost against his ability to afford it and the priority he
gives it. On the other hand, he may realistically anticipate difficulty achieving a fair settlement. In this case he must weigh the
possible cost of an all out fight.

There is a big difference between the two sets of costs. Table
9.3 shows some average prices worked out by a local valuer. They
include the reasonable legal costs incurred by the freeholder and
other interested parties (which the leaseholder is obliged to pay
using the formal procedures laid down by the Act) and they assume
negotiations proceed smoothly. If the freeholder is obstructive the
total cost could easily double. The case has to be taken, possibly
to the county court to establish the leaseholder's eligibility, and
then to the Lands Tribunal to establish a fair price for the freehold if the sides cannot agree. Negotiations at each stage in this
sequence might increase solicitors' fees by £100. To this must be
added up to £50 for representation at the county court, £150 to hire
a barrister and valuer at the Lands Tribunal and, in case of

failure, up to £100 set aside to cover the extra legal costs incurred by the freeholder. All this would make little difference to
a rich man. An increase from say £450 to £800 would merely represent a shift from $4\frac{1}{2}$ to 8 per cent of £10,000 capital. But if he
has only £500 capital (which is probably more than average for
Saltley), then such an increase would put litigation beyond his
means.

TABLE 9.3 Normal cost of buying a freehold

Cost of freehold interests		Legal and valuation costs	
Freehold	£250	Freeholder's legal costs	£30
		Freeholder's survey fees	£25
		VAT	£5
		Resident's legal costs	£40
		Resident's survey fees	£10
		VAT	£5
Head lease	£25	Legal costs	£20
		Survey costs	£10
		VAT	£3
Sub lease	£25	Legal costs	£20
		Survey costs	£10
		VAT	£3
Total	£300	Total	£181

Put simply, the leaseholder has to think about two sets of costs,
the normal costs of enfranchisement and the additional costs of
forcing negotiations to a conclusion. The first can be calculated
more or less independently of the freeholder, but the second depends
upon the freeholder's resistance and in turn upon his ability to
finance such resistance. If the freeholder is as poor as the leaseholder, he will probably not risk being taken to the Lands Tribunal.
If he is much richer than the leaseholder, as most are, then he can
well afford to go to the Tribunal. Even if he thinks he may lose,
he still can use the potential of his economic strength to bluff it
out.
    In principle, to summarise, there are two distinctive cost
limitations on the leaseholder. It is not only his own economic
circumstances which determine his chances of buying the freehold,
but also the relative economic power of leaseholder and freeholder.
In practice freeholders (excluding owner-occupiers) are generally
much richer than leaseholders in Saltley. Most of them are companies or trusts. The biggest in the project area, London City and
Westcliff, is a quoted property company with assets of £95m and a
profit of £4,025,052 in 1973. Leaseholders who use the Act are by
definition individual owner-occupiers. Though the richest of them
may own the leasehold house next door, this is exceptional and most
earn less than the national average. Clearly the economic differences between the two sides is great, making the leaseholder's
bargaining position weak.

On the other hand, the leaseholders are not typically the poorest members of the community: generally they are not on social security or receiving other community help. They represent the backbone of a stable, skilled working class. One of their major priorities is to buy their freehold to gain security, and they have saved up to cover the basic cost. Unfortunately all this makes them ineligible for effective legal aid towards the cost of going to the Lands Tribunal. At the moment there are differences of interpretation within the Law Society which administers the system, but basically most lease-holders are disqualified from substantial help because of the capital they have accumulated to cover the normal costs of purchas-ing their freehold. Normally, in other legal disputes, differential wealth (over a certain minimum) is recognised as inhibiting the case of the poorer man, and legal aid is granted to give him equal access to the law. In our case neither side is considered poor enough to create any inequality before the law.

The project has responded to the leasehold problem at three levels. First is the analysis itself, which takes time and is continually being updated. Then there is neighbourhood work; supporting collective local action to overcome difficulties which flow from in-dividual negotiation. Finally, we endeavour to influence policy - to break down the broader economic, institutional and legislative barriers which prevent any fundamental solution to the problem. Each of the three activities complements the other two. From the beginning we recognised the leasehold issue as one with broader economic and political implications. Neighbourhood activity would lead residents into a more general awareness of the economic dis-advantages they endured. Later as we explored the problem together, links between the local issue and broader economic forces became more explicit. Unequal wealth clearly creates unequal bargaining power. The leasehold issue brings this out vividly.
   Internally the project is geared to feed analysis into neighbour-hood action and into influencing policy, responding in this case to the various components of the leasehold problem. Initially we em-phasised resident organisation to overcome most implementation dif-ficulties, and some of the onus and cost difficulties. It had already got under way on the old Norton Estate before the project arrived. The Estate, which covers about a quarter of the project area, was owned by trustees of the original Norton family until, in 1962, London City and Westcliff bought the freeholds of 809 houses for £80,000. Subsequently they bought many leases also, and they now own over 200 properties outright. Clearly they thought the Estate had development potential and the then chairman of Birmingham Public Works Committee thought so too. It was a time when compre-hensive redevelopment planning had reached a high watermark; any area of Victorian terraced housing was slum clearance potential. But the area is zoned residential and now - in keeping with newer ideas about urban renewal - covered by General Improvement pro-posals. Since it would be nearly impossible for a property company to make a profit by building new houses in such a depressed area, London City and Westcliff have made a series of attempts to get parts rezoned industrial or commercial. Their proposals (the latest in April 1973) have been consistently rejected by the Town Planning Sub-Committee.

The catalyst for community action came in 1967 when London City and Westcliff served dilapidation orders on most of their lease-holders. This the freeholder is legally entitled to do. It requires the leaseholder to put his property into a good state of repair. Though usually enforceable only towards the end of the lease, it nevertheless frightened many residents: poorer and older householders couldn't afford to carry out the work, and they couldn't afford to move because it would cost too much money to exchange their house for one elsewhere. So they formed a residents' association to co-ordinate local resistance. It had twin objectives; first to remove the dilapidation orders, and second, to help members purchase their freeholds under the provisions contained in the Leasehold Reform Bill which was currently passing through Parliament. In a sense they achieved their first aim. Landlords of tenanted property (about 40 per cent of the Estate) were also affected, and by joining with the association, the local MP, Denis Howell, and the Corporation, they were able to suspend the implementation of the dilapidation orders. They were not rescinded, however, and still stand in abeyance. They can be activated at the end of the lease, or when leaseholders ask for an extension under the Act. The threat (as distinguished from an immediate obligation) of having to do expensive repairs still exists.

The association failed to achieve their second, longer term objective. In the six years since the Act only a solitary leaseholder has managed to buy his freehold. The major causes are not difficult to disentangle. On the one hand the freeholder exploited the onus placed on the leaseholder in a way already described - by not answering letters or by asking high prices. On the other, the residents' association fell apart. In the beginning they had a remarkably organised membership. Street representatives collected £5 from each household and this was placed in a fund to be used for fighting test cases. A solicitor was retained and a plan drawn up to pay the legal costs of a small number of residents in their endeavour to settle on a fair price for their freehold. These settlements could then be taken as precedents: other members would follow suit by buying their freeholds easily at a similar price. Using the same solicitor could also cut legal costs. The collective principle is a good one, but the organisation could not sustain it. The chairman, a local councillor, lost his seat and with it interest in the area. The secretary moved away. The solicitors awaited instructions. Individual members, tired of waiting, tried negotiating themselves, failed, and despaired of ever pushing a deal through, even collectively.

When CDP arrived in 1973 the association was about to wind up. Yet resident organisation was needed more then ever. The problem had grown more acute because leases were now six years shorter. The difficulties of implementing the Act had not diminished. We determined then, to reactivate collective action, building on the local tradition of organisation rather than imposing new arrangements. About 175 residents responded to a preliminary leaflet and came to a meeting in March 1973 chaired by a local councillor and attended again by the MP, Denis Howell. It was agreed to re-form the Norton residents' association and fight three test cases in the courts should it be necessary. The objective was broadly as before; to secure by collective action a few freeholds in order to pave the way for individual negotiation by each member. Not only would a few strategic victories establish a level of prices which the freeholder could not resist, but they would also break up his estate and leave him less reason to defend it for comprehensive development. The meeting elected a committee of street representatives and five others. CDP would act as secretary and the old solicitors were retained.

In the past year the committee has put the plan into effect despite a number of false starts. It has meant sacking the first solicitor because we thought him inactive and conservative, but members now feel they have the right combination of professional help. They are well on the way to winning their fight, and just as important, most local people know about it, though naturally there are different levels of awareness. The committee, which meets perhaps every six weeks, knows most. Householders who make up the test cases know nearly as much in general, and more about the legal work which affects them directly. The 160 member households keep up to date with developments through their street representatives or the regular newsletters. Other households get to know on the grapevine, or from the less frequent newsletters which go out to everyone on Norton Estate. There is something like a hierarchy of understanding which coincides with commitment.

Neighbourhood organisation like this eliminates most difficulties associated with implementing the Act, and removes some problems of onus, particularly those of discovering the chain of interests in a property. Residents know where they stand and they get effective service. But such difficulties account for only part of the overall problem. Much more fundamental is both the onus on the leaseholder which allows the freeholder to obstruct negotiations by stone-walling, and the difference in economic strength between the two sides. The first can only be eliminated properly by legislative change and the second, in any general way, only by redistributing economic resources. These are national solutions to a widespread problem and a longer term aim. Realistically we have to think of how to get a local solution quickly. We cannot eliminate the onus, but we can overcome it with cash. We cannot redistribute income, but we can alter the local balance of economic power in the lease-hold equation, again with cash. The freeholder's ability to exploit the situation is considerably reduced if the local leaseholder can afford to follow through the case - to the Lands Tribunal if necessary. The obstructive power of the freeholder depends on his superior economic strength - on his ability to go the whole way to protect his interests. If leaseholders are given temporary economic equality in the dispute, it is more likely that it will be resolved fairly.

Norton residents' association never assumed it would be possible to give all local leaseholders such economic equality. The test case strategy was a device which narrowed down the battle front. If they could afford to support a small number of cases - give them effective economic parity in their negotiations with the freeholder - then other settlements would follow naturally without such support. The Lands Tribunal decisions would be both explicit and public, setting a precedent which the freeholder could not resist.

But even this limited fight requires money; the solicitors advised
it might cost anything up to £500 for court action. When the committee met for the first time they had to choose one of three ways
of raising the money: either (1) CDP funds, (2) legal aid, or
(3) residents' subscription. CDP had up to £20,000 that year for
social action expenditure in the area. Unfortunately the Home
Office had been advised by the Lord Chancellor's Office that using
funds for this purpose would effectively circumvent legal aid provision and possibly preclude association members from using it individually when buying their freeholds in the future. The details
of such limitations were not clarified for the committee meeting,
though it appears (as suggested earlier) that the new legal aid provisions would not have helped many residents anyway. Also, it is
not just a matter of cost. Applying for legal aid takes a long time
and, more important, adopting legal aid procedures and examining
people's means (assessed by Social Security) shifts discussion away
from the public to the private sphere. The committee were not
willing to make this difficult transition and instead opted en-
thusiastically for the third alternative of subscription. They
fixed a figure of £2 a head to be collected by street representatives and by the end of May 1973 had added £150 to the £250 the old
association already had in the bank.

  Solicitors find it difficult to predict even approximately, the
likely cost of court action. But we do know that two cases taken
together are not much more expensive than one, three not much more
expensive than two, and so on. In order to be sure of breaking the
freeholders' resolve we chose ten cases. Unfortunately costs to the
association mounted up very quickly. The original solicitor put in
a bill for £112 and each of the ten cases has just been valued (as a
necessary element in the sequence of negotiation) for a professional
fee of £150. So even before reaching the Lands Tribunal, half the
association's funds had already been spent. Both committee members
and CDP were worried and resolved to see again whether CDP funds
could be released to support the association. It wasn't straightforward. Legal aid provision is in a state of flux and lawyers on
the defensive. The Home Office was in a tricky position. Releasing
funds for this purpose would amount to positive discrimination towards a disadvantaged area much more explicit than the tentative
moves towards community lawyers. It would imply, too, that existing
legal aid is inadequate when the battle hinges, like this one, on
economic inequality, not just on ability to pay normal legal costs.
Finally, it would admit of collective legal action, recognise the
interdependence of a community and blow away the myth that litigation is always about individuals against individuals.

  The Home Office (though with many doubts about the principles involved) did give the association a grant in the end, and this
doubled its funds and sustains action on the Norton Estate. We hope
the money may also be used to fund similar pilot cases in other
parts of the CDP area. The Estate was the project's first focus,
but interest has spread. Our neighbourhood action now incorporates
support for other leasehold groups. More experienced now, we and
the groups of twenty or so leaseholders at a time can do much ourselves. 'Schools' of leaseholders are dispensing with many services
previously carried out by a solicitor and going through the

enfranchising procedure on their own. We can show them how to fill
in forms, advise on reasonable prices, help create a united front,
and generally set the whole procedure in context. In short we are
tackling the implementation difficulties with information and
organisation. But as with our earlier support for the Norton residents' association, this solves only part of the problem. Without
cash it can fail. When it comes to the crunch and a group of residents (however well organised) are offering £200 for their freeholds against the freeholder's final demand of £600, only the Lands
Tribunal can settle it, and it costs a lot of money to take the
action that far.

   That is the extent of our neighbourhood activity. The necessary
ingredients are there for a local solution to the leasehold problem.
The Lands Tribunal decisions should be our major breakthrough, and
thereafter local people should be able to use the Act as it was intended. But we are always conscious that this local action will not
upset the balance of forces elsewhere. Our neighbourhood work will
not itself resolve similar problems in other middle-ring areas of
Birmingham or in other parts of the country. To make more than a
local impact on a problem we have shown to have deep seated structural causes, we are obliged to build on local experience and draw
out its implications.

   In theory we can argue for change at two levels, fundamental or
superficial. And we can wage either of these two at government or
neighbourhood level. We can put forward superficial amendments to
the Act which would shift the onus to the freeholder, or alternatively we can argue for a change in the whole system of land
tenure or for a broad redistribution of wealth, both of which would
make this marginal amendment redundant. We can push for both superficial and fundamental change either 'up-across-and-down' - the
original model of CDP with local projects channelling suggestions to
the centre and across to relevant government departments, hoping
they will churn out sympathetic legislation - or we can take them to
neighbouring grassroots organisations. In practice we have done a
bit of everything and largely failed to make an impact. The evidence is there but no one has moved. We shall have to concentrate
our efforts, and we shall do it knowing that legislative or administrative change through the centre is an unlikely bet.

   To summarise, our project has operated at three levels. Though
these can complement one another running in parallel, in practice
emphasis has shifted from analysis to neighbourhood work, and now to
policy. First we found and analysed the leasehold problem. Second,
we supported neighbourhood organisation to overcome it. Finally, we
are elaborating how its basic causes lie outside our neighbourhood -
in our system of wealth and property.

Chapter 10

THE HILLFIELDS INFORMATION CENTRE: A CASE STUDY

Nick Bond

REASONS FOR SETTING UP THE CENTRE

It is known that certain sections of the population are reluctant to approach formal agencies direct for help or advice. For example, in a 1 in 6 survey carried out by the CDP project in Hillfields in the summer of 1971 22 per cent of the households in the sample said that some member of their family suffered a handicap or disability which prevented them from leading a normal life or restricted their activities; but nearly half of those people, when asked if their names could be passed on to the Social Services Department to see if there was any help they could be given, declined this offer.

It is also known that many statutory agencies effectively ration their services, and consequently under-estimate the numbers of those in need of them, by poor advertising and by off-putting reception and waiting arrangements in inaccessible buildings; by filtering out many applicants at the reception counter (where junior staff often exercise great and arbitrary discretion in their interpretation of the agency's intake policy); and by offering their help through formal interviews where the worker maintains a detached professional role relationship which is bewildering to the deprived client with pressing practical problems.

The Hillfields Information and Opinion Centre was consciously designed to try and counteract some of these features not only because it was felt that this would be desirable in itself but also in order to meet certain aims of the exploratory phase of the CDP experiment. These may be briefly summarised as follows:

1 To establish categories of felt need and aspiration in the study neighbourhood;

2 to discover the kind and amount of need unknown and/or unmet by existing agencies of central and local government operating within the area; and

3 to devise ways of meeting whatever needs came to light either directly or by encouraging residents to seek solutions through collective action.

Additional practical reasons for establishing the centre were to provide a demonstration of concern by establishing a physical presence for the project in a disheartened neighbourhood faced with

imminent redevelopment; to advertise CDP and the fact that it was
concerned to hear residents' point of view and that it had access to
resources; and because no strong community groups reflecting need
existed at that time in the neighbourhood.

From the beginning it was realised that to attract as many
callers as possible, the centre should be as accessible as possible
both geographically and psychologically. To meet these conditions,
a shop was selected in the middle of the main shopping street of the
area and deliberately designed to be as unlike a formal council
office as possible, both in physical appearance and style of operation. It was possible to see through the plate-glass window of the
shop into a pleasant carpeted room furnished with a settee and
several armchairs, and a desk set informally at an angle in the
corner. The downstairs room of the shop was divided by a sliding
partition so that private telephone calls or interviews could take
place in the back of the shop. A small kitchen and lavatory were
situated next to the downstairs room, and cups of tea were constantly available. As part and parcel of maximising psychological
accessibility it was decided not to use the word 'advice' in the
name of the centre to counteract any assumption that the problems of
the neighbourhood necessarily lay in the residents who therefore
needed to be given 'advice'. It was also thought that for someone
to come through a door labelled 'Advice Centre' they would to some
extent have to define themselves as someone with a 'problem', and
that this would be a great disadvantage in attempting to attract as
wide a cross section of local residents as possible. The name
'Information and Opinion Centre' was devised to provide as neutral a
door as possible through which to enter. In an initial attempt to
reach out to potential consumers and to advertise the opening of the
centre posters and leaflets were distributed in pubs, launderettes,
surgeries and other local meeting places and a short article was
placed in the recently started local newspaper the 'Hillfields
Voice' as well as in the 'Coventry Evening Telegraph'.

The specific strategies devised for attaining the aims of the
centre, in addition to the general style described above, were:
1   to offer basic information (initially about the redevelopment,
    and welfare and legal rights) as a resource to residents to in-
    crease marginally their power to bargain for the protection of
    their interests in the city. In one sense information is power;
    in this sense to be deprived of information is, to some extent,
    to be deprived of power;
2   to provide an open-ended informal situation to which residents
    might be attracted to express their grievances, concerns, pro-
    blems and ideas, as a preliminary to stimulating them to con-
    sider ways of solving these problems by their own actions;
3   to place a highly qualified, high-status worker in the reception
    area in an attempt to take the 'presenting problem' seriously in
    the exact terms and form in which it is presented. This was
    also a deliberate recognition that the counter staff whom the
    public first meet often determine the way in which the public
    perceive and respond to a whole institution. This worker was
    briefed to take action on individual problems but also to look
    for the public component of private problems. The aim was to
    link residents with similar problems so that they might consider

whether some sort of collective action might be a more effective way of dealing with them than any individual action taken by the worker.

In a neighbourhood in the throes of redevelopment, information is obviously important for its own sake and it was felt that this in itself might help the elderly, the immigrants, and the inarticulate to cope better with the uncertainties of the situation.   It was also known, as a result of informal contacts made by the CDP action group members living in the area, that some residents simply had not been given any information about the impending redevelopment or what rights they had in relation to it, and that others had not under- stood the information in the form it had been presented to them. However, the emphasis on information and rights was also part of a deliberate attempt to break through the stereotype of Hillfields' residents as 'problem people' in need of special help or advice.   It was also a recognition that ignorance about matters like redevelop- ment and the low take-up rate of certain services and welfare bene- fits were as likely to be related to deficiencies in the manner in which information and services were offered as to any deficiencies in the potential beneficiaries themselves.

THE FIRST YEAR OF OPERATION

In the first four weeks following its opening, there were ninety substantial callers at the centre.   44 per cent of these were re- quests for precise information about the redevelopment plans for their house or street.   Another 14 per cent of the callers came in to complain about the general dereliction of the area.   A further 11 per cent were concerned about the nuisance of prostitution and kerb-crawling.   Other callers asked about improvement grants, offered to help in visiting the housebound elderly, wanted to put their names down for the forthcoming nursery centre and old people's flatlets, and complained about the state of the local parks.   There appeared to be a roughly proportionate scatter of the various nationalities, with immigrants represented in all the above issues.

The number of callers at the centre was slightly smaller than anticipated, but many callers claimed to be speaking for neighbours and friends.   Certainly the above figures only indicate the overt reason for calling and do nothing to convey the strength of feeling expressed by almost every caller about the stress of living under threat of clearance and redevelopment.   The action group was left in no doubt that, at that time (summer 1970), it was the repercussions of this process which loomed as the overwhelming problem in the consciousness of the neighbourhood.   Perhaps more important, the physical environment also seemed to have become the communal symbol for a great deal of bitter resentment and distrust of the council.

After twenty weeks of opening some 350 residents had called at the centre.   Inquiries about redevelopment still formed the largest single category (41 per cent).   Housing problems (i.e. evictions, repairs, homelessness) formed the second largest category (19 per cent) and welfare rights inquiries the third (15 per cent).   On this basis it was certainly possible to conclude that the need for in- formation generally was not being met by existing agencies within

the area and that the centre, at the very least, was performing a
valuable function in bridging this gap. However, in dealing with
inquiries about redevelopment (i.e. dates of demolition, arrangements for removal expenses, choice of rehousing, etc.) the worker
found himself up against the problem that many callers simply did
not believe what he told them, even though this was based on the
latest information available from the planning department. The
whole area was ridden with rumours; many streets were divided by
two or even three compulsory purchase orders with different planned
demolition dates for different parts of the same street; and
several residents complained that demolition dates that had been
given in the past had not been adhered to. The worker was particularly conscious that information he gave might ultimately prove to
be false if plans changed, as they had done in the past. Moreover,
it became apparent that public meetings on redevelopment arranged by
residents' groups (stimulated by an independent community worker)
whilst useful in conveying general information, were inadequate as a
method of solving the individual problems of residents. An additional problem was that several corporation departments might be involved in providing information and help to any one individual resident. The planning department or the public health department
would be involved in giving likely demolition dates; the housing
department in explaining the rehousing positions; and the estates
department in giving information about compensation. It was therefore arranged that the planning department should hold a surgery at
the information centre at specific times each week where residents
could get answers direct from officials,who had this specific delegated responsibility. It was agreed by other local authority departments that planning department officers should deal with all
questions of redevelopment including compensation and rehousing on
their behalf, and that whatever information was given to callers
would be confirmed by an official letter sent to the caller immediately after the visit to the planning officer. By this means it
was hoped to ensure that residents had written commitment from the
corporation, which would encourage any future negotiation to be
direct between residents and one corporation department.

Another problem encountered by the worker in the initial period
was that of getting action on specific problems. It was felt that
in order to attract local residents to the centre it was essential
that it should develop a reputation as a place that got things
done - in contrast to the reputation of many agencies where so frequently residents interpret what happens to them as being 'fobbed-
off'. Hence the worker developed an 'advocacy' style of action,
taking whatever a given caller said was his problem as the problem
to be solved.

During this period several ad hoc groups of residents met various
officials to discuss problems. One group of residents met the
deputy director of the cleansing department to discuss complaints
about dustbin collection, and another group met local police
officers to discuss the problem of kerb-crawling. One residents'
association was started as a result of linking up several residents
from the same three streets with a common concern about play space.
Another residents' association formed as the result of many people
from two adjacent streets calling at the centre in order to find out

the planned demolition date for their streets. In this case the
answer was 'sometime between 1976 and 1986' - much less imminent
than most of the rest of the Comprehensive Development Area - and it
appeared that there was still time for the residents of the two
streets concerned to make their voices heard before the final decision to demolish the houses was irrevocably taken. In this instance therefore CDP was able to engage a qualified planner for
three months to conduct a survey of the residents' wishes in respect
of the redevelopment or improvement of their streets, and at the
same time to produce data indicating the likely uptake of improvement grants should the two streets be declared a General Improvement
Area. The results of this survey were made available to the residents and subsequently a residents' association was formed to
press the council not to demolish the houses but to retain them and
declare the two streets a General Improvement Area. This was eventually agreed to by Coventry corporation and the two streets formed
the first General Improvement Area in Coventry.

    One or two of the other community groups which had been recently
formed with the help of the community worker employed by the
Coventry Council of Churches were strengthened as a result of linking callers at the information centre to them. The eventual result
of this close collaboration between the community worker and the information centre worker was a meeting of representatives of all the
groups which had formed in the neighbourhood. As a result of this
meeting the representatives decided to form a single umbrella body -
the Hillfields Community Association (HCA). This body comprises two
representatives from each of the local groups and residence in
Hillfields is a condition of membership.

    In spite of the gradual emergence of local residents' groups, the
worker at the centre was finding it very difficult to get individual
results for a caller, and, at the same time, to develop in individual callers a consciousness of the potential for tackling problems
collectively. The worker felt that the danger of responding to
callers by first encouraging them to link up with other residents
with similar problems so that they might collectively seek solutions
was that this might be experienced by some callers as being 'fobbed-
off' and the reputation of the centre as a place worth visiting
would suffer.

    The worker sought to handle this dilemma by making it his first
priority to get results for the caller but second to look for the
public component of any resident's private problem and, if possible,
to link people with common problems together. One result of the
advocacy work of the centre was that residents increasingly began to
see it as the place where 'they' get things done for 'you'. Whilst
this was a good thing in so far as it contributed to the aim of
making contact with a large number of local residents it was
counter-productive to another of the aims of the centre - namely to
help local residents seek solutions to their own problems and to
develop means of meeting their aspirations through their own
actions. However, even individuals with individual problems which
the worker solved for them gained some skills in learning how to get
things done. For example, all telephoning was done in front of the
caller and frequently the worker was able to give the caller the
telephone and encourage and enable him to confront an agency direct.

For some callers this was the first time that they themselves had taken such a step.

THE BEGINNINGS OF RESIDENT INVOLVEMENT AND CONTROL

During the first six months several local residents became parti-cularly involved in the workings of the centre. One unemployed young man had been linked up to a group of unattached teenagers and was helping them in planning to start a club for themselves. This young man was subsequently engaged by CDP to do a three-month study of unattached youth in the area, and during the course of this he became more and more involved in the operation of the centre. A middle-aged woman who was particularly concerned about the effects of redevelopment on her elderly neighbours brought many cases of hardship to the attention of the centre and began to develop as a highly articulate advocate in her own right on behalf of this group. Indeed, because she knew them all so well she was far more effective in this than the CDP worker himself. A young unsupported mother also began to learn a good deal about supplementary benefit claims and how to deal effectively with the supplementary benefit commis-sion on behalf of callers. It was decided, therefore, that in order to resolve the problem of the centre developing as a place where 'they' get things done for 'you', and thus hindering the development of the local residents' capacity to exercise more control over their own lives and to seek their own solutions to problems, the 'they' would have to become residents themselves. Moreover, it was thought that handing over the centre to resident control would give the greatest possible opportunity for residents to develop their own style of operation for the centre and to exploit the potential of a fully independent centre to either develop strategies for bringing about changes in the policies and service-delivery systems of those agencies of central and local government which caused problems to the callers at the centre, or to provide an individual advocacy ser-vice for callers, or both. It was also thought that such a move would increase the probability of the centre remaining in operation after CDP had finished.

Accordingly it was suggested to the half-dozen or so local resi-dents who had become involved in the activities of the centre that they should be constituted as an advisory group which would be re-sponsible for the policy of the centre. At the same time - some nine months after the opening of the centre - the young man who had been working with unattached youth in the area was engaged full-time by CDP to operate the centre, and the CDP administration moved out to another office leaving one worker to support and train the full-time resident and offer consultancy to the advisory group. During this handover period the recently appointed full-time secretary of the HCA - a local resident - moved into the information and opinion centre, as a base from which to service the various local groups that were growing up in the neighbourhood, including the information centre itself.

This arrangement proved satisfactory and in June 1971, almost exactly one year after the centre was opened, the CDP management committee agreed to a proposal put forward by the CDP team that full responsibility for the management control and day-to-day running of the information centre should be delegated to the residents' advisory group. This was achieved by the CDP management committee making a grant of £2,985 to the HCA to employ the local resident full-time and to cover the operating overheads of the centre. The full-time resident worker was responsible to the advisory group, and the advisory group was in turn responsible to the HCA. The remaining CDP worker withdrew from the centre but continued to attend the weekly meetings of the advisory group in a consultative capacity.

By the end of the first year there had been over 1,000 callers to the centre. Of these 92.3 per cent came from within the study area (i.e. from within a radius of approximately half a mile of the centre), and 7.7 per cent from outside the area.

Housing problems in general accounted for 25 per cent of the total number of callers; redevelopment problems 21 per cent and welfare rights 13 per cent. The remaining 40 per cent of callers divided themselves fairly equally between inquiries about community activities (lunch clubs, pre-school playgroups, etc.), complaints and suggestions concerning public amenities, complaints about kerb-crawling, and legal advice. Only 3.5 per cent of all callers (41) came in to ask for help from the social services department, who by this time were holding one session a week at the centre. There are a number of possible explanations for this, among them being:

1 that the public nature of the information centre and its style of operation may have dissuaded some people from bringing personal confidential problems there;
2 that people may have hesitated to label themselves as in need of social work help, and preferred to define their problems in terms of concrete external issues;
3 that the residents who staffed the information centre during the latter half of the first year more often defined callers' needs in terms of the immediate presenting problem and did not identify underlying needs;
4 that there are not in fact heavy concentrations in Hillfields of people with personal problems, and that the issues raised at the information centre were an accurate reflection of the distribution of problems in the local population;
5 that the district social work team had not yet become well enough known and trusted in the area to be able to link into the informal networks of communication, or to tap the lay referral system.

Each of these explanations may have some validity and the CDP team felt that the last one certainly warranted further exploration. They argued that although there had been few specific referrals to the social workers on duty for the weekly session there was growing evidence of unmet social need coming to light through casual contacts at the information and opinion centre, through the children using the adventure playgrounds and the summer playscheme sponsored by the HCA, through the activities of the ward welfare committee, and so on. Few of these needs seemed to be presented as specific problems demanding casework help but a number of the field workers felt that social workers would have something positive to contribute if ways could be found of offering their skills at the point of need. A joint working party consisting of representatives of CDP

and the social services department was formed as a result of these
observations, and an experiment to decentralise the local neighbourhood team of social workers was eventually set in motion.

By the end of the first year a weekly councillors' surgery at the
centre had been started; the local health visitors and social
workers were holding weekly sessions there; and a legal advice
session was being offered one evening a week by law lecturers from
Warwick University. Meanwhile, the demand for information from the
planning department had.declined as redevelopment proceeded and information became more widely available, and this direct service was
discontinued, although a telephone link was maintained. A 1 in 6
survey conducted in Hillfields by CDP a year after the opening of
the centre revealed that residents in 76 per cent of households interviewed had heard of the information and opinion centre and 18 per
cent of residents had called there.

Although the centre was originally open during the evenings, experience showed that few people called after six o'clock. By the
end of the year the centre was open one evening a week for the
councillors' surgery and the legal advice session, and since being
handed over to resident control the centre is now also open on
Saturday mornings. The advisory group members take it in turn to
run the shop on the late evening opening and Saturday mornings and
get paid £1.50 for being responsible for each of these two sessions.
Each volunteer thus earns £1.50 every six weeks for this specific
service.

THE COMPOSITION OF THE ADVISORY GROUP

The six members of the initial advisory group consisted of five
women and one man. Two of the women were unsupported mothers, one a
widow, two married to low wage-earners, and the one man was unemployed. Two of this group were the clients of social workers (the
unemployed man and one of the unsupported mothers) and the unemployed man became the group's first chairman. The full-time
worker had himself been a client of a social work agency in the
past. At least two members of the advisory group were old-
established residents of the area, well tuned in to some of the more
important informal networks of communication within the neighbourhood.

Since its inception the size and composition of the advisory
group has fluctuated. After six months the group still comprised
six members, but three of the original six had formally left the
group although they still maintained some contact and continued to
recommend people to call at the information centre. The new members
were one unemployed man (separated from his wife), a widow, and a
young housewife. The full-time resident at the information centre
was briefed to look for local people who might play a role in the
work of the centre. Obviously the fact that advisory group members
need to spend a considerable amount of time in the centre means that
the composition of the group is inevitably weighted in favour of
women and unemployed men. It is worth noting that all the members
of the advisory group are resident in the immediate area, and had
initially been customers of the centre themselves for one reason or
another.

THE SECOND YEAR OF OPERATION: RESIDENT CONTROL

The advisory group decided fairly early on in its existence that the
aims of the centre should be:
1 To help anyone who comes into the shop, regardless of race and
   any other factor;
2 to try and make sure that any local or central government department that exists to help the public is doing its job
   properly;
3 to try and make sure that callers are helped in such a way that,
   as a result of the visit, they learn what to do next time they
   have the same problem.
   Formal meetings of the advisory group are held every week on
Saturday mornings but there is a great deal of informal discussion
(and gossip) during the week as most of the advisory group call in
at the shop every day for some time at least. This means that the
full-time resident worker almost always has someone to cover for him
when he has to leave the shop to visit someone in their own home or
to accompany someone to a supplementary benefits appeal tribunal.
Manning the centre also gives opportunities for the advisory group
members to learn more about legal and welfare rights as well as how
to get things done. This means that as they develop expertise based
on experience the advisory group members themselves are able to develop advocacy skills as well as the full-time worker. The Saturday
morning meetings alternate between a business meeting and a training
meeting. The training meeting has developed a highly pragmatic
approach to learning how to help callers. The technique used is to
take a problem, e.g. 'what do you do if a homeless person calls at
the centre?' and, using the combined experience of everyone present,
to construct a list of all the possible means of helping such a
person. This list is subsequently duplicated and circulated to each
member to go in a loose-leaf reference folder.
   Since the centre was formally handed over to resident control in
June 1971, it has become increasingly apparent that the information
and opinion centre serves at least two functions:
1 that of providing an information and advocacy service for the
   general public of Hillfields and, increasingly, for people from
   outside the area;
2 that of providing a supportive environment for lonely and sometimes disturbed people who come in regularly and often stay
   around for long periods, and who seem to gain support from their
   acceptance in the centre and its generally friendly and informal
   atmosphere.
   Moreover, the volunteers at the centre seem to become involved
not only because they want to help other people, but also because
they recognise that being at the centre is helping them in terms of
giving themselves a role and a friendly accepted meeting place.
   Having people sitting around a great deal has resulted in outside
criticism of the centre from individuals and from one or two key
members of the HCA (e.g. 'it's a place for no-goods, it's a gossip
shop'). This is serious as the success of the centre in attracting
a wide range of callers from the neighbourhood depends on its word-
of-mouth reputation. On the other hand providing support for lonely
and sometimes unstable people is obviously meeting the needs of a

section of the local population which appears not to be catered for
by any of the existing official agencies. The position is com-
plicated because some of the advisory group of the centre are themselves lonely and tend to spend a considerable amount of time there
'hanging around'. During the autumn period the group were forced to
restrict access to the centre to a local 'tatter' who was anxious to
help and needed the friendship and comfort of the centre.

However as he was not always sober and he often interfered in
conversations with clients in the shop front it was recognised that
the image of the centre was suffering in such a way that it might
deter potential callers. This was a painful decision for the group
to take, but a recognition that the primary purpose of the centre is
to offer help to the public at large and that offering a therapy
service to individuals, while often necessary, was a secondary activity for which the physically restricted setting of the information
centre shop front was not ideally suited.

The advisory group members themselves obviously enjoy the informal friendly atmosphere of the shop, the status working there
gives them, and also the fact that they are able to help people get
their rights. There is little doubt too that many members of the
public feel easy about calling into the shop because of the non-
official and friendly atmosphere. However, there are undoubtedly
some local people who have not come to the information centre precisely because of its style, and also possible because local people,
who they may know or may know by sight or reputation, may be visible
in the shop front. From time to time the advisory group themselves
become concerned about this problem, and resolve to make themselves
less conspicuous and also to reduce the picture of apparent chaos
that frequently presents itself to the person entering the shop.
Sooner or later however the more open informal atmosphere reasserts
itself. However, one or two steps have been taken by the group to
counteract the possibility of some people staying away because of
the style in which it is run. These are:
1 providing a large notice stating 'Please ask if you would like a
   private interview';
2 advertising that a social worker is available at the centre one
   session a week, with the implication that private problems may
   be taken to them if wished.

By and large it appears that the more aspirant, upwardly-mobile
the local resident, the more they are likely to be critical of the
'non-businesslike' way in which the centre appears to be run. These
residents may in fact prefer to call at local authority or central
government offices for information. On the other hand since the
number of callers has increased from 25 a week during the first year
to 50-60 during the second, its style is obviously attractive to
many others. In general the centre provides a service for those
members of the community who might be least likely to initiate contact with official departments themselves.

Initially the advisory group found it was difficult to appreciate
that as a group it was responsible for the overall functioning of
the centre. It understood much more easily its role of providing
voluntary helpers in the work of the centre. However, as various
policy issues and crises have come up, like the ones mentioned
above, the group has more and more come to recognise that it has to

exercise collective responsibility in ensuring that the centre runs
in the way its members want.

ADVOCACY AND SUPPORT

The total number of callers at the centre increased dramatically
during the first full year of resident control from approximately
1,000 recorded callers during the year under CDP management, to
approximately 2,000 recorded callers and an estimated total number
of callers of over 3,500 in the first year of resident management.
    In addition to this spectacular increase in the number of callers
at the centre one of the most significant developments since handing
it over to resident control has been that the volunteers at the
centre, as well as the full-time resident worker, have become increasingly expert in their knowledge about callers' entitlement to
welfare rights and in developing tactics to ensure that these rights
are granted. The report produced by the centre on the first five
months of full resident control show that the highest single category
of issues dealt with by the centre was welfare rights (22 per cent
of all cases - an increase of over 7 per cent on the first year
under CDP management), and the largest single category within this
was supplementary benefits problems (18 per cent of all issues dealt
with). The estimated percentage of supplementary benefit inquiries
for the full year of 34 per cent of all inquiries confirms this
trend. These figures suggest that the centre is developing a reputation as a place that gets things done and is worth visiting.
This hypothesis is reinforced by the fact that in the first year of
operation (June 1970 to May 1971) only 7.7 per cent of recorded
callers came from a radius of further than half a mile from the
centre, whereas at the end of the second year (the first full year
under resident control) this percentage had increased to 14.
    In relation to supplementary benefits the centre, and in parti-
cular the full-time resident worker, has developed a fairly aggres-
sive advocacy stance based on a detailed and thorough understanding
of the 1966 Social Security Act. Using knowledge of the Act and
advocacy skills he, or one of the volunteers, will accompany a
claimant to the office in those cases where there appear to be com-
plexities or where it is extremely urgent that the claimant should
receive a payment over the counter. Although the supplementary
benefit commission do not normally pay cash over the counter to
claimants, on every occasion, when the worker has deemed it to be
necessary to meet a claimant's urgent need, he has been able to persuade them to do so. Moreover, the number of supplementary benefit
appeals handled by the centre has been steadily increasing and a remarkably high success rate (92 per cent) achieved. In some eleven
months of operating under resident control the centre has 'won' for
its callers approximately £1,000 from the supplementary benefit commission alone, and this figure does not include any money won in the
form of obtaining free school meals and other welfare benefits, or
grants obtained from other agencies.
    In fact advocacy as a technique for helping people with a wide
variety of problems has developed and expanded considerably since
the centre was handed over to resident control and even local

authority social workers have begun to refer increasing numbers of their clients.

The resident worker at the centre has successfully represented callers at both rate and rent tribunals as well as supplementary benefit tribunals, and the legal advice law lecturer has success-fully appealed before the national insurance commissioners. But in addition to this formal representation at official tribunals a whole variety of advocacy techniques has been developed. Thus landlords who fail to do repairs or attempt to harass tenants have been threatened with legal action; the local newspaper, 'Hillfields Voice', has been used to publicise grievances; councillors have been used to fight for individual callers. In addition, the centre workers have acted as intermediaries with landlords, debt-collecting agencies, the gas and electricity boards and other agencies on behalf of callers. Not only does the centre appear to be more successful than many social work agencies in solving the problems that the customers themselves have said they have had, it also pro-vides an extremely supportive human response to callers with emo-tional and personal problems.

Two of the residents involved with the centre have taken homeless teenage girls into their own homes as a stop-gap way of helping them and also keeping them within the community. A very depressed sui-cidal woman was visited constantly and encouraged to come to the shop during a period of particularly acute depression. In fact a great deal of understanding and acceptance has been given to a whole variety of anxious and troubled people. One member of the advisory group (an unsupported mother) explained, 'When an unsupported mother comes into the shop with a debt I don't have to ask her how she feels, I know how she feels.' In this connection it is probably true to say that all the members of the advisory group have personal problems combined with problems of low income, and that far from hindering them in their ability to help others, their own circum-stances seem to have helped them appreciate the difficulties and have enabled them to respond not only warmly but relevantly. The crucial factor seems to be that if 'clients' or 'people with pro-blems' can be re-labelled as 'helpers' they are able to respond by acting accordingly.

The group of volunteers have proved to be extremely perceptive in their handling of difficult callers. For example, an extremely dis-turbed, attention-seeking, adolescent girl was helped by the group by being accepted and even taken into one of their homes and given a limited role in the centre. But when she started passing out drama-tically in the shop, her behaviour was not reinforced, and she was simply stepped over and ignored until she began behaving more normally!

Often the centre is able to do things that the statutory agency would not be able to do. For example, a local girl of just 16 who had lost her mother a few months before and her father a month later, and who was known to all the members of the advisory group, became pregnant and arranged to get married to her 17-year-old un-employed boyfriend. The girl was well known to the social services department, who had discussed with her the wisdom of marrying so young, and had helped her and the boy to look at alternatives. How-ever, they seemed determined to get married and obtained a special

licence. The boy's mother was living apart from her husband and in
no position to help them. They had no money, no possessions and nowhere to live. The problems seemed insurmountable. The boy was
under 18 and therefore too young to become a council house tenant,
and too young to become a legal tenant anywhere. Being out of work
he had no one from whom he could get a reference to give to a landlord. The problem was brought to the centre on the Monday before
the couple were due to be married on the following Saturday. The
centre took the whole problem on its shoulders: one of the advisory
group took the couple round to look at flats and to negotiate with
landlords on their behalf, and actually found a suitable flat; the
full-time worker went with them to the supplementary benefits office
to get a special needs grant to pay for cutlery, pots and pans which
were not provided by the landlord; a disturbed adolescent girl lent
the bride-to-be her coat to get married in; and the rest of the
group spontaneously organised an enormously successful reception for
them at the centre; several people gave presents, a press photo-
grapher was laid on and the couple were able to invite their friends
and relations.

Although the centre has not developed collective strategies for
problem-solving as fully as it has developed its individual advocacy
work, it has taken up certain general issues in press statements and
in the 'Hillfields Voice', for example, the failure of the city
council to advertise that free school meals are available during the
holidays, and the consequences of the failure of the council to
board up empty properties during the demolition process. Residents
involved in running the centre are presented with a dilemma similar
to the CDP worker who felt that individual advocacy and the stimulating of collective action do not easily mix. However, in terms of
organising collectively to achieve certain 'fun' objectives, as
opposed to 'protest' objectives, the group has been highly successful and, for example, has helped organise a sponsored pub crawl to
raise money for the adventure playground and other similar money-
making activities.

In the absence of suitable meeting places in the area the centre
has become the focal point of community activity and is used by a
whole variety of local groups for committee meetings. The members
of the advisory group are kept informed of the activities of these
local groups through their membership of them, and also through the
secretary of the HCA who is based at the centre.

All the members of the advisory group and the full-time worker
find that they are approached by local residents outside the
centre's opening hours in pubs, launderettes, and even in their own
homes. Thus the service offered is virtually twenty-four hours,
seven days a week which is made even more accessible by the virtue
of the fact that the members of the group are themselves part of the
informal communications system of the neighbourhood and are therefore liable to hear of problems at an earlier stage than might
happen with statutory agencies.

CONCLUSIONS

On the basis of the first two years' experience of a resident-run
information centre, several tentative conclusions may be drawn:

1 That there is an information gap between a wide range of
   national and local government agencies and the population they
   exist to serve, and that information centres, operated in a
   style acceptable to the local population, can help to bridge
   this gap;

2 that poor working-class people from stigmatised areas, who may
   themselves be clients of other agencies, are able to administer
   and run a social agency which relevantly meets the needs of some
   of the most disadvantaged;

3 that the local residents' informality, spontaneity and deter-
   mination to get things done, added to a way of appreciating
   others' problems as a result of being in a similar situation
   themselves, means that the services provided by such resident-
   run neighbourhood centres, and the style in which they are
   offered, are likely to be more relevant and more accessible to
   the community and therefore more effective than the services
   provided by either statutory agencies or middle-class run voluntary agencies;

4 that such centres can be extremely flexible in their response to
   problems and issues and can provide information and action
   'across-the-board', precisely because their activities are defined by their callers' expressed needs and not by a definition
   of agency function which compartmentalises problems as 'appropriate' or 'inappropriate' for the agency to deal with. This
   ability to tackle any problem seems to be especially important
   in a deprived area where the residents are unlikely to know precisely which of a number of official agencies ought to help
   them; where residents are unlikely to complain effectively if
   the agency that ought to help them fails to do so; where there
   is a general suspicion of 'them'; and where needs do not
   usually come singly, in neat compartments, but in combination;

5 that advocacy as a means of helping people in deprived areas
   should be recognised as an especially relevant way of meeting
   needs in such areas;

6 that the funding of such an agency is comparatively inexpensive
   and by tapping other community resources can represent a very
   effective investment;

7 that such centres can become the focal point of local initiative
   and action across a whole range of self-help and protest
   activities;

8 that feed-back from the residents who run such centres could
   form the basis of consumer/client input into social services
   departments as recommended by the Seebohm Committee report and
   could provide an essential component of any city's corporate
   management feed-back system; a component that is all too often
   conspicuous by its absence;

9 there is a strong case for the Urban Aid Programme funding such
   resident controlled centres, and indeed other community controlled projects, direct, since freedom to develop a style of
   operation relevant to the local situation seems to be a clear
   pre-requisite of success.

POSTSCRIPT (SEPTEMBER 1972)

The local full-time worker who had first come to the information
centre as an unemployed semi-skilled labourer in 1970 left the
centre in September 1972 to take up an appointment as a legal execu-
tive with a firm of Coventry solicitors who have appointed him because of their interest in establishing neighbourhood offices. The
management group was able to man the centre with volunteers in the
gap between his leaving and a new appointment being made.

Chapter 11

WELFARE RIGHTS: AN EXPERIMENTAL APPROACH

Jonathan Bradshaw

Much of the writing on evaluation research in social policy is devoted to the problems of carrying it out. The American textbooks on
the subject anguish over difficulties of formulating programme
goals, of finding indicators that measure outcome, of controlling
for intervening variables and maintaining the programme during the
crises of the experimental period and finally, the problems of drawing conclusions from the results (e.g. Weiss, 1972; Suchman, 1967;
Rossi and Williams, 1972)! Yet despite the difficulties inherent in
the method (and the generally pessimistic nature of conclusions)
more and more social agencies in the USA are being subjected to the
scrutiny of the social scientist. In Britain evaluative studies of
social policy have been slower to develop. Most of those that have
been carried out are of an ex post facto type and there have been
very few attempts at social policy experiments or field trials. The
two most notable recent experimental studies in social policy in
Britain have been Goldberg's evaluative study of social work with
the elderly (1970) and the Educational Priority Area (EPA) action-
research study (Halsey, 1972).

When the CDPs were first established it seemed as if they would
provide opportunities for evaluative studies. Early Home Office
memoranda expected that 'the lessons learned can be fed back into
social policy, planning and administration both at central and local
government level.' The projects were to be established in areas of
high social deprivation with an open brief to find new and more
effective ways of meeting social needs. Action and research teams
were to be appointed to each area and there was promise of support
and co-operation from government departments and local authorities.
On the face of it, it appeared to be as perfect a setting as possible for evaluation studies of both existing social provision and
any new initiatives, particularly field trials or experimental projects that might be introduced.

When all the projects have ended a good deal of descriptive and
analytic material will have been produced about the projects as a
whole - what they did, how they did it and what they achieved, but
this evaluation will be based on ex post facto studies or the observations and judgment of the research workers.

Why is this? Undoubtedly people in CDPs have been influenced by

the conclusions of Marris and Rein that the interests of action and
research are so different that attempts to link the two processes in
a single project are doomed to failure (Marris and Rein, 1972).
Town (1973) had also pointed out that in the EPAs 'given the changing nature of the project's activities, it was neither possible to
use the research evidence as a basis for planning action, nor to
evaluate the effects of action in a formal sense by measuring outcome against original intention.' He pointed out that in the EPAs
the original broad experimental design of the projects was abandoned
as the original objectives of the projects changed and it became
more and more difficult to control conditions in the schools. But a
limited amount of experimental work was carried out in the EPAs.
Town was even more sceptical of the feasibility of doing experimental studies on CDPs and Lees, who directs the research in the
Batley CDP has also written about the difficulties of research in
CDPs (see Chapter 7, The Action-Research Relationship).
    The welfare benefits project in Batley was therefore an attempt
to carry out 'hard' evaluative research into the effectiveness of a
trial programme within a CDP. It is the purpose of this chapter to
assess whether the experience of this project justifies the general
scepticism about the viability of experimental research in community
projects.

THE ORIGINS OF THE WELFARE BENEFITS PROJECT

At the end of 1972 the CDP at Batley was established and when both
action and research teams had been appointed they jointly agreed to
embark on a six months' period of exploration before deciding on a
programme of work. The action team began to explore the opportunities and problems in different neighbourhoods of the town while
the research team collected information about housing conditions,
employment and the operation of services across the town. At the
end of the six months' period the action and research teams came together to exchange the lessons that had been learned from their explorations and to consider ideas for action and research and plan
their implementation. One proposal that was brought to these meetings was that the project allowed opportunity for an action/research
experiment around the theme of welfare benefits. There were a
number of reasons why this idea was presented for research at that
time.

1. The social policy context

The Conservative government had come to power committed to selective
social policies and cuts in public expenditure. Two new selective
benefits had already been introduced - the family income supplement
and the attendance allowance - and others were in the pipe-line -
rent rebates and an increasing reliance on supplementary benefits
envisaged in their pension proposals. Other means tested exemptions
had become more valuable as charges for school meals, prescriptions
and dental and optical treatment had been increased. The government
had set great store on the success of their selective strategies and

were already spending large sums encouraging people to claim. Yet what little evidence there was showed that large numbers of those eligible were failing to apply for benefits, that whatever the aspirations of the national government, at a local level, benefits were difficult to claim because of their complexity and because of the way they were presented to the public and because many people remained ignorant of their availability.

2. The research context

Although means testing has become an increasingly important part of the income maintenance system since the war very little evaluation has been carried out of its effects. The government had carried out surveys in the 1960s that revealed that large numbers of those eligible were failing to claim benefits. There had been small scale studies of various aspects of means testing since that time but information on how many people failed to claim was sparse and information on why people failed to claim was non-existent. Academic discussion of social policy in this field as in many other fields was preoccupied with needs. The needs were being repeatedly identified by research; in this case poverty. Governments were passing legislation devoted to meeting these needs but few people, least of all the government, seemed concerned with evaluating those policies - observing how they were transferred into regulation, implemented by organisations and delivered - or too often not delivered - to the public. Little research was being done on what was happening at the interface between the agency and the consumer.

3. The Batley context

Early explorations have revealed that poverty was a pervasive problem in Batley. It appeared to be a town without a middle class, with very high levels of unemployment. Those who did work earned low wages in a rapidly declining textile industry. There were many more large families than elsewhere, larger numbers of immigrants, higher rents, more children on free meals and more old people. Yet in this arena of deprivation, advice or advisory agencies were non-existent. There was no advice centre, the CRO was at odds with the immigrant community, the supplementary benefits commission had closed its local office and removed its staff to Dewsbury. The social services department had no office in Batley, the trades' council was moribund and the textile unions ineffective, there were no tenants' associations and the only neighbourhood organisation of any impact - the working men's clubs - were determined to remain a refuge from social conditions. The inner core of the city had been converted from slums to a derelict wilderness and its inhabitants rehoused on new estates inaccessible to shops and council offices. With a population of 40,000 Batley seemed a perfect experimental ground.

4.   The CDP context

One of the difficulties in CDPs is the wideness of the brief.
Unlike workers in the EPA programmes who at least had education as
their central theme, CDP workers are placed into a strange environment with a general brief to find new ways of meeting social needs.
What do they actually do? The action teams in Batley espoused the
overriding principle that what they should do should come up from
the grass-roots. But given that they all arrived in Batley with
different backgrounds and different areas of expertise it was not
surprising that what 'came up from the grass-roots' coincided pretty
closely with their own interests. Thus an ex-planner identified
urban dereliction and improvements grants as opportunity for action,
an ex-teacher resolved to work on social education projects with
schools and an ex-social worker to support the development of pre-
school provision.
     For the research team these decisions posed certain difficulties.
They could observe how these activities proceeded, but how could
they evaluate them? There were no clear objectives to evaluate.
How could they get out of these not particularly original activities
new lessons for social policy? True they might produce interesting
case studies in the community work process. They might reveal problems in administrative structures; but was this enough? The ideas
that came up from the action team were concerned to alleviate immediate and obvious problems in Batley. They were not designed with
evaluation in mind and it was not clear how these initiatives could
be researched. Was the research team member to travel after the
action personnel recording every word and every deed? Was it only
for this that highly paid and qualified social scientists were
appointed for three years? The research team's career investment
might well have remained unfulfilled. If the action team had spent
three years floundering around looking for a role, then the research
team would end up describing an action team floundering around looking for a role.
     What better opportunity than in a CDP to introduce the one re-
search method that combines measurement and observation with action
- the experimental method? If the backing of the action team could
be obtained the research teams could not only study how welfare
benefits were administered but actually try out ways of administering them better to discover whether as a result they became more
acceptable to beneficiaries.
     When the idea was presented to the action team, no one was very
enthusiastic. They were reluctant to be associated with a project
concerned with testing whether means tested benefits could work. It
was too limited a goal for radical community workers. Their orientations were not towards programmes that made agencies more effective but to strategies that would increase the power of people in
their neighbourhoods. No one on the action team felt they had the
expertise to carry out the action programme.
     In the event however, the project was accepted as one of the pro-
grammes of the Batley CDP. The exploratory studies had revealed the
need for some kind of advice agency in the town. They were attracted to the idea that the project might produce findings of some
national importance to social policy. The following statement went

into the Batley CDP report 'The First Six Months' as one of the proposed initiatives.

The development of an advice and information campaign, with a worker based in the area Social Services department. This Campaign will explore and evaluate methods of disseminating information about all welfare benefits and increasing the rate of take up. An advisory group of local people will be established for this specific programme.

THE IMPLEMENTATION OF THE ACTION AND RESEARCH

The aim of the welfare benefits project as stated, was to discover how far a locally based and concerted campaign of education and publicity could increase the uptake of a range of selective social benefits.

The research proposals went on:

All these benefits are available to the poor if they apply for them but despite considerable expenditure on a national publicity campaign it is clear that many eligible families are still not claiming. Very little is known about why people do not claim but three factors are thought to be important causes of non up-take.

(i) Ignorance of the availability of the benefits or that the individual might qualify for them.

(ii) Complexity - difficulties of getting leaflets and forms, understanding them and completing them deterring applicants.

(iii) Stigma of having to prove poverty with a test of means.

Evidence from earlier studies suggests that stigma is a highly complex phenomenon and it appears that it may not be so much an abhorrence of undergoing a means test that deters claims, but an unwillingness to perceive oneself as poor enough to qualify for the benefit. Thus ignorance and stigma may be closely associated.

The hypothesis of this study is that all three factors can be overcome by a local information access and advisory service - ignorance can be tackled by bringing information home to people where they live, work, worship, play and learn. Complexity can be tackled by improving the knowledge of the helping professions and the performance of the departments administering benefits. Stigma can be overcome by urging the entitlement to benefits.

Selective social policies have not been successful to date - can they be made to succeed? This is a key question in social policy and the central question of this research.

When the research design was written the null hypothesis appeared more likely to be upheld. (1) The results of the action would probably show that some change can be made to take-up rates but that it would probably show even if a special effort is made to encourage people to claim, means tested benefits remain unacceptable to a large number of beneficiaries.

The action-research proposal went on to outline the ideas for the action programme.

ACTION PROGRAMME

There will be an open ended programme of work pursued at different levels over a two year period. It will be mainly carried out by a 'welfare benefits worker' attached to the area office of the Social Services Department but he or she will work closely with the rest of the action team. To appoint such a worker to the Social Services Department with this role is a new idea and as such the method of work will have to be developed by trial and error; however, these are some of the types of activities in which he or she will be involved.

1. Improvement of the information giving of existing agencies:

The following agencies will be involved: Education department and schools, Housing Dept., Borough Treasurer's Dept., Health Dept., and Clinics, Hospitals, GPs' Surgeries, Employment Exchange and Social Security Offices, Library and Post Offices.
  The aim is to increase the output of information from these agencies - not just of their own benefits but also benefits of other departments. At every contact point the public should be able to get information about all the benefits available.

2. Improve the skills and knowledge of helping personnel:

This would not only include the staffs of statutory and local authority agencies (social workers, health visitors, teachers, clerks etc.) but also other people who come into contact with the poor - clergy, trade unionists, employers, voluntary workers and leaders of community groups.
  This could be done in a number of ways: special training courses, the distribution of leaflets, claim forms etc., and the production of a welfare benefits guide for Batley.

3. Improvement of the knowledge of the general public:

There are a variety of methods of doing this:
(a) Leafletting and door to door knocking.
(b) Mobile advice service.
(c) Talks and discussions with all the organisations in Batley
     that may contain claimants.
(d) Education and training of the members of these organisations
     and other groups formed out of other CDP initiatives so that
     they can give advice and information on benefits.

4. Provision of a focus for skilled advice and advocacy:

It is proposed that the focus for this work will be in the Social Services Department where the worker will be available to provide skilled advice and advocacy. As a result of other action group

strategies a shop or support centre may be established and if it
is appropriate this might also be used for information and advice
on benefit matters.

5. Consultation:

It is an essential feature of this project that the welfare benefits worker is sensitive to the needs and aspirations of local
people. It is therefore proposed that a group of local people -
claimants and non-claimants will be established to act as advisers and consultants to the project.
The decision to base the worker in the social services department
was taken for three reasons (a) the action team wanted to build up
links with the social services department and based as they were in
the education department, communication was proving difficult;
(b) there were already moves to appoint such workers to social services departments and the Batley project provided an opportunity to
explore how someone with this role operated in such a setting;
(c) as much of the action design involved co-operating with existing
agencies it was felt that co-operation would be easier to get if the
worker had an official status within the local authority department.
The provision of a consultative body of local people was not envisaged in the original design but was tacked on by the action team
in order to maintain the theme of grass-roots involvement.
The research programme was outlined as follows:

RESEARCH PROGRAMME

1. A statistical analysis of take-up before, during and after
    the two year period. It will not only be necessary to do
    this for Batley but also for other towns to act as a control.
2. Description and analysis of the methods used to encourage
    take-up.
3. Sample Surveys:
    (a) At the beginning of the project a survey designed to
         provide information from claimers on how they found out
         about the benefits and their experience of claiming and
         from non-claimers why they do not claim.
    (b) A small depth study of the general population and of
         claimants to assess their beliefs, knowledge, feelings
         and attitudes to benefits, their recipients and the
         agencies administering them.
    (c) (a) repeated to identify if any significant changes have
         taken place.
4. A cost/benefit analysis of means tested benefits in Batley.
    This then was the action-research design that was accepted by the
action team. Once it had the support of the action director the
Home Office readily agreed to provide the extra finances for the
project and with the Home Office paying 75 per cent of the costs the
West Riding social service committee agreed to the appointment of
the welfare rights worker.
    Having interviewed the applicants for the post, the action

director decided to appoint two people instead of one. They were a
man aged 28 and fresh from a post-graduate social administration
course at Bristol where he had learned his welfare rights in the
local CPAG branch, and a 57-year-old miner who had worked for the
National Council of Labour Colleges and the TUC and was now an unemployed organiser of claimants' unions. In the event, one worker
took up the joint appointment with the social services department
who refused to take on the other as well and he was paid and housed
directly by the project. Both men started work in late autumn of
1972. Meanwhile a research student had been recruited by the university to work on the project and another research student had
volunteered to work on it. One of the research staff at Batley took
on substantial responsibility for the research programme. A research director had been appointed and took over direction of the
research.

What conclusions can be drawn from this experiment of an action-
research project? Has the investment of money and manpower paid
dividends? Does our experience suggest that it is impossible to do
hard evaluative research in this type of setting?

It is perhaps too early to answer these questions finally because
although the experimental period is nearly at an end, analysis of
the results of the project are still in progress. Yet it is possible to indicate what the action and research personnel have decided is worth writing up. If these proposals are set against the
original intention, it becomes more clear what will be achieved and
what will not.

1. The results of the sample survey will provide information
about the take up of means tested benefits and the incomes of people
in Batley. It will also produce statistical estimates within
reasonable confidence limits of the proportions of the population of
Batley claiming rent rebates, rate rebates, free school meals and
supplementary benefits. The sub-sample of FIS families was not
large enough to extrapolate from.

2. Sub-samples of claimants and eligible non-claimants for three
benefits were followed up and re-interviewed to establish whether
they had applied for the benefit as a result of the campaign. It
will therefore be possible to check whether the campaign got across
to these people and made any impact on their behaviour.

3. In the case of rent rebates and allowances and rate rebates,
claims for benefit have been monitored before, during and after the
campaign in Batley and a similar monitoring operation has been
undertaken in six 'control' towns. It should be possible to tell
from this exercise whether take-up rates increased significantly in
Batley as a result of the campaigns.

4. The position of immigrants and the special problems that they
have with benefits is being studied separately.

5. An in-depth study of non-claimants of benefits is being
carried out to examine reasons for not claiming.

6. The experience of the welfare rights workers will be reported
and analysed and put together with experience of those in similar
appointments elsewhere and should produce a comprehensive picture of
the opportunities of this type of role in the social services.

7. The records of the cases that the welfare rights workers have
handled will be analysed and a sample of these visited to produce an

assessment of how effective they have been in their advocacy work. A considerable amount of information has been collected in these records about the operation of the supplementary benefits commission and this will be used to point to areas of reform. It will also include an analysis using test cases of different methods of case advocacy.

8. An assessment will be made of how the agencies viewed the project and what influence it had on their operation.

9. Finally what actually happened will be described - what the welfare rights workers did including what groups they helped to establish, how these groups have operated and what they have achieved and how the project operated within the context of the whole CDP.

Although these achievements go a considerable way in fulfilling the intention of the research design, they leave a considerable amount left undone and particularly those aspects of the project which used the experimental method.

There are two types of explanation of why not all the original aspirations of the project will be fulfilled.

(i) There were a number of difficulties that the research team encountered in setting up the research design that could be described as technical problems. Thus, for instance, a sample survey which had to be carried out in order to establish the base rates had to be completed quickly before the action got under way. Yet it was one of the most difficult types of survey to do, requiring detailed information on income and household circumstances. It had to be a large sample in order to identify adequate sub-samples of claimants and non-claimants.

In addition the action team had asked for the questionnaire to be extended to include many questions not relevant to the welfare benefits project.

It was also found very difficult to obtain statistical information on take-up. The local authority departments co-operated quite freely - but their statistics were rarely collected in an easy form for analysis for research purposes. The control towns were also very helpful but to get co-operation from DHSS required extensive negotiations at national level backed up by the Home Office. In the end the DHSS agreed to trace FIS claims from Batley but only for a period that was too short to evaluate the campaign. The supplementary benefits commission finally agreed to separate Batley claims from the rest of claims to the Dewsbury area office but only from March 1973 by which time the action project had been going for five months.

(ii) The other difficulties that occurred in the project were much more significant and arose as a result of the setting of the project in the CDP and the orientation of the people engaged to work on it.

The most important single factor in the project and one that pervaded the whole operation was the mode of work that the welfare rights workers developed after they had been appointed. They had been given a fairly broad brief to try out a range of different methods to increase the take-up of means tested benefits. This brief involved working with and improving the operation of benefit agencies, improving the skills and knowledge of the helping

personnel, trying different methods of publicity and information including the development of self-help groups and the provision of a
skilled advice and advocacy service.

Partly as a result of choice and partly by force of circumstances
the range of activities they engaged in narrowed. Very little work
was done in a co-operative way with agencies: one of the rights
workers soon found his basis in the social services restricted his
style and independence and he joined the other worker in the project
offices. Dialogue with the local supplementary benefits office
became more and more acrimonious as they both advocated hard on
behalf of individual cases; communication with the educational welfare officer ended abruptly when the project as a whole began to
cross swords with the council (one of the EWOs was a councillor); a
similar situation arose with the community relations office and
little contact was made with rent or rate rebate offices except for
discussing forms and publicity material. At a meeting called by the
regional controller to discuss the tactics of the action team in
pressing claims for discretionary benefits, the officials complained
that no mention of their local office had been put on the action
team's FIS leaflet. 'After all we are administering the benefit',
they said. In taking the side of 'us' the action teams found it
more and more difficult to communicate with 'them'.

Work to improve the skills and knowledge of helping personnel was
no doubt hampered by these cursory relationships. Talks were given
to different groups and welfare benefits information was distributed
but little priority was given to this work which would have required
a considerable input over the period of the project to produce dividends in increased claims.

The publicity campaigns became one-off six week leafletting and
postering and advertising exercises, unrelated to the other parts of
the action programme. They were not generally backed up with talks
to local groups and potential intermediaries, nor was there any
attempt to canvas claims door to door, run a mobile advice service
or try out different methods in different areas of the town. The
time scale of the take-up campaign was drastically shortened. Concerted campaigns started in January and took in rent allowances,
FIS, rate rebates and rent rebates and the whole operation was completed by August.

The two parts of the original brief that were developed most by
the action workers were the provision of skilled advice and advocacy
and group formation.

The action workers were partly forced into concentrating on group
formation and individual case advocacy. They started work in the
aftermath of the upheaval of the implementation of the Housing
Finance Act. As in many towns at that time, militant tenants'
associations had developed to organise opposition to the implementation of the Act. Having failed to stop the implementation of the
Act in Batley the tenants' association decided to establish an
advice centre. The action workers were forced initially against
their will to support this venture and to help it become effective.
They soon found they were having to take on a load of advocacy of
individual cases. As their reputation grew, more and more claimants
came to them for help until they were almost overwhelmed. At the
same time the advice centre became a central issue between the whole

project and the Batley council. The project wanted to develop an
advice centre run by an unemployed ex-tenants' association member.
Batley council opposed this man and wanted a more formal CSS type
organisation with representatives on its management committee. This
became a major issue of dispute which, although interesting in its
own right, diverted the attention of the welfare rights workers from
their brief.

But this movement in emphasis in the welfare benefits project
also arose from the workers' own inclinations. They both had backgrounds of militant action in favour of claimants and they both
found it difficult to combine confrontation strategies with the
public relations, education and detailed administrative requirements
of their role.

The result of all this is that there has not been a broad based
programme of work to encourage the take-up of means tested benefits
and thus to some degree the hypothesis that was originally set up
has not been tested. We still do not know whether a concerted campaign on different levels over a period of time could increase the
take-up of means tested benefits. All we are going to be able to
say about take-up is that when some imaginative publicity is used in
short-term drives, it does not have an impact on take-up.

As a result of the way in which the action team operated, the research team had constantly to adapt their research programme to
changes in emphasis in the project.

A cost/benefit analysis of the operation had been built into the
original research design because it was thought that increases in
take-up should be assessed in the context of the effort required to
implement them. As it became clear that the action team were not
going to invest a lot of time and money to increasing take-up the
proposal was dropped.

It has also been the intention of the research team to carry out
a second sample survey at the end of the experimental period to
assess the changes in take-up that had been achieved during the experimental period. Evidence from the follow-up of the non-claimers
in the first survey showed that the campaigns that had been carried
out had made little impact. It was therefore not worth measuring
how little, given that the results would be subject to sampling
errors and changes in benefit and wage levels.

As well as discarding the parts of the original research design
the research workers have had to adapt their work and follow up and
monitor lines of activity that had not been given emphasis in the
original design - for instance with the welfare rights workers
putting such a lot of emphasis on case-work with supplementary benefits claimants (2) a research worker has had to spend time analysing
their records and following up the families they have visited. No
doubt useful data will be produced both on the methods of case advocacy, its effectiveness and on the workings of the supplementary
benefit scheme but none of these were envisaged in the original
design and it is not easy for a research worker to be as flexible as
this.

Town (1973) has suggested that experimental action-research is
fraught with practical difficulties which are normally articulated
as conflicts between practitioners and the research worker. Certainly there have been conflicts of orientation and value in the

welfare benefits project but they were resolved by adaptation on both sides. Much of the experimental nature of the original design had to be adapted to pick up the opportunities afforded by the action. The action workers had to agree to put some effort into testing out the hypotheses that the research had prepared to test. The experimental setting had to be flexible yet the action workers had to retain some discipline and planning in their work. Although this represents a compromise, it goes further than description and post facto analysis or research totally unrelated to action which are the alternative possibilities in this type of situation.

Experience of the welfare benefits project in Batley suggests that this type of field trial is feasible within CDPs and that if it is not too late some of the newly established projects should be encouraged to establish them. This does not gainsay that mistakes were not made in the Batley welfare benefits project or that CDPs are necessarily the best setting for this type of research project and so it is worth ending this chapter with a few prescriptions.

Future projects should beware of being too ambitious and committing all their research personnel too early in the experimental period. Research workers in Batley were so taken up analysing the mass of data that had been collected from the sample survey, the follow-up studies or statistical returns, that they had no capacity to respond to interesting developments by the action team in the later stages of the project.

Action-research projects should be directed by one person who has his primary allegiance to applied research. For these projects to be doing interesting and useful experimental work, the director must know what is feasible. Having established a programme of activity that is researchable they have then got to try to let the experiment run its course without major upheavals and reorientations. In the CDP context with the action and research role split, it is difficult to get a commitment from an action director to research goals: they are not primarily interested in the research outcome as their reputation rests on the success of the action programme. A director with his primary allegiance to research goals would be more prepared to accept the 'failure' of a project.

The CDP setting is the cause of other difficulties for experimental research. Both the research team and action team have many opportunities to be distracted from work on an experimental project to other activities - not least the continuing debates within the project about its direction and purpose. The CDP setting has not turned out to be an easy environment to execute calmly a predetermined research design and anyone who has worked in a CDP knows the difficulties of concentrating on one programme of work in a highly charged emotional climate of conflicting personalities and priorities.

But it should not be forgotten that there are unique advantages in the CDP setting for evaluative work. CDP are generously financed and staffed, are independent and provide unique opportunities of access for local authority and central government co-operation with an open ended brief. These opportunities are not available elsewhere to university research workers and it ought to be possible to carry out more experimental studies into the effectiveness of social policy within CDPs.

NOTES

1   For a summary of current research on the subject see Peter
    Townsend, 'The Scope and Limitations of Means-tested Services in
    Britain', Manchester Statistical Society, 1973.
2   Over 500 recipients of supplementary benefits in Batley have
    been helped.

Chapter 12

A NOTE ON COMMUNITY EDUCATION

Eric Midwinter

A busking violinist, cap of dimes at his feet, was playing in a New York gutter, when someone asked him how to get to Carnegie Hall. 'Practice, son,' he answered resignedly, still fiddling, 'jest practice.' As we struggle toward that Carnegie Hall of community development - a reformed social and economic context, replete with participation - it is perhaps the task of education to provide the skills (through, as it were, constant 'practice') rather than to specify the direction (in answer, as it were, to the inquiry about how to get there). Many months of connection with CDPs, and other like-minded ventures, including a two-year educational consultancy for the Home Office, during which I visited several CDP areas and met many of the personnel, convinces me that some community developers have not yet drawn that distinction.

The community education movement, in regard especially to disadvantaged areas, has the Halsey Report as its credo. No educational report has been heartier or clearer in spelling out the limitations of institutional education, both in terms of its lack of success as a change-agent and its constantly being the victim of circumstance. The child's education is often dictated by his socio-economic context, and then the schooling he obtains does not enable him, even if he so wished, to alter that context. Many community developers have taken this great truth to heart. They have not as avidly grasped to their bosoms the other truth revealed in the Halsey Report, namely, that one of the reasons for the inefficiency of the education system apropos social change has been its own inherent characteristics. Some of these favour a stationary and ascriptive society, or, at least, are neutral on the subject of change. Briefly, those tendencies which help preclude change are precisely those which involve the alienation of the schools system from its host communities. Conversely, as schools, as several are doing, pay more and more regard to local needs or aspirations and strengths or weaknesses, they are able to relate more closely to their catchment areas.

Some CDPs have attempted to search out a place for education within their activities, notably with John Rennie's Community Education Programme being developed with liveliness and aplomb in Coventry. But there is also a fatalistic view of education. If education, the arguments run, does not contribute to social reform and is itself subject to the strong influence of social factors, then it is hardly worth the appropriately proverbial ball of chalk. Further, this reasoning continues, the efforts of community educators might, at best, be wasteful and, at worst, fraudulent. They might distract activists from the real struggle - that for social and economic reformation - or even give the impression that something brave and fruitful is being done.

This defeatist view of education within the pale of community development has considerable support. In practice, it encourages all shoulders to be placed against the big wheels of, say, housing or employment, leaving schooling, with only, at most, long term and indirect effects, strictly alone. Instead of demanding that they watch with the wise virgins, it would abandon educationists, in the words of the old schoolboy howler, to sleep with the foolish ones. And foolish indeed this would be, for time-lags between advancement on any community-based fronts can be dangerous and critical.

This negative school of educational thought is founded on a simplistic viewpoint of community development; a kind of black and white or see-saw analysis, whereby community-type activities are either fully for us or completely against us. It is only when a more subtle cyclic model of community development is envisaged that the naivety of the see-saw view grows apparent. There is a sense, of course, in which all community development is educational, in that the awarenesses of the public are sharpened by contact with communally-based action and involvement. Herein lies the point. Community education is that element in community development which most lucidly emphasises the growth in skills of community management.

Visualise two likely and oft-repeated possibilities in the community developmental circle. The first possibility might be the arrival, through central or local legislation, of additional resources or services, capable of altering some aspect of the socioeconomic context. Question: does the citizenry have the skills and capacity to utilise the newfound bounty as fully and beneficially as possible? The second possibility might be the opportunity arising for joint action on the part of some group of tenants or other category. Question: does the group have the skills and capacity to turn such an opportunity to proper advantage? It is arguable that, in such situations, the inadequacy of skills has sometimes been inhibiting. To use a common example, it is often quoted that, by and large, the socially disadvantaged are less able than the socially advantaged in terms of organising and articulating and grasping fruitfully at such rights as do exist.

A fully-fledged community education programme embracing adults as well as children, and embracing adults, as adults, as well as in their parent capacity, could provide links in this circular chain. It could assist people both to make the best possible use of resources when offered and to create the kind of organisation and pressures that might be necessary. Conversely, the spiral might run the other way, with resources frittered away and chances wasted or unnoticed through lack of educational in-put.

To underpin this circular effect, one must also emphasise that the education system is inextricably bound up with the rest of the

social whirl of everyday life. It is necessary to stress this
truism, for part of the see-saw analysis is somehow to see the
schools separately from the remainder of the community. The effects
of the outside world on actual educational attainment require no
more rehearsal here, and there is, in fact, a kind of educative
climate throughout the whole of society, influencing what children
do or do not do in school. Again, the school is a common denomina-
tor in the community, for, of all social services, it is one of the
most generally used. Everyone has attended school; many people
have children or relatives presently in school; schools are
familiar landmarks in any neighbourhood, and the idea of the school
having some focal place in the locality is neither new nor modish in
many people's eyes. There is even a pleasing irony regarding this.
In my own experience, I have found many parents in socially deprived
areas who have a high affection for the school, precisely because it
is frequently the only agency that works. In districts of under-
employment, with old housing or redevelopment causing problems, with
public transport and environmental amenities insufficient, with the
social services occasionally unintelligible and a lack of play-space
and so forth, the school stands supreme. It takes one's child
exactly as promised, aged 4 or 5, and, between the contracted hours
and on the contracted days, it caters for the child, giving him,
where appropriate, refreshment as well as more scholarly nourish-
ment. Many children enjoy school and see it as a stable point in
what perhaps are buffeted existences. Many parents have a firm
regard for the efforts of the teachers who, on the whole, keep their
official promise.

This is not a whitewashed picture. There are many problems,
especially where post-adolescence and schooling meet. It may, at
worst, be no more than a superficial sustenance of the official
promise to educate one's child. But, relative to some of the other
difficulties that exercise the minds of a disadvantaged clientele,
education is not high on the list of priorities. Thus it is sometimes hard to persuade parents that, without their active support,
the education system, solidly though it may appear to be operating,
could be unable to offer the children very much. Once more the circular motion of community development is evident. Schools need to
help parents to assist their children educationally; so that the
children might grow more socially efficient and knowledgeable; so
that they might more fruitfully seize chances of improving their lot
and that of their locality; so that, for instance, the locality
might procure better equipped and socially livelier schools, so
that, with the help of a next generation of parents, themselves
imbued with an extended perspective on such matters, the children of
the next age might lift society to a higher level of social effectiveness and good practice.

It is essential, too, to underline the role of the child as a
member of the community. The see-saw viewpoint, tends to observe
the school as manufacturing a human product, who somehow escapes the
pressures of social and economic circumstance until he has been
'prepared'. It is always salutary to recall that the child is a
junior citizen, already beset, from varying angles, with many of the
issues - housing, consumerism, services - afflicting his adult com-
patriots. He is already in the community; his major grouping or

contact-point with others in the community tends to be the school. It would be wise not to ignore this.

There are, therefore, two lines of argument for including community education within community development. The second is the unavoidability of it, the sheer presence of an educative dimension, institutional and non-institutional, in the community. The first is the lubrication argument, the need for an oiling of the wheels of community development, so that participatory processes might improve and improve. I have found community developers taking a dangerously casual or, perhaps worse, romantic view of people's capacity to indulge in successful decision-making schemes. They sometimes seem to expect village Hampdens to rise untutored from the streets by some process of spontaneous combustion. This, of course, is not unknown, but one should be wary about basing a national movement on the likelihood of such a fortuitous incidence continuing. I have heard it said that education for participation and social awareness is 'patronising' and that the professional intervention of the educator is stifling. The ones who say this are often the ones who equally argue that the present educational system and climate train people for an ascriptive rather than a developmental community. They cannot have both the nascent John Wilkes, freely coming to a belief in fighting for communal rights, and desk-slaves, bound to the existing set-up by the ties of an oppressive schooling.

It would be illuminating to know to what extent Wellington really thought that Waterloo was won on Eton's playing-fields, or, more poignantly, Lenin felt that Russia's Bolshevism was based in the British Museum. Community education fulfils, then, a similar lubricant function for community development, and one should remember that hardly any major movements in history (irrespective of whether we personally approve of them or not) has lacked training-schools. Community development is lop-sided without them, and has little hope of more than a transient or short-term success - just as, admittedly, the community educator can only operate in the knowledge that, without major reforms in the communal context, his endeavours are in vain. Let us not see our pet interests so exclusively; community development is or should be interdisciplinary; it should not eschew the second-phase questions of practice in a too rigorous presumption about the first-phase question of direction.

Chapter 13

CURRICULUM DEVELOPMENT AND THE COMMUNITY APPROACH

Ray Lees

In the search to provide a curriculum that is more directly relevant to the lives of most people in an urban society, a number of educationalists have recently proposed a radical reorientation towards education based in and on individual communities (Raynor and Harden, 1973). Only through community based education, they usually argue, can the majority acquire the necessary knowledge, understanding and skills to comprehend or improve their environment. One difficulty with the community approach for the less committed educationalist is that the concept of community can be interpreted in a variety of ways. This ambiguity has been adequately discussed at an academic level (Hillery, 1955), but little is known of its consequences in educational practice. This chapter reports a modest effort in the community approach to curriculum development in one secondary modern school. From the research point of view, it is little more than a pilot study. However, the findings are useful in suggesting some of the difficulties that may occur in introducing community education in schools.

The study is concerned with an experimental course in community education given to pupils in their last year at a girls' secondary modern school. The programme occupied one day of school over a period of ten weeks. Eighty girls were registered for the course. Five teachers were involved out of a staff of sixteen. In addition six students doing a community education teachers' training course at a college of education participated in the planning and teaching. Members of a government sponsored CDP, operating in the locality, were also involved.

There are considerable difficulties in evaluating this kind of short-term innovatory programme. Early observation suggested that the different groups involved tended to perceive the venture in differing and sometimes contradictory ways. In this kind of situation there is no commonly accepted criterion for success against which to measure the project. Given this ambiguity, the research approach attempted to identify the differing perceptions and interpretations of what the course was, or should have been about. The method was partly by participant observation in staff group discussions and some teaching sessions, partly by separate interviews with key actors, and finally complemented by a questionnaire administered to seventy of the girls who participated as pupils.

STAFF PERCEPTIONS

Amongst teachers at the school there were significant differences in perception of the community education approach between those who participated in the programme and those who did not. Those who helped to initiate and run the course tended to see the community focus as offering an opportunity to develop a curriculum that would be more relevant to the needs and interests of pupils than the convential subject-orientated approach. They chose the theme of employment and used various teaching devices, including outside speakers, visits to people and places of interest, taped-interviews conducted by pupils, small group discussions, task-orientated projects and free expression periods. The teachers were young members of staff who felt that their previous classroom efforts had been largely received in boredom and apathy. They wanted the community initiative to provide a means for more effective communication between teacher and pupil, to promote confidence and more effective self-expression amongst the pupils, and for pupils to become better informed on matters considered relevant to their own environment.

Most non-participating teachers, on the other hand, felt that the project was harmful to the on-going work of the school. Some believed that any community emphasis should involve all pupils and staff, thus strengthening the sense of belonging within the school. This view regarded any initiative concerned with less than the whole institution as divisive. Others felt that the community approach should involve some form of social service, such as visiting the elderly in the locality of the school. It was pointed out that the project was not forging links between home and school. The day each week free from regular studies was further seen as interfering with CSE and 'O' level preparations. Others challenged the view that a conventional subject syllabus need necessarily be taught in a narrow and uninteresting way, and tended to regard community education as a 'trendy but short-lived gimmick'. The freer atmosphere believed to be associated with the community venture was widely felt to be having an ill effect on discipline within the school generally. There was also some underlying resentment of the special attention and responsibility that had been given to a group of junior staff members.

The student teachers who participated on the course were also critical, but for very different reasons. They believed that community education should involve pupils in defining their own interests and needs with support, but not direction, from teachers. From this perspective, they felt that participating staff teachers tended to be directive and authoritarian, preventing spontaneous educational experiences from developing. Community education to this group required a situation where pupils should have 'a real and not a token share' in decisions which affect them, should be able to act openly and fearlessly with teachers on terms of equality, and should be completely free in matters of personal self-expression and taste. Any overall direction should emerge only from full 'democratic' discussion to which all individuals could contribute.

AIMS OF COMMUNITY EDUCATION

In his discussion of curriculum development, Halsey (1972) identified the following aims that guided experiments in four educational
priority areas:
1 Improvement of skills by treating traditional subjects in new
   ways;
2 to provide a more enjoyable and intrinsically satisfying
   curriculum;
3 to promote in children a critical understanding of their
   environment.
   Our study of one effort to promote community education suggests
that aims can be interpreted and defined in additional ways. For
example, the staff teachers who participated in the programme also
expressed the following concerns:
4 to provide a curriculum more relevant to the everyday experience
   of children, but not necessarily critical of this environment;
5 to provide for more effective communication between teachers and
   children.
   The student teachers, on the other hand, stressed the critical
element and would agree with Midwinter (1972) that children should
be given 'the social competence to examine the depressing reality of
their world, in the hope they might learn to repair or change it in
ways agreeable and pleasing to them'. This radical orientation suggests further aims:
6 to break down authority distinctions in the teacher-pupil
   relationship;
7 to promote democratic decision-making within the school.
   Finally, the non-participating teachers conceived that community
education should be concerned with social responsibility within the
school, and between the school and its locality. To this group the
aims of community education should be:
8 to promote a sense of responsibility within the school
   community;
9 to provide a form of appropriate social service to people in
   need within the locality of the school;
10 to promote a more meaningful relationship between school and
   parents of pupils.
   The differing perceptions of community education that emerge from
this study are not exhaustive. A further approach, for example,
might seek to promote local involvement in the school process or
even some form of direct community control. In a situation where
meaning is ambiguous in this way, differing expectations can lead to
frustration and conflict. This tendency was apparent in the project
under discussion, with evident tension between the three groups
whose attitudes have been described. Disagreements became apparent
over approaches to discipline and teaching method, the content of
the course, the need for an open-day to display project work, the
desirability of designing a CSE syllabus in community education and
how this should be done, the possibility of creating a post of responsibility for community education in the school, and the relationship of this kind of initiative to the rest of the school
activities. Since underlying aims were usually implicit and often
conflicting, the issues could not be talked through or resolved to
everyone's satisfaction.

PUPIL PERCEPTIONS

Our main approach to understanding how pupils viewed the project was to administer a questionnaire. This took place after the course had been going for eight weekly sessions with two weeks left to run. Seventy girls were involved out of the eighty who were registered for the course. Some questions provided for a range of responses whilst others were open-ended. Girls were assured that their replies would remain anonymous and most seemed to co-operate with enthusiasm. Whilst not claiming to be more than impressionistic, responses do give some indication of pupil perception of the subject.

The girls were asked their opinion about the success of the course both from their own point of view and based on what they imagined the teachers thought. The results were as in Table 13.1.

TABLE 13.1

	Own viewpoint	Staff viewpoint
Very successful	24	20
Fairly successful	42	37
Rather unsuccessful	1	5
Very unsuccessful	-	1
No answer	3	7
Total	70	70

Thus it can be seen that overall the girls thought that the staff were slightly less pleased with the course than they were themselves. When they were asked whether they enjoyed the project more or less than normal school activities, 48 said that they enjoyed it more, 18 that they enjoyed it about the same, and 2 that they enjoyed it less; 6 girls mentioned its usefulness in terms of thinking about their future employment, 6 appreciated the more relaxed atmosphere, 3 felt that they had learned more about the community and 2 that they had gained confidence in talking with people. Ten girls thought that there was no difference between the project and normal school work.

The 25 girls who were taking 'O' levels or CSEs were asked if they felt that the project was interfering with this preparation. Of these, 17 felt that the project had not interfered whilst 7 felt that it had.

A considerable majority (60) thought that discipline was less strict than in normal school activities, but 7 of these felt that this was not a good thing; 29 thought that discipline should have been more relaxed. A minority (9) felt that there was no difference in discipline between the project and normal school experience. Over half (38) of the girls wrote that they found the student teachers more easy to talk to than the regular staff. These largely believed that the students were 'less stuck-up'. On the other hand,

22 felt that their presence had made no difference to the course, 8 found them harder to speak to than regular teachers, and 5 of the girls thought the course would have been more of a success if the students had not been there.

CONCLUSION

From this selection of responses it emerges that most of the pupils felt the project to be a success in a general way, but there were differences in evaluating particular aspects of the programme. Certainly the project was viewed as successful by the authorities. For example, speaking at the school speech day, the headmistress commented on the community education project: 'Our fourth year girls have clearly enjoyed this new type of education. The opportunity to exchange views in smaller groups is clearly what they are ready for. Their self-confidence has developed rapidly and they are formulating informed opinions.' In the light of such assessment the project has since become a regular feature in the school curriculum.

Whilst not wishing to deny that the project was a worthwhile initiative, it remains difficult for this study to pinpoint exactly what it achieved in relation to its goals. One reason for this difficulty is readily apparent. If one wishes to evaluate the effectiveness of a project in achieving a goal one must specify that goal. However, as has been shown, community education is likely to have multiple goals, some of which are mutually incompatible. This points to the need for a rigorous examination of aims before introducing this kind of innovation into the school curriculum. If this preparation does not take place then there is likely to be confusion and possible conflict over aims.

A second obstacle to successful innovation resides in the differing perceptions, feelings and value orientations of individuals and groups towards the planned change. It is also possible that innovation in curriculum will be resisted or disliked because of the supposed or real effect on status of staff. Such differences will not simply melt away under the pressure of increased intellectual rigour. It can be argued, therefore, that understanding and resolving these kind of difficulties requires social psychological insights and what have been called 'the skills of social interaction' (Smith, 1972). As Shipman (1973) has pointed out, 'innovation must not be presented on a plate to schools.' If community education is to play a vital role in community development, as Midwinter has argued in Chapter 12, it is certainly not self-evident what form this activity should take.

Chapter 14

SOCIAL NEEDS OF AN IMMIGRANT POPULATION

Morag McGrath

INTRODUCTION

One of the aims of CDPs is 'a better understanding and more comprehensive tackling of social needs'. This chapter briefly examines
the concept of social need and relates it to the differing perceptions of the social needs of immigrants in Batley, a town in the
West Riding of Yorkshire. Data on the perceptions of local
authority officials, councillors, members of the community relations
council and teachers - collected through interviews, the examination
of official documents and observation at meetings - is compared with
the perceptions of the immigrants themselves as expressed by immigrant leaders in interviews and in a wider survey of immigrant
households.
6.4 per cent of the 42,000 population of Batley are immigrants
(1971 census). An estimated 70 per cent are Muslim Indians origi-
nating from a small area in Gujerat. The remainder are West
Pakistanis, also Muslims. (The latter are at an earlier stage of
settlement than the Indian population with a higher proportion of
all-male households.) The population, particularly the Indian, is
mainly concentrated in one ward of the town, in owner-occupied
terraced houses, many lacking basic amenities. Cultural identity is
strongly maintained. The close village and kin networks, the
compact area of the community near the mosque and Indian shops and
religious customs of the Muslims all assist towards this. While
there are some Indians who do not conform to strict Muslim practice
the life of the majority is closely associated with the mosque. The
interests of the immigrant population are officially represented in
the town by the Muslim Welfare Society (MWS) whose main function is
religious teaching although another important aspect of the
society's work is the welfare of individual immigrants.

SOCIAL NEED

Two broad categories of social need can be distinguished:

1. Those recognised by society - 'normative' need

Normative need exists when conditions fall short of administrative or professional standards such as overcrowding in houses, or standards of literacy. Although these standards are arbitrary - for example, overcrowding is conventionally taken as being over 1.1 persons per room - it gives an accepted base line.

2. Those recognised by individuals and/or groups - 'felt' need

Felt need has the attraction of relating more directly to the issues an individual feels are important rather than imposing external standards. Community work is traditionally based on felt need reflecting both the principle that priorities should be set by the 'neighbourhood' group and the practical point that people are more likely to become involved in an activity they feel is relevant. Emphasis on this aspect of need is regarded as essential in CDPs. However, if need is being examined in order to relate it to policy decisions, felt need has the disadvantage that people tend to identify and compare themselves with groups among whom they live and work rather than the wider society. An immigrant may accept the low pay of the unskilled textile worker as a norm rather than the average pay of manual workers in Britain.

NORMATIVE NEED

The recognition of social need will differ with the perspective of the individual. The local authority officials' views of any minority group is likely to be primarily influenced by how that group affects their own work. In a report to a county working party on immigrants the Batley town clerk raised first the difficulties of language and communication which affected all departments. Even with volunteer interpreters 'one cannot be at all sure that what is being asked or given in explanation is fully understood'. In turn, the public health department mentioned the problem of different standards of public hygiene. The department accepted that non-statutory overcrowding was common although gross legal overcrowding was rare. The MOH's main comment concerned the higher incidence of TB, lack of family planning and high birth rate and inadequate nutrition in younger children. The housing department reported that immigrants in general did not seek council housing considering the rents to be too high. Problems of communication arose in slum clearance schemes, restrictions in LA housing and over the area required. It was estimated that approximately 40 per cent of council mortgage loans went to immigrants. These views derive from the professional standards of the local authority officer and describe normative need.

The general attitude of the town council can be seen in three references to the immigrant population in the council minutes from January to September 1973. First, an application for the mosque and its surrounds to be included in the extensive environmental improvement was accepted although the MWS were not included in the original

list of people invited to participate in the scheme. Second, a
letter was received from two committee members of the MWS writing as
individuals, expressing concern over the housing shortage and asking
for vacant land near the area of immigrant concentration to be
utilised for residential development, making houses available for
sale. There was no implication that the houses should be for immigrants only. The letter was unfortunately misinterpreted as a request from the immigrant organisation for development land for their
own use. Faced with this misunderstanding the matter was dropped by
the two Indians. Lastly, the chief public health inspector was
asked to discuss with the community relations officer what steps
could be taken to alleviate the problem of litter and refuse constantly left outside some immigrant properties. This issue had been
discussed solely in the context of the immigrant population. The
community relations officer (CRO) was later asked to translate a
letter on the subject into Urdu. This view of the CRO's role had
also been demonstrated in previous years when the CRO with housing
visitors carried out an investigation for the housing department of
immigrants in council houses with the subsequent reporting of any
'irregularities'.

The predominant approach to community relations in the town is
reflected in the work of the CRO. This has consisted of organising
various schemes to improve race relations - public lectures, holiday
camps for immigrants and non-immigrant boys, organising language
classes (both English and Gujerati) and helping individuals with
sundry problems. Cases of discrimination reported are virtually
non-existent. The CRO has been hampered by a breakdown in communication between the CRC and the MWS since his appointment. Contact
with the Pakistani population is more successful especially as he
speaks Urdu. The MWS regard the language classes for women initially organised through the Christian church as unacceptable. In spite
of this the home-tutor scheme was established with twenty-five
volunteers at the start although the number had dropped to as low as
three at one time. Other needs of the immigrant community mentioned
by the CRO were a community centre, youth club and playgroups. The
CRC recommended to the council in August 1970 the need for pre-
school playgroups and a supply of books in immigrant languages in
the library. The librarian had already begun a collection of relevant books but the playgroups never materialised.

Participation by immigrants in both the home-tutor scheme and
holiday camps demonstrates that the CRO is meeting the needs of a
number of immigrants in these areas. In general, however, the immigrants' needs are seen essentially in terms of improving race relations or in dealing with individual problems rather than in meeting the needs - either felt or normative - of the immigrant population as a whole. As discussed in detail by Hill and Issacharoff
(1971), this approach is common to many CRCs.

In January 1973 one primary school had 75 per cent immigrant
pupils, another over 60 per cent and a further three between 15 per
cent and 40 per cent. The boys' secondary school and one of the two
girls' secondary schools had 20 per cent immigrant pupils. With
many children starting school unable to speak English, language
difficulties are obvious.

At the secondary level the language problem is less severe than a

few years ago now that most new entrants have come up through the
primary schools. The special immigrant classes for boys whose
English is inadequate are diminishing in size. However, few pupils
thought in English and many found considerable difficulty in passing
English examinations. Official figures on language difficulties of
immigrant pupils reflect only the different perceptions of teachers
on the problem. Of two primary schools containing the highest proportion of immigrants, one reported 75 per cent pupils with language
difficulties and the other none. In the former, the difficulties
are seen as a definite problem which requires extra facilities and
staff. In the latter, the difficulties are accepted as part of the
everyday work of the school.

Apart from language difficulties the problem of children coming
to school tired after spending two hours every evening in religious
instruction at the mosque and trying to cope with homework, were
mentioned. The secondary schools were aware of the tension and
stress incurred by some immigrant adolescents. Views about the
needs of immigrant pupils at primary level varied from those
teachers who saw no problems at all, maintaining one could not distinguish immigrants from non-immigrants to the few who thought positive efforts should be made to help each culture understand the
other. With a few notable exceptions the attitude of the schools
towards the Muslim culture seems to be one of passive acceptance.
Children have to attend morning assembly but usually do not participate at the secondary level. The assembly at primary schools is
seen as basically secular by the teachers. At the boys' secondary
school Islamic teaching in Urdu is offered to CSE classes. One
primary school with a high proportion of immigrant pupils has
appointed a teacher working solely with immigrants including home
contacts. Another primary headmistress runs English classes for
immigrant mothers as part of a mothers' group and also employs an
Asian auxilliary in the nursery school (see also Yates, 1973).

The youth employment officer finds difficulty in placing immigrant boys in skilled jobs. He suggests the causes are partly discrimination but more important is that boys leaving school at the
statutory age have inadequate English and those leaving late are too
old to enter an apprenticeship. In 1971-2 71 per cent immigrants
and 40 per cent non-immigrants stayed on beyond the statutory school
leaving age. In 1970-1 about 79 per cent of immigrant school
leavers took semi-skilled or unskilled jobs compared with 30 per
cent non-immigrant boys. 18 per cent of the former and about 60 per
cent of the latter entered apprenticeships. In 1971-2 no immigrant
secured an apprenticeship compared with 50 per cent non-immigrants.

COMMUNITY DEVELOPMENT APPROACH

The immigrant population was seen by the CDP as a disadvantaged
group with whom contact should be made. The homogeneity of this
population and the fact that it was represented by one organisation
only, the MWS which had broken off relationships with the CRC placed
the project in a dilemma. There were a number of possible strategies - to work solely through the CRC, to work with the MWS leader-
ship or to attempt community work in the immigrant area outside the

MWS structure. It was decided that given the short-term nature of the project the second was the only feasible initial strategy.

In the summer of 1972 a Gujerati-speaking Indian student was employed to make contact with the immigrant population. She interviewed some of the MWS leaders and also spoke to women and teenagers. Following from this, there were a number of meetings between CDP and the MWS leaders mainly concerned with the religious needs of the group - extra priests, premises for religious classes, marriage laws. During these discussions it was agreed that the two organisations should co-operate on a survey of immigrant needs. The MWS leaders recognised a number of problems but lacked adequate information on the attitudes of the whole population. The CDP was interested in helping the MWS leaders to increase their knowledge of immigrant needs so that these could be made more public and might enable the leaders to recommend action.

A questionnaire was drawn up after discussions with the action director and the MWS. Two threads ran through the discussions - first, that immigrants should benefit from and be able to contribute to British society more fully, and second, the recognition and maintenance of the Muslim religion. The questionnaire covered the areas of need as seen by the MWS leaders - language, education, including pre-school and further education, employment, housing, health services, welfare rights and links with the non-immigrant community. Questions on race relations suggested by the CDP were excluded. The MWS leaders felt such questions might be seen as antagonistic.

A random sample of 69 immigrant households (14 per cent total immigrant addresses) was taken from the electoral register. Excluding empty houses and non-contacts, 55 households were approached, which resulted in 43 completed interviews (34 Indian and 9 Pakistani). The needs of the Pakistani and Indian population will largely overlap but given the different stage of settlement and nationality status, the Pakistani households are likely to have needs which were not revealed in the 9 interviews. The interviews were carried out by pairs of interviewers, one from the MWS and the other from CDP. Despite the inevitable methodological shortcomings of the survey the results give a good overview of felt need among immigrants.

To provide some comparative data, a sample of 49 non-immigrant households was interviewed. The small control sample is not put forward as representative of the non-immigrant population. However, it gives some indication of the different needs recognised by immigrant and non-immigrant households.

FELT NEED

Householders were asked which of the needs discussed they saw as presenting the greatest difficulty. Table 14.1 summarises the results. (The figures are not directly comparable as language is an extra factor for the immigrants.) Language and/or education were mentioned by 21 of the 30 immigrants who thought difficulties existed. Housing and/or employment predominated as areas of need for the non-immigrant households. The MWS leaders' views on the needs of immigrants were largely confirmed either in terms of felt need and/or normative need. Language problems are more strongly expressed and religious education less emphasised by the sample than by the leaders.

TABLE 14.1 Social needs of immigrants and non-immigrants

Area of need	Number of households mentioning problem	
	Immigrant households	Non-immigrant households
Language	18	-
Education	7	-
Housing	9	17
Employment	2	17
Religious needs	4	-
Transport	-	2
Need for		
Advice facilities	4	5
Play facilities	5	4
Youth Club	2	3
Other	4	8
Claiming to be without problems	13	4
Total	43	49

1. Language

Language is seen as the major difficulty facing an immigrant by nearly half the sample, the problem emerging in all sections of the questionnaire.

(a) Men: 21 expressed difficulties in speaking and understanding English, 5 would welcome any opportunity to improve their English. Most, however, implied that organised tuition was not required, some giving time or shift work as a constraint.

(b) Women: only 7 of the 40 wives spoke English. A number of consequences were mentioned - social isolation, inability to visit schools or deal with town hall officials.

(c) Pre-school children: the most common reason for sending children to playgroups or nursery school was to learn English.

(d) School children: nearly a fifth of parents with primary school children and nearly half those of secondary school children considered there were language difficulties at school and that extra tuition was required.

2.   Education

(a) All except one immigrant father wanted their sons to stay on
at school, usually to improve their English and/or gain qualifica-
tions for technical training. 8 of the 10 non-immigrant fathers of
secondary school boys thought their sons would leave at the statutory school-leaving age.

(b) The jobs of boys who had recently left suggest the aspirations of immigrant fathers for further education are rarely realised
and there was some feeling that more could be done for immigrant
school leavers. None of the 12 immigrant boys aged 15-20 appeared
to have received any further training apart from one who had left an
apprenticeship after three months. 3 of the 7 non-immigrant boys
are apprenticed and a fourth is a trainee manager. These figures
are supported by the youth employment office data.

(c) In general there was greater ignorance of the education
system among the immigrant parents, particularly further education.

(d) There was considerably less contact with secondary schools by
the immigrants.

3.   Housing

(a) 9 immigrants and 17 non-immigrants regarded housing as a
major problem. The immigrants saw housing need as a scarcity of
houses in the immigrant area and to a lesser extent an emphasis on
the need for larger, more modern houses in the same area. Some felt
that the council would prefer to see the immigrant population dis-
persed. The non-immigrants were concerned particularly over the
lack of choice of council houses in both type and area, and over the
shortage of houses in Batley, particularly those in the cheaper
price range. There was criticism from both samples of the lack of
building, especially council houses in the case of the non-
immigrants, in view of the large-scale demolition programmes in the
past.

(b) The immigrant sample included 40 owner-occupiers, 2 local
authority tenants (both rehoused from slum clearance) and 1 private
tenant. The houses are mostly terraced, frequently lacking the
basic amenities e.g. no inside toilet in 17 houses. The average
rateable value of under £24 reflects the standards.

(c) Overcrowding was considerably more common among the immigrant
households. Taking a density of over 1.1 persons/room as the conventional definition of overcrowding, 28 of the 43 immigrant households are overcrowded compared with 7 of the 49 non-immigrant households; 24 immigrant and 20 non-immigrant households want one or
more extra bedroom.

4.   Employment

Only 2 immigrants gave employment as a major problem compared with
17 non-immigrants. This was seen either as the lack of jobs in
Batley and/or the low wages of the area. Over a quarter of the
immigrant men, mainly those with previous training expressed

dissatisfaction with their present job. Only 10 per cent of the non-immigrants were dissatisfied with jobs. There was considerable interest in further training among the younger men from both groups particularly the immigrants.

5.   Information and rights

The need for further advice facilities was mentioned by both groups. A higher proportion of immigrants than non-immigrants are unaware of eligibility to welfare benefits.

6.   CRC

Immigrants were asked what they knew of the CRC. 27 men claimed they knew nothing of the CRC or CRO. 4 men had contacted the CRO for assistance. There was a feeling among those who knew of the organisation that the CRC and CRO were more concerned with the question of 'assimilation' than with the problems seen by the immigrants themselves.

7.   Discrimination

We know from feedback to the MWS that experiences of discrimination were under-reported. 7 men said they had been discriminated against in employment. There is general agreement that it is at the level of foreman or chargehand that discrimination occurs rather than at management level. 2 of the 5 complaints of housing discrimination in the private market came from people who had taken action which again suggests an under-estimation of discrimination in housing. The evidence suggests that relatively few immigrants expose themselves to the possibility of direct discrimination over employment and housing. There is a tendency to apply for unskilled textile jobs with firms known to employ immigrants. Similarly houses are most sought after in the area where there is a high immigrant concentration.

This account of immigrant needs could be paralleled in many Asian communities in Britain - concentration in overcrowded low standard accommodation, predominance of unskilled and semi-skilled workers, difficulties of school leavers, lack of knowledge of how the system works in relation to school, welfare rights, exacerbated by language difficulties (Krausz, 1971; Patterson, 1969).

Immigrants were not asked specifically about the maintenance of the Muslim culture but discussion showed the attitude to various aspects of the question. Most immigrant parents disliked their children attending morning assembly at school. Some felt strongly that separate morning prayers and religious education classes could be held for Muslims in those schools with a high proportion of immigrants. Others were concerned about the effect of the 'permissive' atmosphere in schools on adolescents. (The single-sex secondary schools of Batley are an advantage in this context.) Four men emphasised the desirability of keeping the immigrant community

together when discussing the shortage of houses in the area. There
was the request that all factories should recognise the Muslim fes-
tivals as do the main employers of immigrants. In general, there
was implicit recognition that the Muslim community was a distinct
one whose members related mainly to others in the community and to
the home areas in India.

DISCUSSION

The survey results provide a wider perspective of the immigrants in
Batley, enable a greater emphasis to be placed on the immigrants'
views and also allow a comparison between normative and felt need.
    A number of recommendations can be listed based on discussions
with the immigrant leaders and the survey results including English
classes for adults, extra resources and expertise in the schools for
English teaching, explanatory leaflets in Gujerati and Urdu of the
further education system, welfare rights, house improvement grants,
facilities for further training of adults, encouragement of house
building and the provision of social facilities like community
centre, youth club, play areas. This excludes the problem of discrimination and of employment, controlled mainly by national policy.
    The MWS leaders had two basic aims. First, that immigrants
should benefit from and be represented in British society and,
second, that the Muslim culture should be maintained. Overcoming
language difficulties is of prime importance as far as the former is
concerned. Inadequate English removes an element of choice in many
circumstances in which immigrants may find themselves, and enforces
a social and cultural isolation even where this may not be desired.
    Organising English classes for adults can be difficult and they
are often poorly supported. Classes arranged in the town next to
Batley where there is also a large immigrant population had to be
abandoned becuase of the low response. Castles and Kosack (1973)
discuss the problems involved with an emphasis on the time constraints such as shift work, cultural habits of Muslim women and the
difficulties of finding trained teachers. They conclude that the
most effective system is classes during work hours which, without
government compensation, most employers will not consider. The
House of Commons Select Committee on Race Relations and Immigration
place a low priority on adult education (1973). The need for improved language teaching in schools has been documented many times
by Hawkes (1966), DES (1971a). More dramatically the Select Committee report on immigrant education confirmed the urgent need for
extra resources in the school. Until the language problem is dealt
with more adequately the immigrant school-leaver seems trapped between inadequate English if he leaves school at the appropriate age
for an apprenticeship (or other skilled work) and being too old for
one if he waits until his English has improved.
    Most of the needs outlined would be accepted by LA officials and
some, for example nursery provision, are extensions of present
policy. It is easy to draw up a list of social needs for any 'disadvantaged' area or group and to point out the shortcomings of local
authority departments, most of whose actions are influenced by
government policy.

Public policy tends to be geared to normative need and to dis-
regard felt needs that cannot be described in objective terms.
Prior to the survey the CDP sent data on overcrowding in nursery
schools and numbers of pre-school-aged immigrant children - current
and projected - to the education department suggesting the immediate
need for more nursery provision. Differences of opinion over the
extent of language difficulties in the schools seem to have arisen
because although normative need is accepted, there is in fact no
established standard for measuring it other than a pupil's academic
attainment in normal school examinations and class work. This point
is made in a DES (1971b) report which found a strong demand from
teachers for appropriate methods of assessing linguistic competence.
It should be possible to apply tests to children leaving primary
school to establish how great a need there is for extra tuition at
secondary level. Similarly other felt needs could be translated
into normative need if standards were agreed, for example the need
for further training facilities for adults. The official recognition of felt need where no normative need is seen may require a
change in policy such as the introduction of playgroups or Islamic
education in primary schools.

Assuming a need is recognised, two main factors will determine
which of the various ways of tackling any particular immigrants'
problems is most favoured.

First, the extent to which a need is viewed as being peculiar to
immigrants. Some councillors objected to the amount of time spent
with immigrants by the CDP because they did not consider their problems to be different from other working-class households. They
felt the project should serve the community as a whole. The sample
of non-immigrants shows a considerable overlap of needs expressed
with those of the immigrants. Difficulties over the health service,
lack of knowledge over welfare rights and the education system,
housing problems, need for play facilities are found in both groups.

The second factor is the extent to which it is thought the immigrant population should be assimilated into the host community.
While some teachers saw their role as increasing the understanding
between two cultures, others felt that assimilation should be the
school's policy towards immigrant pupils. Apart from helping disadvantaged non-immigrants with linguistic difficulties, language is
accepted as a specifically immigrant need at the present time. The
other specifically immigrant need was the concern of the MWS leaders
to maintain their own culture and religion. A case could be made
for a more positive acceptance by schools of this culture and
religion.

The crucial element, however, is housing. There were 71 immigrants in Batley LA housing (August 1973). Although many immigrants
believe correctly that it is council policy to disperse immigrants,
in practice this is stated as desirable rather than being a policy
which is positively enacted. There are two possible controls available to the council. The first is the provision of mortgage loans
of which many immigrants have taken advantage. The second is the
allocation of council houses, for which very few immigrants apply.
Most of those in council property are from slum clearance areas and
many would move out if suitable property near the main immigrant
area was available. As in the schools, the policy is a passive

acceptance of the presence of the Muslim population. The housing situation in the area and indeed elsewhere in Batley could be improved by encouragement of private building, building council houses (although this would be of limited value to immigrants unless they were for sale) or the encouragement of co-ownership.

This desire by the immigrants to remain in one area is a felt need not totally acceptable to current ideas. There is an assumption that high concentrations of immigrants are largely the result of lack of choice in the housing market and with time there will be dispersal. While this may be true in some areas of Britain, and is an element in the Batley situation, it seems likely that a majority of immigrants will wish to live in close proximity for many years. This is not to deny that dispersal will occur eventually but to suggest that voluntary dispersal is likely to be an extremely slow process and to be slower than among less homogeneous populations.

CONCLUSION

The acceptance of 'cultural diversity' in Britain is not necessarily reflected in official policies. If the right to maintain 'cultural diversity' is granted then the necessary corollaries of recognition within the schools and spatial requirements should be accepted. This is not to advocate racial discrimination either way in housing, but to be prepared to encourage house building in immigrant areas and to cease regarding concentration of particular nationalities as undesirable in themselves. The Cullingworth report (1969) for example considers that 'Dispersal of immigrant concentration should be regarded as a desirable consequence but not the overriding purpose of housing individual immigrant families on council estates. The criterion of fully informed individual choice comes first.' Deakin and Cohen (1970) after discussing the advantages and disadvantages of dispersal recommend that policies are developed to make choice over housing area by immigrants a reality. As Rose (1969) pointed out, 'The idea has rarely been entertained that British society might move . . . towards a chequer board pattern in which class and ethnic differences divide society horizontally and vertically.'

I regard 'choice' as the key word. Although it is possible to demonstrate that certain needs - felt and normative - are common to many of the immigrant population, individuals will also differ widely in their needs and aspirations. At present, in those policy areas relating to the maintenance of their own culture such as recognition within the schools, and housing policies, the felt needs of the immigrants are largely ignored - they have no choice. Equally in those policy areas which affect the ease of integration or even assimilation, particularly relating to language, the lack of resources and limited views of the problems by policy makers again vitally restrict the choices open to an immigrant. (Here many of the problems do overlap with those of the non-immigrant.) When discussing social needs of minority groups, authorities are receptive to needs which fit into the present system and can be looked at as normative needs but seem reluctant to concede policies that recognise felt needs specific to the distinct culture of immigrants.

The Home Office brief for CDP with its emphasis on both felt need and the necessity for improved communication and increased responsiveness to such needs by local authority and government departments implies some recognition of this general point. It remains to be seen whether Batley CDP can demonstrate how this might be achieved - whether, for example, the CDP can succeed in feeding back their main conclusions from the study and involve the MWS or other sections of the immigrant population in pressing for changes which would establish more efficient channels of communication, including the CRC and allow a greater response to the felt needs of the immigrant population.

Chapter 15

JOB-GETTING AND JOB-HOLDING
Glyncorrwg CDP

The Glyncorrwg CDP has focused much of its attention on the linkage between economic and social problems, more so perhaps than any other of the CDPs. That this has been the case is not surprising. The majority of the CDPs are concerned with situations in the inner city; however, the Glyncorrwg CDP is based on a number of small, former mining communities, now an integral part of industrial South Wales, which is facing all the problems associated with an older industrial area where the traditional economic base is undergoing change. The needs of the communities in the Glyncorrwg CDP have become of some concern when seen in the context of recent changes in the social and economic structure of the area. The 1951 population of 9,240 had stabilised at 9,370 in 1961; however by 1971 had fallen to 8,640, a total loss of some 700. As the natural increase during the decade 1961-71 was 800, the size of outward migration in this period has been 1,500. Since 1966 all three collieries in the valley closed, the railway line taken up, and a major redundancy programme implemented by the largest (and only) firm in the area. The valley has been faced, therefore, with a rapidly declining industrial structure (600 jobs in 1971 compared to 3,000 in 1961) with few lost jobs being replaced by new employment opportunities. The relatively 'closed' community has been 'opened up' with people seeking access to jobs outside, mainly in the Bridgend/Port Talbot/Swansea growth point. In every sense of the word, the communities in the upper Afan valley are 'marginal' to these growth points, and present a challenge for social planning. (1) In 1973 the employment position improved when Glyncorrwg itself benefited from a period of improved national economic activity and attracted a small but significant number of jobs.

Economic problems such as persistent and high unemployment, rising prices, and inadequate income, among certain groups, are now known to form the basis for many of the most difficult traditionally described social welfare problems as well as the most difficult issues in the provision of social services. However, while a classification of fields of study into economic and social policy may be useful for identifying the needs and aspirations of a community, it must be recognised that these phenomena often act in combination, and it is sometimes difficult to allocate them as either

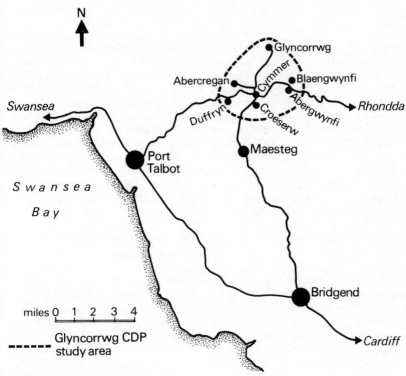

FIGURE 15.1

economic or social. In many cases, phenomena, such as unemployment,
have both an economic and social dimension, with a loss to the community of industrial output, together with individual and family
hardship.

AN ASSESSMENT OF THE EMPLOYMENT PROBLEM

The nature and extent of the problems involved in gaining and holding jobs in Glyncorrwg is illustrated by an analysis of the current
performance of the local economic base. With plenty of time and
resources a number of techniques can be used to analyse the functioning of a local economy. However, in the short term, there does
exist a set of social and economic indicators which can be applied
quickly to assess the vitality of an economy. The CDP team has used
a comprehensive range of social and economic indicators to identify
local needs. In the context of job getting and holding the most relevant yardsticks are those of unemployment, employment growth,
activity rates, migration, and dependency of the community on social
security payments. One of the problems involved with economic analysis at local level is the paucity of data, particularly on
personal income and expenditure. However, some work has been done
by the project to overcome this particular deficiency.

UNEMPLOYMENT

The most obvious measure of poor economic performance and under-used
resources is unemployment. Rates of unemployment that are persis-
tently and substantially above the national average are confined
almost exclusively to the Development Areas. The economic aspect of
unemployment is of concern at both national and local level. At
national level, the government's regional policies are specifically
geared to reducing regional differentials in rates of unemployment.
At local level, just as at national level, the extent and nature of
unemployment has a significant effect on the level and rate of
economic growth. The social aspects of unemployment are also central; to the individual worker and his family, unemployment can be
anything from a temporary inconvenience to a crisis. In its mildest
form, unemployment may represent a week without work; at the other
extreme unemployment may mean absence from the labour force for more
than a year. In January 1973, 33 per cent of men unemployed in
Glyncorrwg had been out of work for more than a year, compared to
27 per cent nationally.

Table 15.1 illustrates the level and rate of unemployment in
Glyncorrwg in recent years. While the actual numbers of people unemployed relate to the employment exchange area (which is synonymous
with Glyncorrwg UD) rates of unemployment are available from the
Department of Employment only for the travel-to-work area. Rates of
unemployment based on a single employment exchange can be misleading
due to travel-to-work patterns. However, some attempt to calculate
a rate of unemployment has been made as this is clearly an important
piece of information.

TABLE 15.1   The level and rate of unemployment in Cymmer EE

	Total	%*	Great Britain %
Jan. 1965	142	4.2	1.6
July 1965	130	3.6	1.2
Jan. 1968	259	7.3	2.7
July 1968	158	3.5	2.2
Jan. 1971	221	3.7	3.0
July 1971	226	3.9	3.3
Jan. 1973	259	4.1	3.5
July 1973	201	2.9	2.4

Source: Department of Employment.
* In July 1968 unemployment rate given for Port Talbot travel-to-
  work area, and not Cymmer/Maesteg as previously.
NB Rates of unemployment calculated after October 1972 by Department of Employment exclude the temporarily stopped.

A conventionally based unemployment rate of unemployed: employees in employment for Glyncorrwg yields a figure of some 30 per
cent (220 unemployed/700 employed). However, given the travel-to-
work context of the area, a more realistic calculation is the ratio

of unemployed/economically active at work both within and outside
the community (some 2,800 according to 1971 census figures), which
gives a figure of 8 per cent; this is still a very high rate of unemployment when compared to the 1971 Great Britain average figure of
3.3 per cent.

The ratio of unemployed persons to vacancies is some measure of
the demand for labour in an area, although it does not necessarily
illustrate the availability of labour. The figures shown in Table
15.2 emphasise the low level of demand in employment terms within
the community.

TABLE 15.2   Unemployment/vacancies ratio (adults)

	1971		1972		1973	
	Jan.	July	Jan.	July	Jan.	July
Glyncorrwg	205.0	213.0	325.0	262.0	259.0	201.0
Great Britain	4.6	5.4	8.9	4.9	4.1	

Source: Department of Employment.

In the period 1971-3 for the months selected (at random, being representative) there was only one vacancy notified and remaining un-
filled in the Glyncorrwg labour market, and this was in January
1971; none in the remainder of the period. While this is some
measure of the absence of job opportunities in the community, it
must be remembered that many job seekers and job notifiers may not
use the official employment exchange system. This particular aspect
of the labour market has been examined by the project and is referred to later.

ACTIVITY RATES

Apart from reducing the level of unemployment, and utilising the
growth of the population of working age, an important contribution
towards increasing local income might be made by reducing non-
participation in the labour force and thereby bringing into employment hitherto inactive persons. An activity rate is defined as the
proportion of people of working age who work.

$$\text{ACTIVITY RATE} = \frac{\text{Economically active}}{\text{Population aged 15}} \times \frac{100}{1}$$
years and over

The level of activity rates in Glyncorrwg are shown in Table
15.3, and have important implications for the community. Localities
with a skewed employment structure, weighted heavily to the coal or
steel industries, afford few job opportunities for women. Local
income is a function of employment, and with relatively low activity
rates the level of income is depressed. While male activity rates
in Glyncorrwg are similar to those nationally the female rates are
still substantially below the national level. If female activity

rates can be increased in Glyncorrwg extra income will be injected into households and the community.

TABLE 15.3   Activity rates 1961-71

	Male 1961	1966	1971	Female 1961	1966	1971
Glyncorrwg	85.4	80.5	76.2	22.2	27.7	30.2
Wales	85.0	81.1	78.5	28.1	33.4	35.7
Great Britain	86.3	84.0	77.3	37.3	42.1	41.2

Source: 1961, 1966 and 1971 censuses of population.

INDUSTRIAL STRUCTURE

The preceding issues of unemployment and activity rates are closely linked with Glyncorrwg's industrial structure and recent changes in employment. Table 15.4 illustrates the economic base of Glyncorrwg in 1961 and 1971 and the dramatic changes which have taken place.

TABLE 15.4   Employment structure 1961-71

	1961 Nos	%	1971 Nos	%
Primary	2,407	80.8	86	11.5
Manufacturing	52	1.7	248	33.3
Construction	121	4.1	113	15.2
Services	398	13.4	298	40.0
Total	2,978	100.0	745	100.0

Source: Department of Employment.

Table 15.4 shows quite clearly the dominant position of the coal industry as the main source of employment in the area in 1961 and the virtual absence of any manufacturing industry. By 1971 the situation had changed dramatically; the serious loss of jobs started in 1966, since when all three collieries in the community closed (Duffryn Rhondda in November 1966, Avon in September 1969, and Glyncorrwg in May 1970). A further blow at this time was a major redundancy programme begun in late 1970 by the only manufacturing plant of any size, which led to a reduction of its labour force by some 300 to a current figure of 70 persons.

The impact of the loss of jobs in Glyncorrwg during the period 1966-72 has been relatively greater than even the 1973 proposals to reduce by half the steel industry jobs in Ebbw Vale. In this latter case, while central government established a task force to find new jobs, no such help was forthcoming for Glyncorrwg. The recent

changes in the employment structure of the community have been
staggering; the 3,000 local jobs of 1961 were reduced to 745 by
1971, and this has been further reduced to somewhere in the order of
600 jobs, as the redundancy programme of the major firm in the
locality had not been completed by June 1971, which is the latest
date for which Department of Employment figures are available.

The extent to which recent changes in the industrial structure of
Glyncorrwg is a matter of concern can be assessed by the use of an
economic analytical technique known as the 'shift ratio'. In this
technique, employment changes which have taken place in the national
economy over a period of time are applied to the local economy.

TABLE 15.5 Shift ratio applied to employment growth

	1961	1971	% change 1961-71
Glyncorrwg	2,978	745	-75
Great Britain	22.68 million	22.71 million	+ 0.4

Source: Department of Employment.

The shift ratio applies changes which have taken place in the
national economy 1961-71 to the 1961 employment structure of
Glyncorrwg; this has produced an estimated employment structure for
1971 which is then compared with the actual 1971 situation. As seen
above, the national economy grew at +0.4 per cent 1961-71; if
Glyncorrwg had grown at this national rate of growth 1961-71 there
would have been 3,000 jobs in 1971 instead of the actual 745. Thus,
due to poor local growth rates 1961-71, Glyncorrwg lost 2,250 jobs.

At the time of the colliery closures in the valley there were
1,500 men on the books, of which there was some voluntary wastage,
retirement and redundancies; however, almost 1,000 men were transferred to other collieries in adjacent valleys. Information
supplied by the National Coal Board illustrates the extent to which
the once coal-dominated community now has few miners left let alone
no collieries (Table 15.6).

TABLE 15.6 Men resident in Glyncorrwg who work in the coal industry
1961-71

Date	No.
1961	1,720
1966	1,480
1971	534

Source: Censuses of population, and National Coal Board.

POPULATION CHANGE AND MIGRATION

The 1970s may prove to be the most crucial period yet for the future
of the South Wales valley communities. This is particularly the
case for the communities in the Afan valley where their very existence is being threatened; a central issue in this situation is the
relationship of job-getting and job-holding to the process of
migration.

Between 1961 and 1971 the population of Glyncorrwg UD fell by 700
persons to 8,600 despite a natural increase of some 800 people. In
total, therefore, the rate of net outward migration has been in the
order of 1,500 over this ten year period. Despite the tenuous
nature of the 1966 census of population data it appears that the
major impetus behind migration gained momentum after 1966, the time
when the valley's economic base began to be eroded. A new threat to
the stability of the size of the communities has come in recent
years with a fall in the rate of natural increase; the rate of this
reduction has been well above the national rate. While the annual
rate of natural increase throughout the 1960s was on average about
100, for the past three years the figures have been:

    1969-70   +39
    1970-1   +48
    1971-2   + 8

If the rate of outward migration experienced in the period 1961-71
continues, there will be no buffer of natural increase to support
the total population. The Glyncorrwg CDP is undertaking a considerable amount of research into the issue of migration as it is
fundamental to the future of the community.

One of the most serious aspects of loss of population is the depletion of community resources through migration of the economically
active. The position for Glyncorrwg is illustrated in Table 15.7.
Between 1961 and 1971 there has been a fall of 600 economically
active persons; while some part of this may be due to higher rates
of unemployment recently, the main factor has undoubtedly been the
migration of economically active persons. The slight increase in
the number of economically active females can be more than accounted
for by recent increases in female labour activity rates.

TABLE 15.7 Changes in number of economically active persons in
Glyncorrwg 1961-71

	Males	Females	Total	Total change 1961-71
1961	3,060	810	3,870)	-600
1971	2,344	942	3,286)	

Source: censuses of population.

The work of the project team has shown that there are strong cause and effect links between the number and nature of so-called 'social' problems of the communities and the ability of families in them to be financially self-supporting, and, therefore, self-determining (self-supporting means, in this context, having financial budgets that include margins for 'investments' of various kinds, as well as just enough money to pay for essentials).

A central theme of the project's approach to social planning has been that the number and nature of local 'social' problems can be reduced by increasing the number of families that are financially self-supporting and independent of government social security benefits. The project's current research, supported by the Department of Health and Social Security, has shown that some 2,760 people are partially (many wholly, although the degree of dependency is difficult to determine) dependent on public funds for their support; this amounts to a weekly income bill of £23,000 per week into the community, and accounts for one in three families.

While the project team has used a wide range of social and economic indicators to identify local needs, this yardstick of the extent of community resources has been found to be the most comprehensive in coverage and penetrating in its identification of needs.

ACTION PROGRAMMES ON JOBS ISSUE

In the Glyncorrwg CDP, the approach in providing solutions to the problems of financial self-support and depletion of community resources has focused on a series of adjustments to existing social and economic policies and practices which may be grouped into three main categories:

1   those which improve job-getting and job-holding capacities of individuals, families and communities, through better information, education, training, and retraining;
2   those which improve accessibility to a wider range of employment and other opportunities at growth points (Bridgend, Port Talbot, Swansea, and Baglan Bay), whose remoteness has been created by decisions of central and local government to rationalise investment and the location of new services, jobs and social facilities at a number of theoretically highly accessible points;
3   those which increase the range of local employment opportunities by extending the incentives already available to new and expanding employers and/or helping in the realisation of local initiatives and resources.

While it is possible to identify here the job-orientated action programmes of the project, it is feasible to cover only a selection of them in any depth. Before this is done, however, it is important to recognise that the solution of a local problem may require action and adjustments to policies at a range of levels; while some solutions may require only local action, others may also involve access to decision-making at the regional and national level.

1. Schemes concerned with better information, education, training, and retraining

A wide range of programmes have been followed by the project on this aspect on job-getting and job-holding. Of particular importance might be cited the participative employment service, community resources centre, and a range of projects in the education field.

In areas like Glyncorrwg, employment exchanges (at present undergoing a welcomed change of emphasis in their function to an employment 'shop' service) are the least successful medium for residents finding new jobs. The reason for this lies partly in the close knit social nature of old industrial communities, and also in the growing practices of new firms to make private (prior) arrangements with others to exchange staff according to their respective contraction and expansion programmes. Employment exchanges seem rarely involved or informed, and vacancies (as already shown) rarely arise. All this reduces the chances of the unemployed entering the labour market and it is more difficult for employment offices to provide an effective service for those in the labour force, and also produce an accurate picture of labour vacancies plan appropriate training programmes. The CDP has therefore operated a scheme which aims to strengthen the existing formal and informal jobs service in the valley by extending the community resources centre at Glamorgan House (the base of the project team at Cymmer in Glyncorrwg UD) to include an employment service.

The community resources centre has been particularly involved with a programme of social and language development for school children. This scheme has been operated by CDP in association with the Primary Extension Programme of the National Council for Educational Technology, and run by a full-time person. While the centre has been available for the prime use of schools in the project area, this is now being extended in the direction of further and wider community uses. Clearly, the role of education is a critical factor in enhancing both economic and social opportunities for young people.

2. Schemes concerned with improving accessibility to a wider range of employment and other opportunities at growth points

In a situation where most of the job opportunities for job seekers and holders in the community are to be found at the growth points in the South Wales coastal belt, accessibility has become a key issue. However, the availability of transport for travel to work forms only a part of a general problem of mobility deprivation. Action strategies to deal with this need are discussed in detail in a later chapter.

3. Schemes concerned with increasing incentives to new and expanding employers and aiding the realisation of local resources and initiatives

Action undertaken within this heading concerns a number of schemes including a critical examination of the actual and potential

benefits available under the 1972 Industry Act and central government's regional policies; subsidies for industrial freight charges
where these are a decisive factor in locational decision making;
house and area improvement through use of the provisions of the 1969
Housing Act; a local resources study to examine the nature and
extent of local resources, initiatives and entrepreneurship, for the
creation of new jobs; and finally the Welsh miners' museum scheme.
     While each of these schemes could be the subject of some examina-
tion, attention will be focused on the miners' museum scheme. In
September 1972 the Welsh miners' museum committee, based primarily
on local initiative, asked for CDP's help to develop the idea to
establish a Welsh museum of mining at Glyncorrwg north and south
pits. The original idea has now been expanded into the concept of
an 'industry country park' which would be the first of its kind in
Wales. The scheme has attracted a great deal of support from many
agencies and individuals. One of the main objectives of the museum
scheme, in addition to preserving Welsh architecture and industrial
heritage, and a place for tourist and educational interest, is to
directly reduce local unemployment. This may be made effective not
only directly through the facilities and services required but also
by the substantial indirect or 'multiplier' effects envisaged of
spending on a tourist industry.

SUMMARY AND CONCLUSIONS

The issue of job-getting and job-holding is a key feature of the
Glyncorrwg CDP, and linked closely to a wide range of social and
economic problems. While the project has been involved with a wider
range of issues than just that of jobs, community development in
older industrial areas must grapple with this central problem. It
is the hope of the Glyncorrwg CDP that its work, in identifying
local needs, and the solutions it has been able to offer, may have
replicative value for other communities in a similar situation, of
which there are likely to be many, not only in South Wales, but
other parts of Britain and perhaps in other countries.
     There appears to be no easy or quick solution on the jobs issue.
The extent to which the Glyncorrwg CDP has managed to be an agent of
social change itself, and within the process of government and administration generally, has required action and research on a broad
front at national, regional and local levels. The relevance of
action and research on a mix of social and economic policies and
practices has become an integral element of the comprehensive social
planning approach adopted and pursued by the project.

NOTE

1   For a fuller discussion of the problems of social planning in
    marginal regions, see the report of a seminar held at Swansea in
    April 1972, 'Marginal Regions - Essays in Social Planning',
    edited by M. Broady, Bedford Square Press, 1973.

Chapter 16

MOBILITY DEPRIVATION
Glyncorrwg CDP

The need for mobility, for residents in the upper Afan valley, has become of increasing importance in view of changes that have taken place in the spatial organisation of activities. Naturally, the distribution and arrangement of activities in space is a prime determinant of the nature and direction of interaction.

The communities in the upper Afan valley currently experience a situation which is in marked contrast to its former state. The 'raison d'être' for the valley was the exploitation of coal. During the hey-day of the industry, when the valley was prosperous and thriving, a high degree of self-sufficiency was apparent in terms of most activities - employment, housing, social and community infrastructure.

Housing agglomerated around the collieries and the concomitant social and community provision was also attracted, i.e. shops, chapels, pubs. Concentration was a feature of activity opportunities - they were internal to the valley and locally based. Consequently, physical access to most activities was not a great problem to residents of the valley.

The demise of the valley's economic base, together with its replacement by the coastal belt of South Wales as the new locational centre of activity in the region, has destroyed this self-sufficiency. The newly emerging industries of the Welsh economy do not have the same locational pre-requisites as the coal industry. Their needs are best fulfilled at the valley mouths and in the coastal towns e.g. Llantrisant, Bridgend, Port Talbot, Neath, not in the physically restricted and remote valley heads.

The rapidly disappearing jobs in the collieries in areas like the upper Afan valley have not been compensated by alternative, locally-based employment opportunities - the majority being attracted to the coastal plain. Public and private investment has also been steered to the expanding coastal towns. New housing has developed in good environmental conditions and a high quality social and community infrastructure has emerged - schools, roads, shops, hospitals, etc.

The upper Afan valley has correspondingly declined. Population levels have fallen with the loss of local employment opportunities. Social infrastructure has declined and not been replaced and the thresholds of viability of many services and facilities have been crossed causing the remaining standards of provision to be poor.

In brief, the number of activities that can now be satisfied locally has been drastically reduced.

In terms of employment, in 1969, there were still 1,944 local jobs in the upper Afan valley, but in 1971, only 745. Whereas in 1969, one-half of the valley's economically active persons were employed in the coal industry, the corresponding figure for 1973 is one-fifth. Although the coal industry is still the largest employer there are no local mines and work is found in the adjoining valleys - particularly the Ogmore, Garw and Llynfi valleys. The other major sources of employment are also located outside the valley in Port Talbot, Maesteg, Neath, Kenfig and Bridgend. Local opportunities are few.

The distribution of industry is an example of concentration and rationalisation occurring at a sub-regional level. However, because the small and scattered distribution of settlements is not sufficient to support a full range of services, many of the remaining activities in the valley have also been concentrated and rationalised. Cymmer is acknowledged as the 'strategic' centre where local investment is guided.

Secondary education (to the age of 16) is, therefore, provided at the comprehensive school at Cymmer. Also present at Cymmer is the health centre, employment exchange, library, youth wing and fire and ambulance station. Sixth form education is not provided in the valley, nor is any type of further education or government re-training centre. Port Talbot is blessed with these functions.

The nearest hospital is at Neath and the better shopping and commercial activities at Maesteg, Port Talbot and Neath. The range of shops in the valley is not extensive (usually of the convenience type) and prices are high. Professional and personal services are few as are high quality recreational and entertainment facilities.

The two-stage concentration and rationalisation of activities has been supported by local and central government strategic policy-making - either explicitly as 'growth point' policy or simply by default and neglect.

The overall result in mobility requirements is far removed from the former situation where most needs and activities were satisfied locally. Now, the quality of mobility is an essential and important feature governing the ability of persons in the upper Afan valley communities to take advantage of, choose between and participate in the many activities that sustain human existence.

TRANSPORT INFRASTRUCTURE

Given the spatial distribution of activities as described in the last section, the crucial question is, how far does the available transport infrastructure serve the mobility needs of the upper Afan populace? Does the transport system effectively ensure that individuals have unrestricted physical access, and therefore choice, to the range of activity options?

All the grand predictions relating to universal car ownership and unconstrained personal mobility do not hold true in the upper Afan valley. Car ownership levels are low and well below the national average. The 1971 census of population calculated that the percentage of households without a car was 66 per cent in Glyncorrwg, compared with 48 per cent in Great Britain. A recent transport survey undertaken by the project team in Abercregan confirms this variation with a massive 70 per cent of the total number of households without access to personal transport.

Crude indications of present and predicted levels of personal income leads one to conclude that car ownership levels are not likely to rise rapidly in the near future. Access to personal transport will remain the prerogative of a relatively small section of the community.

The car owning clientele are able to achieve reasonable access to the main centres - down the valley to Port Talbot and Neath, northwards to the Rhondda valley and eastwards to the Llynfi valley (Maesteg and Bridgend). It should be observed, however, that physical and climatic conditions attain more than usual significance, e.g. steep hills, inclement weather conditions.

These conclusions on the mobility levels of the car owning households do need to be qualified by two, usually concealed, considerations.

These were readily made apparent in the Abercregan transport survey and are:

1   a large majority of the car-owning households have only one driver (invariably, the wage-earner). This means that during the working day, the remainder of the household (housewife, children) are without access to the car and effectively in the same situation as non-car owning individuals;

2   figures indicating the quantity of vehicles in a particular area generally make no reference to quality of vehicles. In the case of Abercregan, the quality of the vehicles (measured by age) is low and unreliability combined with fairly rigorous physical and climatic conditions is significant, e.g. inability to reach work on time.

The low level of car ownership in the upper Afan valley places an added burden on the public transportation network. The system available, however, does not live up to expectations.

Formerly, the Afan valley was served by good rail communications to the adjoining valleys and to the coast. The decline of the coal industry and, more recently, the effects of the Beeching Report, have brought about the disappearance of the railway. The last train seen in the valley was in 1971.

The alternative form of public transport - the bus - has likewise not fared particularly well during the last decade owing to the county-wide increase in car usage. In common with most bus operators, the local subsidiaries of the National Bus Company have been placed under great pressure.

There has been a decline in route mileage for the county of Glamorgan and also in the number of passenger journeys. Although the decline has slowed recently, the companies claim that there are many services which, as an economic proposition, are not viable. These services account for about 18 per cent of the total NBC route mileage in Glamorgan and include all the services using the upper Afan valley.

The nature of the existing system is best discussed under three headings:

1. Availability

Six services enter the valley but they are routed and scheduled in such a manner as to create a differential service in each of the constituent communities. At the one extreme, Cymmer being the focal point of the area benefits from all six services which run through it - to Maesteg, Port Talbot, Neath and Swansea; but at the other, Abercregan has no service at all. Glyncorrwg has direct services only to Maesteg and Port Talbot - other journeys involve changing and considerable waiting-times, usually at Cymmer.

2. Frequency, timing and duration

There is much disquiet about the frequency and timing of the services in the valley. Most of the individual services operate at hourly intervals but, with the routing described above, many journeys are a much more difficult proposition. Changing and waiting-times are a great inconvenience. The duration of journeys to the main centres is considerable (e.g. 35 minutes from Cymmer to Port Talbot, a distance of eight miles) and coupled with infrequency of operation creates many problems.

3. Cost

Cost of transport is a particularly important factor in usage. Fares are generally high and reflect the high and marginal costs of economic operation. A single journey from Cymmer to Port Talbot is 21p (£1.89 weekly); Glyncorrwg to Maesteg 17p (£1.53 weekly) and Blaengwynfi to Neath 24p (£2.16 weekly). Internal travel is also costly: Glyncorrwg to Cymmer 11p; Blaengwynfi to Cymmer 12p and Cynonville to Cymmer 12p.

Small and limited income households are readily susceptible to costs and it should be noted that one in three families in the upper Afan valley depend on some kind of social security benefit - indicating a low level of self-support.

Some of the inadequacies of the public bus service have been plugged by private operators. The foremost of these include:

1 The local education authority which provides contract services for school-children residing above the statutory walking distances.
2 The National Coal Board which arrange contract services for their labour forces between home and workplace.
3 Some private firms in need of Afan valley labour supply provide contract buses, e.g. building contractors such as Scotts Ltd, Wimpey.
4 There is a case of a privately arranged contract service by workers of the Borg Warner factory at Kenfig and a private bus operator.
5 Many health and welfare agencies are obliged to provide special transport, e.g. meals-on-wheels, mentally handicapped to day workshops, etc.

In general, the transport infrastructure at the disposal of the

residents of the upper Afan valley is inadequate. The implications
of this in relation to the spatial distribution of activities leads
to forms of 'mobility deprivation' which the following section
outlines.

THE DIMENSIONS OF MOBILITY DEPRIVATION

The quality of urban life is enhanced by maximising the range of
activity options available to all residents. The transport system
should therefore ultimately aim at maximising the frequency and
variety of activity options. Deprived of his mobility, due to an
inadequate transport system, a person's propensity, both to participate in and choose between a full range of activity options, is
arbitrarily restricted.
    'Mobility deprivation' is apparent in the upper Afan valley. The
car owning households are few and the majority of residents are not
availed of this personal transport that gives such great freedom of
movement. Rather, a large proportion are forced to rely on public
transport (the bus) and can be regarded as 'captives', i.e. they
must use public transportation regardless of cost or level of service. Furthermore, these persons are captives of the existing
public transport configuration and can travel only in those sections
of the space-environment, at those times and with such frequency
that public transportation is provided.
    The range of opportunities and spheres of influence of persons
are limited and sometimes determined by the peculiarities and nature
of the public transport - availability, cost, timing, frequency and
convenience being the key determinants.
    It is the case with public transport 'captives' that the existing
pattern of their movements may not necessarily be a true indication
of their real needs - demand being constrained by type of supply.
The concept of latent demand has been introduced to describe an individual's real demands. The concept may be defined as the demand
for a good not now being exercised but which may be exercised in the
future. It is, of course, a relative concept and is given meaning
only with respect to a set of community goals and objectives which
might vary over time.
    The quality of overall mobility in the upper Afan valley is low
but the severe implications can be observed on particular groups of
individuals within the community. The CDP's approach to mobility in
the project area has been characterised by an identification of
these 'disadvantaged' groups and an assessment of their peculiar
circumstances.
    The true character of 'mobility deprivation' can be usefully
illustrated with reference to three such groups in which the project
has become involved.

1. Young unemployed and employed

When young persons (those aged between 16 and 18), living in the
upper Afan valley communities, leave school and seek employment they
are immediately placed at a disadvantage because of accessibility

problems. In the first instance, the one agency that assists such persons in finding suitable employment, the Careers Office, is located in Port Talbot (only partly offset by facilities being provided in Cymmer one day per week). More importantly, young persons are not re-imbursed for any transport costs incurred in attending job interviews. As it is highly probable that any job interviews offered will be held outside the valley, the cost and inconvenience of getting to them may well have an influence on the person's ability to attend and, therefore, his job-getting capacity. Where considerable costs are incurred, a prohibitive burden may be placed on some personal/family budgets, causing a reduction in the amount of participation in other activities.

Even when young persons are in full-time employment, it appears that transport costs are of some significance. A pilot survey sponsored by the project team calculated that a considerable percentage (15-20 per cent) of young person's gross wages were disappearing on transport costs to and from their place of work. This situation prevails because the level of wages is low (e.g. junior wage rates) and the majority of jobs that are available are found outside the valley and require travel.

In fact, the differential, in income terms, between working (having subtracted transport costs, canteen costs and National Insurance) and not working (receiving state benefits) was found to be marginal, and in some cases, negatively so. Job motivation is hardly enhanced in such circumstances.

The level of transport costs as a proportion of gross wages offered must have a very real influence on the range of job opportunities available to young people living in the valley.

2. Adult employed

A high proportion of the valley's labour force (about 120 workers) have found employment in the Borg Warner factory at Kenfig (near Port Talbot). Realising that public transport was inadequate betweeen the valley and the factory, the workers took the initiative to arrange a contract bus service with a local private operator.

The original bus operator withdrew in the face of various operational difficulties and although he was replaced by another firm, the service has again been found to be an uneconomic proposition.

The alternatives to this direct service are few. Only a fortunate few of the labour force have cars and the public bus service is grossly inadequate. The journey would involve at least two changes (three if from Glyncorrwg), the cost would be about £3 per week and the duration of the journey, two hours per trip. It is also impossible to reach certain shifts and to return from others.

Consequently, if the private contract service is not supported, a large percentage of the labour force would become unemployed. This example is one of the most severe, but it does illustrate the very real limitations and difficulties a person has in gaining access to employment, overwhelmingly concentrated outside the valley.

3. Internal accessibility

A youth wing attached to the comprehensive school in Cymmer offers high quality recreational provision (e.g. gymnasium, swimming pool) to the youths of the constituent villages of the upper Afan valley - an example of concentrated local investment. An evaluation of the utilisation of this resource pinpoints the fallacy that it is strategically located and, therefore, each person in its hinterland has an equal opportunity to use it.

Membership figures, analysed by village, reveal a clear distance-decay function, i.e. the youth wing is under-utilised by youngsters in the villages farthest away. Cost of transport appears to be the main factor in prohibiting youths from attending the centre. The fare from Glyncorrwg to Cymmer, for instance, amounts to 22p for one visit. In terms of a family budget, this amount reaches significant proportions in cases where more than one youth is involved or where more than one visit per week is contemplated, not to mention the cost of membership and entrance to the youth wing and expenditure on refreshments.

These three examples clearly indicate the character of 'mobility deprivation' as experienced by particular groups in the community. These cases are by no means exclusive and the project team has piloted further investigations into other 'captives' e.g. handi-capped, OAPs, unemployed, school-children.

A STRATEGY FOR ACTION

The climate of opinion coupled with recent administrative and legis-lative changes offers a potentially amenable environment in which the CDP can work towards highlighting and solving problems of 'mobility deprivation'.

Given the spatial separation of urban activities and the compre-hensive nature of a family's activity options, there is an enlarged domain of public responsibility to increase and/or improve the over-all level of mobility. In order to maintain the quality of urban environments, access to activities should be provided to a much greater degree than the minimum required to meet essential needs. It is important to have a range of choice, even if that choice is infrequently exercised or deferred.

There is a growing awareness along these lines that public trans-port should be seen as much a 'social service' as an economic propo-sition - that even though the car may increasingly account for the majority of trips undertaken, there are groups of people and whole communities who are, and will continue to be, dependant on a public transport service.

Section 34 of the 1968 Transport Act is a statutory recognition of these beliefs. This section makes provisions for local authori-ties to offer financial assistance for the purpose of securing 'the provision, improvement or continuance of any bus service . . . if in the opinion of the council . . . that service is or will be for the benefit of persons residing in rural areas.' Glamorgan county coun-cil have taken steps to support many services within its area with the aid of these provisions - including all those existing public services in the upper Afan valley.

A further significant principle incorporated in the 1968 Transport Act acknowledges that particular groups in the community are at a greater disadvantage than others and require special provisions to compensate for their circumstances. Section 138 provides for local authorities to offer travel concessions to certain specified groups. The breadth of these categories is at present limited - being confined to OAPs, blind persons and persons whose ability to walk is severely impaired. The principle of special groups to whom discriminary action should be accorded has, however, been established.

An administrative revolution is occurring in transport planning. Section 203 of the 1972 Local Government Act has, effectively for the first time, made one agency responsible for transport planning. It gives the county councils an entirely new responsibility to develop, in consultation with the public passenger transport operators, policies to promote a co-ordination of operations. There is a statutory obligation for all public passenger transport operators to co-operate with each other and with the county council. Circular 5/73 (DOE) outlines the broad policy areas which the county council will be required to consider. These include levels of service, co-ordination of passenger transport, co-ordination with other authorities and fares (including concessionary fares).

These administrative changes have been supported by a radical alteration in the system of giving grants for local transport, outlined in Circular 104/73 (DOE). In view of the comprehensive approach to transport planning that is being encouraged, the existing multiplicity of transport grants, at different rates, some payable to operators, some to local authorities, is considered unsuitable.

It is intended that many of the existing specific grants are replaced by a unified system covering current as well as capital expenditure and public transport as well as roads. Also, the grant is not to be based on the actual cost of individual schemes, but on county programmes of estimated expenditure backed by a comprehensive statement of transport policies for the area (TPPs).

The onus for transport planning is squarely in the hands of local authorities and should reflect to a high degree the individual needs of each area.

THE ROLE OF THE CDP

The above organisational changes come into effect in April 1974 and the CDP offers the opportunity for testing the practicability and efficacy of the county council's new responsibilities.

The project team has increasingly informed the county council of the situation in the upper Afan valley and the existence and implications of the so-called 'mobility deprivation'. Its work has focused on the plight of specific groups in the community and its intention has been to indicate to the relevant agency, by way of experimental action projects, the most applicable and effective policies.

The last section made reference to the workers at the Borg Warner factory whose jobs were in jeopardy if a contract bus service were

allowed to be discontinued. The project has succeeded in sponsoring
a scheme whereby the bus service in question is subsidised to the
extent of the deficit between actual revenue and costs incurred.

The essence of such projects is that they are evaluated during
their operation, to determine the degree of effectiveness, so that
the responsible public agency may accept their necessity and, perhaps, deploy such a policy in other similar situations, i.e. replicative value.

In this particular case, the evaluatory tools are partly self-
evident. The costs of a bus subsidy are being compared to the costs
(both social and financial) that could be incurred by the state in
supporting families if workers became unemployed as a direct result
of the axing of the bus service. Such an economic assessment is an
extremely powerful argument with which to convince a public agency
of the usefulness of the subsidy.

The example of 'mobility deprivation' outlined in respect of the
youth wing has also become the subject of a CDP sponsored experimental project. The basis of the scheme is that eligible youngsters in
the outlying villages are offered free travel to the centre.

Apart from the equality of opportunity argument, a straightforward evaluation can be made in terms of the cost-effectiveness of
a unit of investment. The costs of giving travel concessions to
young people may be more than offset by the benefits of increased
use of a facility. An added consideration in this case concerns the
possible increased use of an already heavily subsidised public bus
service.

The CDP's strategy, therefore, has been to identify cases of
'mobility deprivation' in specific groups within the community and
to promote solutions through experimental projects inculcated with
evaluatory measures with which to judge effectiveness and
applicability.

'Mobility deprivation' is a little acknowledged or realised form
of social deprivation. It is all too evident in the Glyncorrwg CDP
as this chapter has described. However, with an increasingly responsive administrative and statutory climate, the project team has
proceeded to draw attention to the issue and offer solutions for its
eradication.

Part four

ACTION AND RESEARCH STRATEGIES

Chapter 17

CDP AND THE URBAN PROGRAMME

Richard Batley and John Edwards

Compared with previous government action on deprived areas, the Urban Programme and the CDPs offer a potential of concentrated and cross-service co-ordinated action. In their conception, they extend the scope of positive discrimination to cover all services, focus attention on areas of need rather than individual problems and offer the possibility of integrated action by departments working together at central and local government level. Together with this potential for comprehensive action they share an ultimate concern with 'urban deprivation'.

UP FUNDS AND PROJECTS

Since October 1968 and until April 1974, the Home Office jointly with other government departments has put out twelve circulars inviting applications from local authorities and (except in Phase 1) voluntary organisations. Table 17.1 shows the total sum approved for England and Wales for each phase up to the ninth. Of this sum,

TABLE 17.1 Urban Programme expenditure and projects, Phases 1-9, in England and Wales

	Capital expenditure £000s	No.of pro-jects	Revenue expenditure £000s	No.of pro-jects	Total expenditure £000s	No.of pro-jects
Phase 1	3,935	184	23	6	3,958	190
Phase 2	4,347	286	770	235	5,118	521
Phase 3	4,770	290	619	247	5,390	537
Phase 4	-	-	518	264	518	264
Phase 5	6,272	235	-	-	6,272	235
Phase 6	-	-	72	111	72	111
Phase 7	4,067	232	1,816	488	5,884	720
Phase 8	-	-	125	214	125	214
Phase 9	3,636	160	930	269	4,566	429
Total	27,027	1,387	4,873	1,834	31,903	3,221

central government meets 75 per cent and local government the remainder. The table shows at cash prices the funds committed for the
first year of projects ignoring the fact that the UP normally meets
up to five year's running costs on projects.

Over the life of the UP, the government has been committing
itself to about £5 million of new projects per year, and the annual
cost of these commitments to the government is running now at about
£12 million for England and Wales. Table 17.1 shows that a total of
£32 million of fresh commitments has been shared between more than
3,000 projects. Somewhat more revenue projects (staff and rents,
etc.) have been funded than capital projects (building and equipment) but the balance of approved expenditure has been heavily in
favour of capital.

Up to and including Phase 9, voluntary organisations had received
about 43 per cent of total revenue but only 7 per cent of total
capital funds (see Table 17.2). The proportion has grown over
recent years and seems likely to continue to grow with an increasing
awareness of the UP on the part of voluntary groups and freer access
to its capital funds.

TABLE 17.2 Proportion of funds going to local authorities and
voluntary organisations, Phases 1-9, in England and Wales

	Capital			Revenue			Total		
	LA %	VO %	Total £000s	LA %	VO %	Total £000s	LA %	VO %	Total £000s
Phase 1	100	0	3,935	67	33	23	100	0	3,958
Phase 2	99.7	0.3	4,347	69	31	770	95	5	5,118
Phase 3	99.5	0.5	4,770	58	42	619	95	5	5,390
Phase 4	-	-	-	64	36	518	64	36	518
Phase 5	93	7	6,272	-	-	-	93	7	6,272
Phase 6	-	-	-	49	51	72	52	48	72
Phase 7	85	15	4,067	52	48	1,816	75	25	5,884
Phase 8	-	-	-	56	44	125	56	44	125
Phase 9	77	23	3,274	52	48	875	72	28	4,562
Total	93	7	27,047	57	43	4,817	87	13	31,919

Each UP circular has placed special emphasis on certain types of
project. The bids made by local authorities and the approvals in
each phase have to some extent reflected these emphases, but
throughout the life of the UP the vast majority of projects approved
have been of the same type from year to year. On the capital side,
these have included for example: nursery schools and classes, reception and language centres for immigrant children, day nurseries,
adventure playgrounds, community centres, and family advice centres.
More recently, housing and legal advice and aid centres have been
promoted and approved, but, in the case of the legal centres, in a
very small way.

On the revenue side, there have been, for example, community
workers, playgroups, staff for advice centres, family planning

services, literacy and language schemes, volunteer organisers and grants to voluntary bodies. Table 17.3 shows the proportion of funds going to the different types of project.

TABLE 17.3 Proportion of funds going to project types, Phases 1-9, England and Wales - capital and revenue funds

Type of project	Funds £000s	Proportion %
Nursery schools and classes	8,287	27
Day nurseries	4,785	15
Other child care	2,835	9
Care of the aged	1,452	5
Housing aid centres, etc.	790	3
Community centres	2,573	8
Family planning	394	1
Advice centres	1,012	3
Playgroups	666	2
Other play schemes	1,359	4
Other education	1,752	6
Miscellaneous	4,798	15
Neighbourhood schemes	300	1
Holiday projects	241	1
Total	31,249*	100

* Total excludes certain once-only funds.

The funds have been spread across a wide range of projects and project types. Few large scale projects have therefore been funded: in Phase 7, for example, 61 per cent of all approved projects cost less than £5,000 (90 per cent of revenue and 24 per cent of capital projects) and only 5 per cent of capital projects cost over £40,000. Sums are not only small but scattered widely between authorities. In the first phase, 34 local authorities were selected on the basis of criteria relating to concentrations of immigrants and overcrowding. Since then the identification of areas of 'special social need' qualifying for UP funds has been left very much to local authorities; so far 216 authorities in England and Wales have benefited.

THE CONCEPT OF URBAN DEPRIVATION IN THE UP AND CDP

No definition of the nature of 'urban deprivation' or 'special social need' is simply located in either programme. Both the UP and CDP have been affected by the fact that the nature, form, extent and parameters of urban deprivation have never been articulated and, indeed, have never been elevated above 'common knowledge' and a 'gut feeling' among politicians and administrators.

The problems that these two programmes were established to tackle, and the goals they were to aim for have remained vague and nebulous, and this has resulted in a failure on the part of both to

develop a robust strategy or a clearly defined machinery by which
goals might be achieved.

This lack of clarity and failure of definition has perhaps
created more problems for the CDP than it has for the UP. The UP
can be seen as a resource delivery mechanism by which additional ex-
chequer funds are channelled to local authorities to establish projects in 'deprived areas'. While the Home Office has given some
guidance in circulars about what sort of projects might be suitable,
the onus has been firmly placed upon local authorities to interpret
the aims of the programme, identify 'deprived areas' and the problems therein, and to devise projects which they think are relevant
to meeting the needs of those areas. It could be argued therefore
that since this is essentially a local authority programme, it is
only right and wise that the definition and refinements of the problem it is designed to tackle should be left to local authorities in
the light of the wisdom and knowledge they have gained in operating
major service programmes. This does not excuse central government
however from formulating any policy other than a purely administrative one. The CDP, on the other hand, has attempted more direct,
complex and intricate forms of action. If the UP is predominantly a
channel for additional funds, the CDP is predominantly an action
programme in which project leaders are charged with the task of developing new strategies for action. The absence of a clear definition of problems and strategies from central government has clearly
therefore had a greater impact on project teams.

The terminology which has explained the UP and invited local
authorities to apply for grant aid, has been vague. The areas at
which the UP is aimed are 'areas of special social need' or 'areas
facing acute social problems' or 'areas . . . where living conditions are particularly poor and pressure on social services
severe'. Again, references to the aims of the programme have been
grandiose and unspecific - as John Greve (1973:7) has said of the
aims of CDP, 'they are, indeed, little less than re-assertions of
the fundamental ideals of social policy and of democratic politics.'
The then Home Secretary stated in the House of Commons, 'The purpose
of this Programme is to supplement the Government's other social and
legislative measures in order to ensure as far as we can, that all
our citizens have an equal opportunity in life' (Hansard, 1968: col
41). And again, David Lane (1972), Parliamentary Under-Secretary of
State at the Home Office: 'Our primary aim (with the UP) is to re-
lieve acute social need so that the quality of life of those in deprived areas is improved significantly.'

Such statements illustrate how the term 'urban deprivation' is
used interchangeably with others such as 'special social need',
'acute social problems', 'poor living conditions', 'severe pressure
on social services' and provide little guidance to the form the UP
should take.

If the definitions of deprivation are lacking in specificity, its
alleged manifestations as far as the UP is concerned have at times
been embarrassing in their abundance - but so inclusive as to provide no more concrete clues about the nature of deprivation. The
programme's first circular listed the following manifestations:

Notable deficiencies in the physical environment, particularly in
housing; overcrowding of houses; family sizes above the

average; persistent unemployment; a high proportion of children
in trouble or in need of care
and the ninth circular partly reiterated and added to the list:
overcrowding, poverty, high levels of unemployment, delinquency,
mental disorder or of children in care, old and dilapidated housing, inadequate community services, and a rundown and poor
environment.

The implication is that not only are these the indicators by
which UP areas might be identified, but since they are the forms of
social need, that they are also the problems that the UP seeks to
remedy or at least alleviate. It need hardly be said that such a
list represents an ambitious agenda for a programme of the size of
the UP. Such vague terms as 'multiple deprivation', 'special social
need' and 'acute social problems' on the one hand, and the mis-
cellaneous collection of social ills on the other, betray a lack of
clarity, and indeed a confusion about what urban deprivation is -
and by implication, what machinery is required to tackle it.

There is a continuum of meanings and interpretations laid upon
the concept of urban deprivation. At the one extreme, it is interpreted as 'social malaise' or 'social pathology', at the other, as
a disadvantaged position in a power structure.

The 'social pathology' view of deprivation sees the deprived to
be those who are handicapped in one way or another - mentally or
physically, and who, because of their handicap are less able to cope
with the pressures of urban life than their fellow men. The growth
of the 'social indicators' movement in this country (the means by
which deprived areas qualifying for additional resources might be
identified) has tacitly assumed and fostered this view of deprivation. 'Social malaise' indicator studies tend to have focused on
the kind of local authority and census data which assumes that the
roots of deprivation lie in personal inadequacy, illness or
villainy.

The 'power' structure model of deprivation on the other hand,
holds that urban deprivation is the result of competitive forces in
three important markets. It is the structural inability to compete
effectively in those markets which most affect people's life chances
- the employment, housing and education markets. This conception of
deprivation assumes that the means by which certain societal resources, like housing, education and employment are distributed, are
competitive means and are therefore referred to as markets.

Each of these markets (housing, education and employment) represents a situation of competition and conflict where a few win hand-
somely, most manage adequately and some fail miserably. Unlike most
competitions however, not everyone starts with equal chances, some
are set for success and others doomed to failure almost before they
are born.

The three markets are closely interlinked, such that disadvantage
in one will often determine disadvantage in the others. If a
child's parents are poor and live in an inner city area of decay,
the chances are that he will go to a poor school: his education
will be deficient and the opportunities for advancement through
examination success will be low or absent. He will progress to perhaps the lower streams of a secondary modern or comprehensive school
and will likely emerge at the earliest opportunity to take up a job

which offers low pay, low security and no future. His social position and lack of money will effectively disqualify him from competing effectively in the housing market, and in areas of acute housing
shortage he may well end up once more in privately rented accommodation in the inner city area - if he ever left. The similarities
between this formulation of deprivation and the 'cycle of deprivation' formulation proposed by Sir Keith Joseph, is more apparent
than real. In the latter formulation, the cycle is regenerated
through an inadequate socialisation process; in the former, by the
interrelation and continuance of discriminatory factors in different
resource allocation markets.

The implications for social policy and the formulation of effective programmes to counter this kind of deprivation are of course
far reaching. It is doubtful that the type of positive discrimination programmes which have been developed thus far (UP, CDP, EPA)
can go very far in solving this problem. Their content and the
mechanics of their operation are more suited to the role of a rather
patchy second safety net to major welfare programmes, whereby some
of those who fall through the welfare net (and many of these will be
the handicapped) can be caught and heaved back into it.

It seems a logical consequence of defining urban deprivation in
terms of social structure and process (as has been the case above)
that solutions must be sought in terms of intervention in those processes - and specifically the processes of resource allocation.
Thus one might query whether institutions such as building societies, estate agents, flat agencies and private landlords are appropriate agents for the allocation, in one way or another, of housing;
whether the financial and social rewards accruing to some jobs are
not insufficient and for others far too sufficient; and whether the
present priorities in the allocation of educational resources ought
not to be seriously re-thought.

Between the two interpretations of urban deprivation lie a number
of combinations (or confusions) of the two, and to the extent that
there has been any (tacit) underlying notion of deprivation to the
UP and the CDP, then it is of such an intermediate kind. Thus, in
the Phase 9 circular of the UP, among the forms which social need
may take, are the following: children in trouble or in need of
care; delinquency; mental disorder ('social pathology' interpretations), and poverty; unemployment; overcrowding ('power model'
interpretations). As has been noted above, the solutions to, and
the machinery to be used in achieving these solutions are quite different for the two types of deprivation and any programme that con-
fuses and attempts to combine the two will necessarily achieve less
than success in either.

Of the CDPs it can be said that at least in conception they were
concerned more with boosting self-help in communities as a substi-
tute for statutory welfare services and with attempting to make
these services more aware of local needs and better co-ordinated
than they were with actually altering the distribution of resources.
Nevertheless, what marks the CDPs out from the UP is that as action
research projects they hold out the possibility of a better understanding of the processes which have actually caused people in a
certain area to be deprived. This has taken the CDP teams well
beyond a purely local concern into matters concerning regional and

national industrial, housing and social service policies and processes. They have the capacity to demonstrate to government in concrete terms that local problems are often the consequence of outside
forces. The danger is that as small scale experimental projects,
government may be able too easily to dismiss action on their findings on the grounds that they are of limited applicability. We may
also doubt whether community action, which is the other major distinguishing feature of the CDPs from the UP, can bear any relation
to a far reaching analysis; in other words, whether there is any
action at community level which can really affect structural
deprivation.

The concern of CDP with the 'small area' ranges beyond the administration of any particular set of services, allowing it with the
research to attempt an explanation of local deprivation in structural terms even if there is no likelihood of government response in
the same terms. The UP apparently shares the area approach with CDP
in its focus on 'areas of special social need'. The difference between the UP and the CDP is that while the CDP defines areas as
parameters for study and social action and then looks at them in
their totality, the UP assumes an advance knowledge about the location and problems of deprived areas. The UP talks of 'needlepoints'
of deprivation as if (i) they can be precisely defined, and (ii)
it offers a solution which somehow with minimal expenditure will go
to the roots of deprivation. But in spite of its definition of the
problem, the UP scatters its remedies both widely and thinly. Some
of them serve small areas; others go well beyond any needlepoint to
cover whole authorities.

The UP is conceived in terms not of experiment but of service
provision. The point was not to learn lessons about the nature of
deprivation and to indicate the way to fundamental reform but to add
resources to local government and voluntary organisations on a selective basis. There is an implication in the very setting up of
the UP that existing services and organisational structures were
failing in at least some respects to get to the roots of the problem. But the dependence of the UP on these organisations' own
identification of their problem areas and ideas for remedies indicated an assumption that the failure was believed to be in their inadequate resources rather in the perceptions and interrelations of
these organisations.

The UP, then, tends to have identified areas in pathological
terms (a potentially endless list of problems and of groups thought
to have problems) and to have offered remedies in terms of additional services. The only doubt is whether within this service-
orientated framework the UP is expected to solve the problem of
urban deprivation, to catalyse developments in social service provision or to palliate the situation by providing more of the same
services.

The steps from 'pathologism' to 'structuralism' go from additional service provision (to those who are regarded as physically,
mentally or culturally handicapped) to service reorganisation and
co-ordination and from there to more fundamental changes in the
operation of markets which distribute basic resources. On this continuum, the UP, as it has been implemented, stands near the beginning: it does not merely provide more of the same services but

has gone a little way towards stimulating new ones and towards concentrating action in selected areas.   The CDP stands further along
the continuum, somewhere between the reorganisation of service
delivery mechanisms and a more fundamental examination of the causes
of deprivation.

Chapter 18

COMMUNITY DEVELOPMENT AS A PROCESS OF EMERGENCE

Samuel H. Bailie

I understand the word 'development' to contain at least, the ideas of 'process', 'emergence' and 'change'. Although this chapter is not intended to be a study in conceptual analysis, nevertheless it is important to distinguish different notions. 'Community development' itself is a confused notion. Thus 'community development' is used sometimes to refer to a better provision of services. At the other extreme it is taken to be solely a strengthening of local politics or even further the imposition of idealistic societies. It is true that there are terms which distinguish different approaches to social intervention such as 'community provision', 'community action', 'community service' or 'community relations' but often they are lumped together under the title of 'community development'.

I intend to discuss 'community development' under the three component headings 'process', 'emergence' and 'change' to distinguish it from other approaches to change within a community, though there are always border-line cases which could readily fit into more than one compartment. One could select examples of actions which may be described either as 'community action' or 'community service' and so on.

Broadly speaking, 'community provision' is concerned with physical amenities normally provided within statutory obligations by statutory bodies to compliant recipients. 'Community service' is often voluntary work done by people for other people, who are usually considered to be incapable for various reasons of doing it for themselves. 'Community action' usually implies a desire within a community to win a battle over a particular issue affecting the community, whilst 'community relations' is normally taken to mean 'race relations'. I am aware that short, terse, descriptions like these, often caricature or misrepresent ideas, but I am at pains to point out that there is a difference and it is useful to know (and to examine) what is being done, or what it is hoped to achieve.

The importance of this analysis lies in the strategy of intervention which is being adopted, and the role of the worker within that strategy. In other words, what are the objectives and how are they to be achieved? What are the basic assumptions upon which the strategy is based? The assumption, objectives and strategy of the worker determine, for example, whether he takes the role of a social worker, an organiser, a leader, a director, an imposer, an advocate, a teacher or a preacher.

Thus one can ask whether one is engaged in activities which will produce better amenities, better people, a better society? One can also ask what is meant by 'better' and whether these activities are once-off engagements or on-going? Whether this is a battle or a war, an issue or a process?

CHANGE

I begin with the idea of 'change'. If one mentions 'change', it involves changing both people and things. To change people is education, to change things is politics. If worthwhile and lasting change is to be effected it means also a change in the people who use or do things - a change in how people do or see things.

When one talks about change, one is also talking about the values which are held by different people and different sections of society. By what criteria can these values be assessed and by what right should a value or set of values predominate? Should the inherent conflict between values be supported, treating situations of confrontation as inevitable, or is there a method by which differing values may be reconciled if not in principle at least in practice? The assumption of the latter solution is that different values can be understood, respected and accommodated. It is the work of community development, as I am trying to describe it, to ensure that all concerned are properly represented, taken account of when decisions are made and that they compete on equal terms.

The fact that there are alternatives simply shows that there is no ideal or perfect solution to any problem even assuming that the problem has been correctly identified. Let it be met and faced on its own terms and not solely on rigid or pre-determined lines of action which may have little relevance to the present except that it has been done elsewhere.

The putting forward of alternatives to safe or accepted ways of doing things or to previously unchallenged value systems often raises resentment and hostility based on fear and insecurity. It is akin to having a mat pulled from under one's feet. In a sense this is what it is, but providing there is someone behind and that another mat is offered this may not always be a dangerous exercise. Even the experience itself may be worthwhile.

Thus the community development worker must be aware of what he is doing in this respect, and therefore he is not surprised that he is involved in conflict situations. In fact, he expects this as an integral part of the job, and he must take account of the full range of feelings. A community development worker who is surprised that people do not always co-operate as he expected, even when they ask for his help, is either naive or inexperienced.

This is the point of conflict which raises all the issues with which community development is concerned. What should a community development worker do to ensure that problems are dealt with in what he considers to be an effective manner? This raises a·dilemma for workers employed within a local authority. Do they represent the authority or the community? In truth, of course, they represent no one but themselves, and this provides a way out of what is really a non-existent dilemma.

Which of the interested parties needs to have their view of the problem changed or enlarged? What re-identification of the issues would produce an acceptable solution? The enlarging of horizons and the development of the critical faculty are educational processes. These call for educational methods to put them into effect. Education is concerned with communication, the development of the understanding, modification of attitude, self examination.

Therefore the methods used must produce changes in people which will lead to increased discussion, understanding, co-operation and experimentation.

Pressure group activities can produce short term success on particular issues. Usually nothing much else is achieved except a build-up of a greater degree of resentment and hostility between the contesting parties. 'Might is right' becomes the philosophical basis for resolving disputes.

PROCESS

I have been trying to distinguish between 'once-off' successes or conflicts, and the process of working out solutions to problems by the people who experience them, as distinct from imposed solutions. I have laboured to point out that people hold different values and that there are no 'neutral' criteria for assessing their worth. Even if there were rational arguments which could list priorities, there is no method by which anyone can be made to accept them. Values and moral judgments have this in common that no conclusion follows logically from premises of fact. No matter how sound the argument may appear, or how rational the case, it still remains to find a means of convincing the listener. Two parties may agree that a particular neighbourhood is lacking in various facilities. They may not agree that it is 'deprived'. Even if it is agreed that an area is deprived, there may be dispute over priorities or in allocating resources. One cannot convince the other on these points; it is just how they feel about the problem. It is the work of the community development worker to produce situations, in which there is a possibility that feelings can be changed. This is done by ensuring that a problem is examined in different ways and is seen and understood in its different facets.

From what has been said it is obvious that a CDP sited within a local authority and backed by government funds must take account not only of the problems of the people in the community, but also those of officials of local and central government and elected representatives. In addition there are the many voluntary agencies. Within this context, one can emphasise the experimental nature of CDP.

The strategy being put forward here has to be tried and assessed over a period of time. The assessment itself is another matter. I am inclined to the view that the success of a project should be based on whether it is continued, albeit in some other form, by consent and desire.

The total view of problems then, involves working at five broad levels: people in the community, elected representatives, government officials, people from voluntary organisations, and the staff of the community development agency itself.

Within the community there must be concern for its problems, an understanding of its difficulties, and a confidence to do something about them. Sometimes feelings of general frustration have to be put into concrete terms, and the issue broadened to take account of the barriers that have to be overcome.

EMERGENCE

The work of community development as presented so far sounds a bit piecemeal, action being based on response to pressures within the community - a picture of a worker being led rather than leading. The picture is not completely true. The worker is led to some extent because the issues with which he is involved are issues which the people identify as important. However, sometimes the worker has to help clarify what the issues are. Action by a community group will result only if the members are convinced that the analysis of the problem is correct.

The piecemeal response - as it appears - begins to take shape. Local community groups are formed over particular issues. The community group broadens its view of the problem by action and it often becomes clear that their problem is part of a larger one, and that other people are experiencing similar kinds of difficulties. This leads to the desire to forge linkages with other groups or neighbourhoods to achieve their objectives.

They are seeking a common identification of their difficulties, resulting in joint action to produce solutions. This calls for resolution of conflict within and between communities. It entails a sharing of ideas, an ability to learn from one another and the acceptance of criticism of one's own point of view. Learning is a slow and painful process, but it is an accelerating process and the experience of the process develops both confidence and competence.

Amalgamated groups are also looking for consultation with authorities and agencies. This is the development of communication channels, and communication entails both the ability to express oneself and the ability to listen. It is often at this level that conflict arises. If a community worker has concentrated all his efforts on the community, the breadth of vision of the community groups may exceed that of department officials.

Some officials through experience may have come to regard themselves as being loyal to some anthropomorphic institution, as beneficent providers to people whom they are supposed to serve. It is foreign to such thinking that people should be consulted over issues that affect them. What is being asked by the community is a share in the decision-making process, regarded sometimes as the prerogative of chief officers. This is not an issue of rights, rather it is an acceptance that people are experts in identifying their own needs, and that they are capable of meeting some, though not all, of these needs without external assistance. All this adds up to a shift of control over the quality of life experienced by people into their own hands, control which includes allocation of resources and spending power.

The acceptance of such ideas inevitably raises issues for all professions involved in government or social provision. What effect would public consultation and participation have in planning, education, housing and welfare? It is the work of community development to raise these issues, not in an academic way, but through working them out in practice to help people in the community, with local government officials, elected representatives, and professionals.

DEVELOPMENT

It would be wrong to assume that community development is only a subtle means to achieve control over resources. Development of community means development of people, and this I see as a self-awareness, a conscious exercise of one's personal skills and an acknowledgment of what one lacks. There is also a recognition that one can achieve more, and that the limits of achievement are unknown. To develop personal qualities is to develop an ability to meet the difficulties of living, either to deal with problems falling within one's own competence, or to communicate with those whose duty it is to deal with problems we cannot fully combat alone.

In changing situations people must change to meet new demands upon them. This applies just as much to community development workers as to those with whom they work. Apart from the more obvious things such as improved facilities in a particular neighbourhood or the growth of community structures and organisations capable of handling community problems, the exciting thing about community development is the process of change in oneself and the build-up of confidence in individuals. Often this confidence - this change in outlook in life - leads to a separate development for some people, some into social work, some into higher education, some to politics. It is certain that their experience in community affairs will enable them to put into practice in their new occupations, the human skills that are necessary to produce the healthy society that everyone desires. Only the means is in dispute.

Chapter 19

THE FLAW IN THE PLURALIST HEAVEN: CHANGING STRATEGIES IN THE COVENTRY CDP

John Benington

The original model for the national CDP was based on a belief that there were in our cities small concentrations of people with special problems which demanded special treatment. The Home Secretary in his 1969 speech in Parliament, when he announced the CDP, defined that category of people like this: 'Although the social services cater reasonably well for the majority they are much less effective for a minority who are caught up in a chain reaction of related social problems. An example of the kind of vicious circle in which this kind of family could be trapped is ill-health, financial difficulty, children suffering from deprivation, consequent delinquency, inability of the children to adjust to adult life, unstable marriages, emotional problems, ill-health - and the cycle begins again.' So it is clear that he had a precise view of the kind of people towards whom CDP was to be directed.

The Home Office in its original prescription clearly believed that one solution to, these assumed concentrations of people with special pathology was to tighten co-ordination in the delivery of welfare support services to them. The original job description for my appointment to Coventry CDP in January 1970 was as the leader of a team which was to include a psychiatric social worker, a child care officer, education welfare officer, disablement resettlement officer, and mental welfare officer. It is clear that the problems are seen as those of social cripples and lame ducks. They are to be helped to make better use of the welfare state first by closer co-ordination in the delivery of personal services and second by self-help. In announcing the project in Coventry in February 1969, Richard Crossman perhaps unwittingly revealed one of the underlying paradoxes in these early views of the experiment:

> It is not just a matter of helping to get these people back on their feet by gearing up the social services for them in a fully co-ordinated way but of helping them to stand more on their own in the future by their own efforts without having to rely so much on external support.

Greater co-ordination should increase take-up of services and therefore costs, while self-help is designed to reduce demands on the welfare state and therefore limit costs. That is a paradox that was never resolved, or even really acknowledged.

    Experience in the first two exploratory years of the project
forced us to challenge and reject those initial assumptions. First,
it became clear that in spite of its reputation, Hillfields did not
have an abnormal share of families with personal social handicaps.
The most obvious and blatant problems that people experienced were
not internal and pathological but were external. They arose from
the very low incomes people were having to live on and the very poor
housing and environment in the district. These problems were not
peculiar to that neighbourhood; they were the same as the problems
which were afflicting large sections of the working class population
throughout Coventry. They were more acute in their degree but they
were not different in kind. The major factor that was specific to
the Hillfields neighbourhood was the council's intervention with a
comprehensive plan for redevelopment. This again was not a problem
which arose within that community; it was a problem which arose
from the policies of the city towards that neighbourhood. It was
clear that the issues did not just concern a deviant minority within
the welfare state, but large sections of the population as a whole.
We were looking as it were at a microcosm of processes that were
part of the whole city's dynamics and were not peculiar to that
neighbourhood.
    Second, there was little evidence that the problems people ex-
perienced resulted from any obvious deterioration in the patterns or
values of community life. When we arrived to start work in Coventry
at the beginning of 1970, we found that the planners had identified
a grid of 26 streets which was to be the target area for CDP. This
had been selected on the basis of certain assumptions about social
pathology. Different agencies had been asked to identify where
their heaviest problems lay. Some departments had done this in
detail and had plotted their caseloads by marking black dots on a
street map of the city. Others were much more cavalier and just
drew a circle around an area which they believed to have the worst
reputation. The planners brought all this information together on
base maps, overlaid with census information, and eventually chose a
core of twenty-six streets which they saw to be the black spot of
the area. As it happened, we arrived to find that a change in the
redevelopment time-table meant that a large part of this core area
was to be demolished within a matter of months. Ironically this
gave us the opportunity to stand back and ask a lot more questions
about the ways in which the area's reputation as a blackspot had
arisen. We came to see that this was less a reflection of deteriorating standards of local community behaviour, than of processes external to the locality. The area's reputation for prostitution is a
good illustration. Statistics of court convictions for 'loiter
prostitution' would certainly show a heavy preponderance in
Hillfields. But levels of surveillance by the vice squad are also
greatest in Hillfields. A self-fulfilling prophecy seemed to be at
work, whereby the police were more alert to this phenomenon in
Hillfields than in other districts and so their levels of detection
and hence conviction were also greater. In fact, it seems that the
prostitution in the district is almost entirely a commuter business.
It is not local women but women from the West Midlands who come from
as far away as Nottingham to solicit in Hillfields. Their clients
are not Hillfields men either but commuters from other parts of

Coventry or the city region. So the 'malaise' statistics record a
number of phenomena which have little connection with any deterioration of community values in Hillfields.

The third thing that became clear was that local people did not
see more communication leading to better solutions to their problems
at all. On the contrary, they were in direct dispute with the
authorities about the nature of their needs and their aspirations.
They saw the problem as their difficulty in influencing decisions
which affected their lives in the directions which they wanted. It
was not a consensual situation. It was a situation where residents
believed they had a different interest from that represented by the
public authorities. Communication was there in plenty; communication that was only sometimes vocal or articulate, expressed mostly
in informal social settings, but sometimes through the traditional
means of petitions and public meetings and at times of exceptional
frustration, even in minor acts of insurrection. One local resident
was prepared to barricade himself in his house and to put live elec-
tric cables around to keep the bulldozers at bay. That seemed to be
a fairly clear message.

So it became clear to us that the initial prescriptions of CDP
were inadequate to the actual situation. The diagnosis was in-
correct. The solutions for Hillfields could not be looked for in
stronger doses of the medicine that the welfare state had been serving up, or in a better mixing of ingredients in that dose, or even
in a better bedside manner in the administering of the dose. We
were in fact confronted by problems of politics, the problem of conflicts of interests in the city, and the problem of powerlessness in
influencing political decisions.

This led us into our second phase of work. We felt at that stage
that it was important to shift exclusive focus away from the neighbourhood as the source of problems and to concentrate research and
action on the government agencies that appeared to be controlling
the destinies of the people in that area. I say 'appeared' because
later experience led us to see that this was not necessarily where
effective control of all the processes lay. However, we felt at
that time that a local CDP on its own was not in a position to
tackle the ultimate causes of disadvantage which have their sources
nationally in the economy and in government policy. So we began to
map out a series of studies of the agencies which we believed to be
mediating the distribution of public resources at the local level.
We were aware that local government was not the only controller of
people's destinies but we felt that it was at that level that we
could best hope to contribute. So we began programmes of work which
attempted to analyse and modify the processes within government
agencies which sustain and reinforce disadvantage at the local
level. We concentrated on the following main fields: income maintenance, housing and environment, community education, the transition from school to work, and services for the elderly. We were
aware that this ran the danger of breaking the phenomenon of
multiple-deprivation down into isolated parts. We therefore had
another programme, which we called social priority planning, which
tried to take some account of the structures within which the
separate functional services operated. (At this stage we concentrated rather narrowly on organisational and managerial structures,

and were too little aware of the wider political and economic structures.)

We approached this goal in a number of ways and at different levels. Our strategies have included research, promotion of change within the corporation's management system, and direct involvement with particular interest groups in the neighbourhood. They have ranged across the following kinds of intervention:

1   identifying those whose circumstances or conditions make them eligible for existing service provision and helping them to press their claims upon those services;
2   attempting to make agencies more receptive to needs for which they are responsible and to argue for changes in the mechanisms for identifying and categorising those in need;
3   pressing agencies and institutions to consider alternative structures and methods of responding to need;
4   experimentally developing innovatory structures for dealing with problems as a demonstration of alternatives to existing institutional patterns;
5   presenting ways of redefining the problems themselves which may lead to more relevant ways of dealing with them;
6   critically appraising the functioning of institutions and agencies to identify elements of their practices which may act to compound the problems they seek to resolve.

I will try to share some of the general conclusions we have drawn from this experience, first in terms of the functioning of some of these agencies within the urban system and then in terms of our attempts to bring about change. The first thing that became clear to us was that government programmes were not benefiting everyone in the city equally. Even those programmes which purported to be universal were giving benefits to certain sections of the population often at the expense of others. The most obvious example is the ring road in the city. As in many cities this was assumed to contribute to the well-being of the city as a whole, enhancing mobility and tackling a general problem of traffic thrombosis. Car owners certainly benefited. But certain sections of the population actually lost out. It was the inner city areas that were carved up to make way for the ring road. A few people lost their houses and many more were blighted. Furthermore, these were the very areas which had the least proportion of cars so the least number of people that could take advantage of the benefits.

Second, it became clear that even those programmes that were designed to tackle particular problems or to compensate for disadvantage very often had side-effects that outweighed the benefits. Redevelopment is a familiar example. Our observation and experience confirms much other research that on any kind of cost benefit calculation the advantages to be gained by residents of older housing areas through comprehensive redevelopment are very doubtful. First of all, it is not often the original residents of the depressed area who stay to enjoy the benefits of the redeveloped area. Second, redevelopment brings new physical capital into an area (houses, schools, roads, play areas) but often destroys the social capital which residents have invested in their neighbourhood over a long period of time. This is not easily quantifiable, as it is embodied in networks of informal relationships rather than in any formal

institution. However, it can pay a tangible dividend towards the
quality of life.

The third thing that came home to us was that even those programmes which were designed to offer support and help to the so
called disadvantaged groups, sometimes seemed to 'come over' in
quite an opposite way to those on the receiving end. This has been
well documented in the field of social security but less in the
field of the 'caring' services where we have come to believe that
the battery of community care provision for the elderly (meals on
wheels, home helps) in practice may have very different effects from
that which is often claimed. It seems possible that old people may
find it a threat to their sense of status and their independence to
be in receipt of meals on wheels and home helps. If this is so,
then these services, in their current form, may reduce rather than
enhance a person's capacity to maintain themselves in the community.
A study we commissioned on the role of the schools, the youth employment service and employers in helping young people make the
transition from school-life to work-life, led us to a similar kind
of conclusion. It appears that many young people feel that the
careers advisory system in practice serves to sort and file them
into pre-ordained pigeon-holes.

With these kinds of perspectives on the functioning of local
agencies, we began to try to negotiate with them for the development
and testing of programmes which would discriminate positively
towards those who had lost out most and begin to provide services
more relevant to their values and interests. Our experience of
trying to work for organisational change can be summarised crudely
like this. We did gain a positive response from the education and
social services and were able to design substantial joint programmes. We do not think that the responses from these two agencies
was simply to do with their having progressive chairmen and chief
officers. In those fields and those professions, there has already
been debate (Plowden and Seebohm) which has prepared the ground and
which can accommodate the kind of criticism that we developed.
Furthermore, in some ways those agencies stand to gain from evidence
of unmet need. The solutions to unmet need in education and social
services are often presumed to be more staff, more teachers or different kinds of teachers, or more social workers or different kinds
of social workers. So in a sense, those departments have a vested
interest in collaborating with those who produce research about
unmet need, particularly if they are agencies which can also give
them a subsidy to fund programmes which in themselves are likely to
lead to further evidence of unmet need and thus ammunition for increased budgets. However, we soon became aware that our resources
were being swallowed up in experimental programmes which could
easily be restricted to change at the field level.

We have a community education programme going in thirteen local
schools and a decentralised social service experiment, both of which
have put pressure for change on the face to face workers (on the
classroom teacher, on the field social worker). These have resulted
in some 'loosening up' of professional thinking and practice,
greater interaction between clients, professionals and the local
neighbourhood, and in greater relevance in what is offered by these
agencies. However, we became aware that we were in danger of

colluding in humanising services which were still perpetuating more basic inequalities. More sensitive delivery of services is obviously a good thing in itself, but cannot hope to compensate for the massive inbuilt disadvantages which arise from the housing situation, the employment situation and the wider economic structure as a whole. The Coventry education committee has begun to work out some of the policy implications of what is happening in the schools programme and has now committed itself to some positive discrimination in the allocation of per capita and other allowances between schools in the city. So Hillfields children may begin to get a slightly happier education, in schools which are slightly better provided. But it is more doubtful whether any of this has been or will be able to make any significant impact on the real life-chances and opportunities of people in the area. Similarly, in the social services experiment we have been able to increase the level of resources available to the decentralised neighbourhood team. They have a slightly augmented staff, and a resource fund of £3,000 a year which they can use with local people to develop innovatory programmes to meet local needs. But it is increasingly clear to us that the social services are a bottomless pit in the inner city. Resources could be funnelled in endlessly and they would be absorbed like blotting paper, because field workers are constantly having to try to mop up the consequences of low income, poor housing, brutalising employment, and inadequate shares of investment from the public sector.

Our experience in the field of housing and the environment has been very different, but has led our thinking in the same direction - away from managerial and technical solutions. The inner city area, including Hillfields, has been declining steadily since the war. The redevelopment programme has been one of protracted stop-go. Whole areas have been blighted and physical conditions have deteriorated. More houses have been knocked down than replaced, which has therefore decreased the overall supply of cheaper housing in the city. The housing which has been built is of the wrong kind and type to allow families to mature in the area. Private property speculation in the area meant that it was increasingly hard for ordinary men and women to find housing they could afford, and there was a growing problem of homelessness. The identification of unmet need in the field of housing has a rather different effect from that in education and social services. That problem cannot be solved by employing more staff or more housing welfare officers. It puts enormous pressure on the local council and housing department to spell out what their priorities are for the allocation of those very scarce resources. Land and housing are probably the most critical resources in Coventry at the moment.

The only fluid area for further development is the inner city. So it has become a real battle as to whether that land is going to be used for houses for working class people who have always lived there or whether it is going to be used for public sector and private development of a city-wide kind. The area already houses the city's bus depôt, the football ground, the central hospital, a staff hostel for a hotel and a number of industrial sites. So there is competition from the public sector which needs land to develop further central services and also increasing pressure from the private sector which is wanting land to build profitable office blocks and develop night-life entertainment. The local authority is thus bargaining with local people over how their area should be re-developed while the private sector is upstaging them all by being able to pay prices for land that the local authority and local people cannot match.

The corporate planning and management system claims to provide a more rational basis for the allocation of land and housing on the basis of need. Our initial presumption, therefore, was that if we were able to feed in data about unmet need or about the negative consequences of existing policies, this would compete on equal terms with other data about need around the city. However, experience began to suggest that the planning and management system did not respond neutrally. It appeared to have within it a systematic bias in favour of certain interests - a bias which was not altogether within the control of the elected democratic system. We had to begin to account for the fact that a local authority which had managed to build an internationally famous city centre, prestige civic monuments and award winning estates had somehow failed to produce similarly efficient and well co-ordinated operations in Hillfields. For a long time, we assumed that the problems were lack of data, or bureaucratic rigidity, or technical incompetence. But it became clear that the local authority is not incompetent, does not lack technical expertise; it has a highly sophisticated corporate management system which manages to serve certain interests in the city very well. The important thing was to look at whose interests were in practice being served by the operations of that system and whose interests were not - who gained and who lost from the outputs of the local authority. Coventry divides very obviously into a north and a south; a south that has large houses, wide tree-lined roads, attractive parks and open space, and a north which has congested housing, dense industry, little open space - a clear contrast between haves and have-nots. The policies and programmes of the local authority, whatever their intention, did not seem in practice to be compensating for those blatant inequalities. Indeed, in some respects, the already better-off areas and groups within the population seemed to be creaming off the main benefits. The corporate management system operated as if the whole population was homogeneous in its needs, and did not draw effective attention to questions of economic and political distribution. Plans and reports acknowledged 'priority areas' but the data was presented in highly technical, sanitised terms, projected into the future; ten year plans, fifteen year plans, raised to higher and higher plateaux of generality, so that any plan for Hillfields had been pre-related to the plan for the city, for the sub-region, and for the metropolitan area. The conflicts of interest were thus reconciled by being raised to a level of universality where it appeared that all people had interests in common. At the local level, it was quite clear that some areas and some sections of the population were systematically gaining while others were systematically losing.

The third insight brought home to us was the extent to which the technical management system were not really open to effective political challenge even to those who were equipped with alternative data and analysis. I have suggested that the corporate management

system was serving up to the main local authority committees a consensual view of the city based on homogenised data which obscured
underlying conflicts of interest and areas of unmet need. CDP was
serving up to local residents and to councillors a different view of
the city based upon finer-grain data which exposed some of the inequalities and problems. But we found that the traditional democratic procedures did not necessarily provide an effective point of
leverage for alternative views. We have only very small examples of
this but I believe they apply more widely.

After a social survey by CDP, a residents' association was formed
in two streets keen to have their area declared a general improvement area. The local authority set up an inter-departmental team to
implement the GIA and nominated a planner as team leader. The 1969
Housing Act places an obligation on the authority to take residents'
views into account in any GIA. The residents' association had
several sessions with the planner and found him quite receptive to
their suggestions and wishes. However, it became clear that he had
little delegated authority, and their demands kept having to be referred back up the hierarchies of the local authority. Extensive
consultation and modification took place first in the officer system
and then proposals were eventually processed by a variety of committees. Decisions were taking longer and longer and the residents'
association was getting more and more frustrated at the failure to
make progress.

After two years of waiting, they noticed that an area of land
immediately next to their two streets was cleared of its houses and
prepared for new buildings. This was going to be the site for a
hostel for a new hotel which was being developed in the city centre,
by a group which owns a chain of hotels and restaurants (including
the Mirabelle in Mayfair) around Britain. The De Vere group had
approached the local authority about a site for a hostel for their
workers. Hillfields was close to the hotel and to the city centre,
and the area around the GIA was conveniently ripe for development.
The De Vere Hotel had been able to negotiate at rather a different
level and on rather different terms from the residents' association.
Their public participation had been not with the friendly neighbourhood planner, but with the top manager in the planning department
and the corporation's Land Resource Unit. It was not simply a difference in levels: it appeared to the residents that in practice
the planners were taking the hotel's requirements as the independent
variable and that the residents' demands were going to have to be
related to that. It certainly seemed that way in terms of the speed
of decisions and action over the staff hostel. It was the first
noticeable change on the ground near the GIA and to this day remains
the most striking 'improvement' in this area.

This is not an isolated example of the mobilisation of bias.
Hill's Plastics, which makes ashtrays and other plastic mouldings
for Chrysler (in fact is a subsidiary of Chrysler UK) has a small
factory at the end of the two streets in the GIA. Local residents
were in dispute with them about the use of the streets. They wanted
the streets closed off, traffic free, so that they could be
landscaped and improved. Hill's Plastics wanted turning space for
their lorries. The local authority planning department had to
decide. Residents came to feel that this issue was not being

decided in the scientific, cost-benefit terms that the management
system led them to believe but that it was, in practice, a hard
political fight between Chrysler (UK) and a handful of residents
from two streets. The model of the democratic system that we had
been operating with was a naive and false one. We had assumed the
democratic system to be a kind of pyramid in which all are represented but in which some people have less access to the top. Experience of struggle with local people 'demystified' this picture
for us. It became clear that only a very narrow section of the decisions which were affecting the lives of the people in our area lay
within the control of the democratic system, even at the apex of the
pyramid. A much larger and stronger set of variables lay in sections of the economy which were not within the control of local or
indeed central government. The important thing to understand was
the role played by the state in mediating and servicing the interests of the private sector.

THE PLURALIST SNOOKER GAME

A man with the unlikely name of Schattschneider has said that 'the
flaw in the pluralist heaven is that the heavenly chorus sings with
a strong upper class accent.' The pluralist view of the social
system is of a kind of snooker game in which different interest
groups in society are all jostling with each other. The pluralist
view is that the snooker balls are all different sizes and colours
but they are all jostling in the same game. The competition is seen
to be a bit unequal but the rules of the game are basically fair.
The pluralist solution is to help those who are currently losing out
to compete more effectively. In discussing the evolution of our
ideas through experience in CDP, I have alluded so far to two very
different views of the social system: the first is a consensual
view in which it is assumed that all groups in society have similar
goals and similar aspirations; if people are not meeting those
goals it is something to do with their personal handicaps; they can
be helped and educated to achieve better. The second is the
pluralist view of different interest groups competing in a game
which seems to be rather biased but where the rules are basically
fair. There is a third view of the social system based on an analysis of structural or class conflict.

I personally have turned to this explanation not on abstract
theoretical grounds, but as someone who came into the situation four
years ago with fairly 'progressive' social work views but who has
been forced through experience in a concrete situation to look for
more satisfactory explanations. I can perhaps try to develop this
not in terms of some broad theory which would define a particular
political position, but as a personal interpretation of what is and
has been happening in our particular neighbourhood. One of the ways
of looking at what has happened in and to Hillfields, since the
beginning of the century, is not in terms of any preponderance of
families with special personal handicaps or peculiar personal
pathologies, nor in terms of maladministration or imperfect planning, but in terms of the fluctuating relationship between private
capital and the state.

PRIVATE CAPITAL AND THE LOCAL STATE IN COVENTRY

We have come to see more sharply the ways in which the development
and decline of Hillfields is closely tied up with the patterns of
private capital investment in the city over the past 150 years.
Hillfields was built between 1830 and 1861 as the city's first
suburb and was not joined to the city centre until about 1850.   It
was known as New Town -˙a boom community of prosperous ribbon
weavers. The bottom dropped out of this trade during the 1860s and
Hillfields was hit particularly hard. However, the skilled craftsmen quickly adapted themselves and their cottage factories to the
new boom in bicycle manufacturing. This created opportunities for a
new middle class, many of whom came in from outside the city. A
number of individual entrepreneurs came to invest their engineering
skills and their capital in the new markets for bicycles and eventually motor-cycles and cars. Volume production was sought as a
means of realising maximum profits and larger factories became the
dominant production unit in the city for the first time.

The Klondike-growth of the motor and engineering industry in the
first half of this century created opportunities for profitable
mass-production and a massive demand for labour in Coventry. This
was recruited from the depressed areas of the British Isles and of
the Commonwealth. The growth of the engineering industry in
Coventry was accelerated further by munitions production in both
world wars and this created a further demand for labour. The population of the city almost doubled between 1901 and 1921 and again
between 1921 and 1940. Between 1921 and 1937, it rose at a rate
seven times that of the country as a whole (even allowing for the
boundary extensions which more than quadrupled the area covered by
the city during the same period). This rapid and large-scale immigration, largely to meet the needs of the private sector, put enormous pressure on the public sector. The local authority had to provide housing, schools, and basic social and community services for
the incoming population. Furthermore the local authority carried
much of the cost of providing the basic infrastructure (roads,
sewerage, water, electricity, gas) needed by industry to support its
phenomenal and profitable expansion.

Bomb damage during the war imposed massive further costs upon the
city. With the loss of homes and the further expansion of the population expected after the war, the city had an immense problem of
reconstruction. It is estimated that the total public and private
investment in major building and civil engineering construction in
Coventry between 1945 and 1966 amounted to £195 million (at 1966
building costs). However, the rapid growth in population and the
scale of bomb devastation together confronted the local authority
with impossible choices about priorities. The eventual pattern of
investment was determined partly by the continued pressure for expansion from private industry, partly by local political choice, and
partly by the availability of central government grants for particular purposes.

The effect of this combination of factors has been to deprive
older housing areas of the sustained investment which was necessary
to prevent them from decline. Over the past hundred years Greater
Hillfields has thus suffered the pressures arising from

1   the intrusion of industry: the factories in the railway
    triangle provide one-third of all jobs in the city;
2   the successive waves of immigration into the city: the railway
    triangle has functioned as the main reception area for newcomers
    to the city, providing a necessary supply of cheap, rented
    accommodation;
3   the appropriation of land for a number of city-wide services,
    e.g. ring-road, football ground, bus depot, hospital;
4   planning blight, which has led to economic uncertainty, loss of
    property values and deterioration in the condition of both hous-
    ing and the environment. Public labelling processes then helped
    to set in motion a self-fulfilling prophecy in which the area
    gradually came to be defined as a blackspot.

The combined effect of these economic and physical assaults has been
to leave Hillfields as a twilight area, supporting a high proportion
of the most vulnerable sections of the population - elderly long-
standing residents, immigrant families and others with young
children, and claimants and others dependent upon state benefits.
Even the working population are economically disadvantaged. Over 40
per cent of the economically active and retired males of Greater
Hillfields are classified as unskilled or semi-skilled workers.
These sections of the labour-force are not only among the lowest-
paid but also the most 'at risk' at times of redundancy or
rationalisation in industry.

Coventry's relationship with both the engineering and construction industries may now be at a crucial turning-point. The city's
employment is concentrated dangerously in the manufacturing sector
(63 per cent of jobs in the city in 1971, compared with 39 per cent
as the average for Great Britain). Furthermore, there is a concentration on four industries within that sector (motor vehicles, aircraft, mechanical engineering and electrical engineering) which are
particularly responsive to changes in the national economy. When
the latter is buoyant and demand is high, employment in the city
benefits from its narrow concentration, but when the economy is
down, the city's economy is precarious.

Even more seriously, the industry is also vulnerable to the fluctuations in multi-national capitalism. 90 per cent of the work-force
employed by firms employing more than five persons in the manufacturing sector are employed by fifteen major companies. Two-thirds
are employed by ten firms each with assets of more than £20 million.
As the home market for cars nears saturation, and as the motor industry is increasingly challenged by overseas competitors, the
engineering industry has concentrated into larger and fewer combines
in order to remain profitable. The industry has also become less
labour-intensive as firms invest in more sophisticated forms of
technology in order to maximise output per unit cost. There is now
less of a demand for semi-skilled and unskilled labour and these
sections of the work-force are at risk. The period 1961 to 1966 can
be seen clearly as the crest of the boom experienced by Coventry.
Since 1966, there has been a steady decline. A key factor has been
the massive reduction of the aircraft industry in the early 1960s.
This industry has been shedding labour over the whole country (a decline of 18 per cent between 1961 and 1966) but in Coventry the contraction was nearly three times as great (a decline of 50 per cent

between 1961 and 1966). The machine tool industry (which is responsible for about 10 per cent of employment in Coventry) has also been undergoing rationalisation.

For the last hundred years the city has acted as a kind of storage-tank for labour to service the profitable boom in the vehicle and machine-tool engineering industries. Those industries have now saturated and exhausted their markets in the west, and face a major crisis in profitability. Under certain circumstances the city could all too easily become a massive pool of redundant and unemployed labour, a memorial to a spent phase of capitalism. The local authority seems to have responded by trying to support and service the engineering industry in its search for new markets and new contracts (e.g. trade missions of local industrialists led and blessed by the Lord Mayor and other Coventry councillors, to Germany, Russia and China) presumably on the assumption that the city's economic health depends upon maintaining order books and hence jobs. An alternative approach which has been less explored would be to question whether these trends cannot be challenged and whether industry cannot be forced to carry the costs of its cast-off work-force and to compensate the community for its ravishing of the environment in the north of the city.

The city's land has also been plundered, in addition to its labour. The expansion of industry and of the labour force has put increasing pressure on Coventry's land resources. It is now predicted that Coventry will run out of building land within its own boundaries in the next fifteen years. In this situation the older inner-city areas develop a new scarcity value. The council's intervention through compulsory purchase and redevelopment exposes major conflicts of interest over the ownership and use of the land in the inner city. The traditional role of the inner areas (providing a supply of relatively cheap housing for newcomers to the city and for lower-paid and lower-status workers in both the manufacturing and service sectors) is now being challenged by pressures to perform further central area functions. Again it is the ordinary men and women of Coventry who carry the heaviest costs. With the fiercer competition over the ownership and use of land, and for the use of the building industry's machinery and labour, it is increasingly only the large investment companies which can afford to undertake development in the city. While lucrative office-blocks and hotels spring up rapidly, house building slows down and the problem of homelessness becomes more and more acute. The local authority continues to contribute to the 'calculability' of the economic environment for private developers, by assembling land into sufficiently large parcels for development and by processing planning permissions.

DIFFERENT STRATEGIES

The above interpretation of the problems in Hillfields is clearly a long way from the initial assumption of the CDP experiment. The distinction is more than academic. Different diagnoses lead to different kinds of action. Some of these differences can now be summarised briefly in terms of CDP. The early formulations of the experiment implied a consensus model of social change. This is based on the assumption that social problems are 'malfunctions' which can be cured by adjustments and re-arrangements within the existing operating systems. The problems are defined mainly in terms of failures of co-ordination and communication, and the focus of change is thus on management and administration and the non-participant. The central tactic is debate.

Observation and experience in the project areas has led many CDP teams to reject this initial prescription in favour of a pluralist model of social change. This is based on the assumption that social problems arise from 'imbalances' in the democratic and bureaucratic systems. The problems are defined mainly in terms of failures of participation and representation of certain interests in the political process, and the focus of change is thus on politicians, policy-makers and the disenfranchised. The central tactic is bargaining and negotiation.

A growing awareness of 'the flaw in the pluralist heaven' has forced a number of the CDPs towards a structural class conflict model of social change. This is based on the assumption that social problems arise from a fundamental conflict of interests between groups or classes in society. The problems are defined mainly in terms of inequalities in the distribution of power and the focus of change is thus on the centres of organised power (both private and public). The main tactic is organisation and raising of levels of consciousness.

SERVICING THE DISADVANTAGED OUTSIDE THE WORK-PLACE

Analysis of social problems in terms of structural class conflict has often led to the assertion that the only possibilities for change lie in revolutionary change of control of the means of production. That kind of crude reductionism ignores the changes which have taken and continue to take place in the relationship between the traditional classes in advanced capitalist societies. In particular it ignores the changes in the relationship between private capital and the state, and (of special relevance to CDP areas) within the state apparatus itself at the local level. There has been some attention to these changes at the macro-level, but much less study of their impact in the fine-grain.

The study of small disadvantaged areas is beginning to show up some of the ways in which the fluctuations of capitalism have had consequences outside the work-place. The task is to understand better the way the processes have worked to the disadvantage of particular sections of the population in concrete situations; to trace the roles played by the state, both centrally and locally; and to begin to test out some of the strategies for challenging the course of these processes. The trade union movement has traditionally protected its members' interests in relation to inequality and injustice at the work-place. It seems to be much less well equipped to service its members in relation to what is happening outside the work-place. There are as yet few agencies geared up to service the political needs of the disadvantaged working class outside their work-place. Experience in CDP has begun to suggest some of the kinds of service that might be offered:

Information and intelligence

Help to residents in the gathering of information about their own situation (e.g. household surveys, census analyses) and about how decisions affecting their lives are made (e.g. information about the employment and investment plans of local firms; the forward plans and programmes of government departments, etc.).

Hard skills

A pool of expertise to be drawn upon by residents and their representatives on a 'hire or fire' basis. The range of useful skills include solicitor, planner, accountant, public health inspector, income and welfare rights. The aim is to demystify the knowledge which such specialists have and to share it as openly and widely as possible.

Adult education and community development

Helping groups and individuals to identify and define the issues they wish to tackle. Feeding in information and intelligence, and access to a pool of hard skills (as described above). Linking groups and individuals up with other organised movements working for similar changes. Collaborating with groups in learning about their own situation and from their experience of trying to change it.

Chapter 20

ACTION-RESEARCH: EXPERIMENTAL SOCIAL ADMINISTRATION?

George Smith

In braver, brighter days before the white heat of technology had finally cooled, and CDP was as yet but a glint in some under-secretary's eye, grew up the idea of 'experimental social adminis-tration'. The aim of linking social science and government closely in policy development had been long established; but setting up small-scale experimental projects where action and research combine to promote and test new policy was very much a product of the 1960s - with their hard-to-recapture optimism over the power and effectiveness of government action against poverty.

Much has been made of the American origins of these ideas, parti-cularly the 'War on Poverty'. But this is to overlook the form they took in Britain: one that led several Americans to deny paternity. (1) There, at least in educational programmes, the dominant model of research involvement in action, was either the campus-based experimental school with its one-way glass screens and closed circuit TV, or the evaluation of programmes already in full operation - for example the series of national studies on Head Start. The idea of selecting a handful of pilot areas, introducing action and research teams directly sponsored by central government to test out future national policy, though it finds echoes in some of the early American programmes, fits far more naturally into the apparently more centralised structure of British administration.

The Plowden Report on primary education confidently reflects this approach. 'Research', it stated, 'should be started to discover which of the developments in educational priority areas have the most constructive effects so as to assist in planning the longer term programmes to follow.' And the EPA action-research programme was to be 'a preparation for later advance'. If only it could all have been that simple.

Though not the first in the field, CDP was the archetype. In origin it preceded the EPA programme, which was conceived, produced and written up before CDP was fully operational. EPA was closer to a university-based research project, being funded and organised through a university department on a fixed research grant. It had no formal or regular relationship either with the relevant central government department or the local authority where each project was based. In contrast CDP involves central government directly through

the central team at the Home Office, which was originally backed by
a central steering group with interdepartmental representation.
Action staff are formally employees of the local authority; universities and polytechnics are responsible for the research teams.
It is hardly surprising that much of the history of CDP has been an
attempt to get this cumbersome structure to work. Yet in its
original form - with the local action team bringing in the 'local
community' to complete the picture - CDP clearly embodied what were
seen as the necessary elements in 'experimental social administration': a grand alliance of central government, local authority,
specially appointed innovators, the local population, research and
evaluation.

This cathedral-like structure owes much to the views of CDP's
'founding fathers', particularly to Morrell. But it cannot be
written off entirely as an idiosyncracy; for it incorporates many
of the central assumptions about policy development held by both researchers and administrators. As Halsey (1974) notes, 'the challenge' to social scientists and administrators of field testing innovation 'is irresistible'. And the approach has had many imitators
since, though each has naturally tried to simplify the original
model, learning from CDP's often bitter experience. (2)

Action-research is now well established, with most central
government departments involved in at least one experimental scheme,
and more on the way. A significant proportion of people engaged in
social policy research is involved in this type of project, with
some forty researchers in CDP alone, and perhaps as many again on
other schemes. But whether they become a permanent mechanism for
policy development must in part depend on restatement and revision
of the original idea of field testing new policy, which so far has
been handed down from project to project without fundamental re-
examination.

The idea of 'experimental social administration' was attractively
laid out in the early CDP literature. It promised a new relationship between social science and social policy - one where reform
'may be seriously conducted through social science experiment.'
Rational social science inquiry would feed in to a more rational
social policy; politicians and administrators alike would be free
of the need to promote or defend untested programmes; the commitment would be to experiment and inquiry. But there were snags:
'the language of "social problems" may all too often disguise an
underlying conflict of political and social interests' (Halsey,
1970); and the view that these 'problems could in fact be solved by
reform 'may turn out to have been nothing more than a shibboleth of
liberal society in decline' (Halsey, 1974). But these warnings, as
Marjorie Mayo's paper demonstrates, were treated as the inevitable
academic small print and relegated to a mental footnote as CDP was
developed.

The all-inclusive and rational model of CDP that emerged, where
research was first to contribute to the identification of an area's
problems, then participate in developing suitable programmes, and
finally evaluate their success or failure, left little room for the
idea that the social scientist must remain as 'a critic of the
social order', or the possibility that 'the theory of poverty to
which the social scientist is led through his service to a

governmentally financed experiment may call for political action unacceptable to his political masters' (Halsey, 1970). There was no
obvious bridge between the administrators' view of research as a
technical process, and the social scientists' concern to retain a
critical and independent stance.

In practice, as the chapters in this book show, the experience of
CDP has been very different from the 'coolly' rational, tightly
articulated experiment of the original literature. What went wrong?
One response is to point to the cumbersome organisation, the rapid
turnover of staff at the centre, the lack of continuity and the
steady erosion of CDP's importance nationally, particularly when
similar programmes were wheeled out by other departments. Yester-
day's programmes quickly lose their glamour. Another response,
sometimes favoured by researchers as they struggled to apply a text-
book research design, was to blame the type of person appointed to
direct local action - charismatic figures not content to work
through more conventional solutions or apply a programme consistently. If only action men could have been more like researchers,
able to try out a programme dispassionately. Echoes of this argument run through Jonathan Bradshaw's account of the Batley welfare
rights experiment.

No doubt these problems contribute to the difficulty. But as
Town (1973) points out, there has been an excessive tendency to concentrate on the internal problems of action-research, on the inevitable tensions between its components, and see these as the major
cause of the problem. Clearly the key reason, pinpointed in
Marjorie Mayo's and John Benington's contributions, is that the
issues into which CDP was drawn involved conflicts of interest, particularly when projects began to move away from the original social
and community work brief. Here there were no solutions without
costs for one group or other, and naturally resistance to what could
be seen as a partisan approach. The original assumption had too
easily been that the interests of different groups could in the
final analysis be reconciled and technical solutions found, though
they would need high diplomatic skills to be successfully
implemented.

An analysis which recognises basic conflicts of interest is now
commonplace within CDP. It has led at least at a theoretical level
to the rejection of the original model of field-tested innovation,
though this has not yet been replaced by any clear alternative
approach. In practice projects continue to follow a mixed strategy,
adopting some elements of the original package, while rejecting
others. What is now needed is a more detailed examination of the
assumptions which underpin the idea of 'experimental social administration' to see whether some part can in fact be salvaged, or
whether it must be finally abandoned as a misplaced attempt to
introduce a more rational form of policy development to a world
where decisions are solely the product of competing interest groups.

The assumptions underlying 'experimental social administration'
can be grouped under three headings - assumptions about action,
about research, and about the proper audience for any findings. But
they are not independent. Combined they provide an apparently
logical sequence where the appropriate audience is the obvious final
step - a model of tested innovation too easily accepted and

uncritically applied in very different situations.

ACTION

The traditional mode of reform, it was argued, was 'to announce a
nostrum which is held to be certain in its cure' (Halsey, 1970). In
contrast, experimental social administration would bring in objective standards of proof to test these claims. But old ideas die
hard. And a basic assumption has been that social experiment would
reveal which in reality were the 'nostra'. Research would supply
the necessary imprimatur. This might be called 'the crock of gold'
assumption - the belief that somewhere, if only we could find it,
was the 'solution' - a uniquely successful scheme of action. Of
course, none would admit, if pressed, that there are such panaceas;
but the way we set about the search implies that we expect to find
them. Four related points support this argument.

First, action-research is almost always linked with those nebulous, but attractive areas of social policy, where imagination
quickly outruns our ability to translate ideas into practice -
'community education' 'the community school' 'community development'
as an answer to social problems in the inner city, or the techni-
cians' favourite, a 'total approach' to urban management for the
same end. The promise is of dramatic change: the assumption that
experimental action and the 'superior vision' of research will somehow identify the magic ingredient.

Second, there is a heavy emphasis on 'programmes' - a belief that
successful action can be discrete and self-contained. As a result
there is pressure to minimise the importance of the social context
for a programme's effects; one form is the attempt to develop
'teacher proof' materials and kits in education: another when
evaluation grosses up the results from different areas to produce
an overall verdict - win or lose. 'Not so much a programme, more a
way of life' rightly became a catchphrase on the EPA projects.

Third, there is the tough minded response of research to this
promise of dramatic change: one that places the onus of proof on
the programme, and reinforces the success/failure mentality, with
no middle ground - a properly sceptical stance to exaggerated
claims, but it implies that there must somewhere be a programme with
dramatic effects. We cannot set standards of success so high that
none will pass. If in fact single programmes have at best no better
than marginal effects, the wholesale use of tough minded evaluation
would be disastrous. It will sap confidence in reform, and encourage a drift to apparently more radical but vague and untested
ideas. The American poverty programme is full of examples - the
Westinghouse study of Head Start and its aftermath being a classic
case. As an evaluation strategy it would contrast with a more
charitable approach which would screen a range of programmes to pinpoint the more successful. (3)

Finally, search for 'the crock of gold' restricts evaluation to
one or possibly two outcomes, conveniently ignoring what may be important side effects. Rory Williams, in a discussion on the Community Hospitals' evaluation, suggests that this is because 'the
classic method of disciplining the element of value has been to

choose one effect, or set of effects, and concentrate on what pro-
duces it' (Williams, 1974). This is the way to establish causal
links; but in the evaluation of practical schemes, the risk is of
selecting outcomes that reflect the interests of particular groups,
especially those who have commissioned the research. As Williams
points out, medical evaluation has naturally concentrated on the
primary effects on the patient, and the economic costs of treatment,
but not for example on the social costs to the patient's family.
This restricted focus encourages the belief that the purpose of
evaluation is to identify the next step 'on the approach to perfec-
tion', rather than set out the costs and benefits for different
groups involved in any change. Here evaluation would be expressed
'as a trade-off between consequences.'

   This latter way of looking at evaluation has important implications; for it immediately lifts evaluation from a technical
accounting exercise to a far more sociological activity. And it
begins to build a bridge between the social scientist's role as
technician and as social critic. By mapping in the unforeseen costs
and benefits of change, and putting forward the perceptions of
otherwise unrepresented groups, the evaluator is in some small way
adopting a more critical and independent stance; one where he is
beginning to present 'conflicting definitions of reality' (Mills,
1959). Far from providing cut and dried answers, evaluation here
must in most cases serve to heighten the problems of choice: there
are no 'solutions' - unless it is decided to ignore the costs for
one group or other.

   CDP's organisation with its original centre-periphery arrangement - local projects feeding their findings to a central team - reinforced the belief that there would be a series of clear policy
messages piloted in action and tested by research. And CDP's all-
embracing structure promoted the view that conflicts of interest
could be reconciled by the right approach. Both sustained the
assumption that uniquely successful 'programmes' would be uncovered.
This, in turn, led on to two further sets of assumptions.

   The first concerns the question of 'access' - the assumption that
action teams would be able to implement their plans, and research be
free to evaluate them. Nobody, of course, assumed that CDP would
run without snags, but as Marjorie Mayo shows, the tendency was to
play down potential problems, partly to win over hesitant local
authorities and partly to maintain central support. The result was
that far too little attention was paid to the problems of implementation. In the original formulation where team leaders were to work
with staff seconded from other departments, the possibility that
this might have effectively crippled any action was not considered,
though the checks and balances were finely conceived.

   Though an experiment, CDP is not free of the normal statutory
constraints, and therefore cannot introduce changes which would
elsewhere require legislation. Projects are formally part of a
local authority, and may be barred from intervening in areas outside
the scope of their parent body. Projects have increasingly come up
against these checks, as the range of action has expanded. Yet the
problem here is at least open and clearcut, even if there is no
solution. Perhaps more important are the more subtle pressures and
constraints which prevent, deflect, or slow down any action.

Against these, a local project's resources are puny - one reason why a common early element is the need for projects to build a support base among local people, elected representatives or sympathetic officials.

Again the original concern to draw out findings for a central purpose turned attention away from the problems of mounting even pilot action. And though mentioned as a function of research, it was clearly secondary to evaluating the results of the action. The dilemma for research is whether to watch the race, setting up elaborate machinery to record exactly who wins - or whether to study and inevitably be drawn into the jostling and argument at the start, the wheeling and dealing to see whether there is a race at all. These preliminaries may form the main activity in a short life project like CDP. The key question is whether the scheme has been set up according to plan. If it is, the effects are often self-evident.

The second set of assumptions centre on the problems of inter-connection between one piece of action and another at the local level. Again the logic of the original model was that single findings could be drawn out for more general application - an approach conveniently close to standard practice, where a single idea once accepted is universally applied. Yet this ignores interaction at the local level between social context and any new programme, or in CDP, between one programme and another. One scheme may be successful only because it operates alongside another; and conversely the project's links with one group in the area inevitably affect its chances of working with others.

Perhaps more importantly this single focus ignores what in CDP is loosely termed a project's 'strategy' - a recognition that the project is not merely a vehicle to test out an assortment of ideas - some attempt is made to relate one piece of action to another. A strong message of much action-research has been the need for local diagnosis and analysis before action on a wider scale. Ironically, instead of presenting hard generalisable results, and itself withering away, the experimental project argues in effect for an extension of the action-research process. In part this may be the well-known phenomenon where educators see more education as the answer and social workers, social work. Yet at another level it represents an alternative model of policy development, where instead of a single programme applied across the board, there is an attempt to concentrate developments in a single area, to lay down a matrix of related programmes.

Action, then, scarcely resembles the cool intervention of experimental social administration. CDPs operate in a turbulent area where they must trim before superior forces. The sudden effects of new national policies, housing finance or rate revaluation, local clearance or redevelopment, or of industrial change and closure, far outweigh the small resources and power of CDP. It is a major activity merely to analyse and comprehend these changes at the local level, harder still to mount effective counteraction.

RESEARCH

Closely linked to action, research experiences many of the same problems; and there is a growing literature on the tensions in action-
research (Smith and Barnes, 1970; Town, 1973; and Lees, in this
volume). Like action, it was too easily assumed that research would
have free access to observe and measure what happened: as if research was a process with no thickness, its measures truly non-
reactive, the researcher a silent shadow of the action, able at a
glance to take it all in and pronounce a verdict.

Even in research on its own, this is less and less the position,
as more groups become suspicious and organised enough to bargain
over the conditions for research. For a long time this has been the
case with professional groups; now it is spreading as research concentrates on particular minorities, immigrants or the poor. (4)
Perhaps this is one reason why the researcher so readily accepts
that the problems are 'out there', and heads off to set up a survey
of the general population, rather than bargain his way into local
authority or other bureaucracy; at least with the general population he cannot be 'closed out' completely.

With action-research, activity is concentrated in a small area,
and the effects of research on future action cannot be ignored.
Research is inevitably drawn into the complex process of bargaining
that surrounds the development of almost any programme. Access
cannot be guaranteed, however independent of the action the research
team might wish to appear.

A further assumption found in the original model, and taken up by
field-workers in a different form, is the belief in the 'superior
vision' of research: that it could without difficulty discern
success or failure, or that it had techniques to identify problems
and priorities rapidly at the local level. Yet the conventional
weapons of research are cumbersome; heavy field-pieces dragged
slowly into position, and aimed with difficulty, hardly suitable for
the swift moving, rapidly changing targets of an action programme.
There would be danger, too, if in the drive away from the ground
level, research was expected to play the face-to-face role 'on the
door-knocker' - of drawing out an area's problems and priorities;
this could too easily become a simple head count, with little attention to strength of feeling, or the views of key individuals who
mould local opinion.

In the uncertain situation of CDP, the pressure is on research to
provide certainty, by identifying the central problems and picking
out the answers. But researchers have hardly learnt to operate
under these conditions, and cannot fill this role adequately. The
risk is that by failing to deliver the complete solution, the role
of research in action will be demoted. This would ignore the contribution research can make, in offering alternative definitions of
the situation, exploring the social context of the action programme,
monitoring its progress from a slightly less involved standpoint and
making selective formal studies and evaluations. Much of this can
only be done in close dialogue with the action team - and is not an
independent technical process.

AUDIENCE

Given the central structure of CDP the audience was naturally at the
centre - and the original central steering group, comprising central
and local government representatives was the mechanism. Its role
was to consider 'recommendations to central government/local govern-
ment/voluntary organisations regarding the organisation of the
social services in the light of the project's success, and make reports accordingly to the appropriate Ministers.' Marjorie Mayo's
chapter traces the rise and fall of this apparatus; in practice it
was never really put to the test, as it was set up before local projects were in operation, and fell into disuse before they were well
established, partly perhaps because there was no steady stream of
'findings' to be digested and sent off to the relevant authority.
And many of the early recommendations, instead of being demands for
innovation on a wider scale - more information centres, more community workers - where there might have been less resistance, dealt
with existing policy that had negative consequences for project
areas. The steering group was for projects a route to other government departments when local contacts had failed. And as many of the
issues raised touched central points in other departments' programmes where there was little chance of ad hoc change being made,
the mechanism was largely ineffective.

The 'up, across and down' method (Green, 1974) of lodging results
depended on the other assumptions about action and research being
met; that projects would come forward with well tested and clearcut
programmes, technical solutions which would be immediately acceptable. The assumption too was that this central forum would translate any such findings into policy recommendations for all levels of
the system, in many ways a reversal of existing practice where
statutory authority frequently takes over and formalises the initiatives of voluntary groups. CDP itself represented central government intervention into an area where there was already rapidly expanding voluntary activity. The model of central dissemination of
results, too, ignores the distribution of power in the system, at a
minimal level the power to block developments. Again the assumption
was that the findings would be self-evident and uncontroversial, and
therefore there could be no reason for opposition.

But the experience of CDP has been very different. As projects
expanded their work beyond the original social service brief, they
became involved in areas where conflicts of interest were open and
acknowledged; they began increasingly to resemble other pressure
groups in the same line of business, though with the ability to
assemble data effectively, and argue their case from strong local
experience. For such pressure groups the internal 'up, across and
down' approach represents only one possible audience, and not
necessarily the most effective, as CDP's national importance was
eroded.

One small example, almost a field test of the effectiveness of
the two different approaches, illustrates the change. In
Birmingham, a large proportion of the project population is from
Pakistan and was affected by the 'Pakistan Act' under which they
must register as British citizens or become aliens. Naturally with
language difficulties, complex forms and documentation, the

procedure of registration caused difficulty. The project carefully
assembled evidence on the problem, particularly the difficulty of
getting reliable advice on how to complete forms. With additional
evidence on the regional and local distribution of Pakistanis, this
was presented 'up and across' to the relevant departments (within
the Home Office) to argue for the very limited objective of de-
centralising some part of the information services - all of which
was based in Croydon. After some pressure for a response, a meeting
was held between the project team, other groups concerned with immigrant problems and officials from the department. Again the case
was presented as a rational argument for change in response initially to a clear local problem along the lines of the original CDP
model. But it was immediately clear that the department for its own
internal reasons was not prepared to accept the change: and there
presumably the matter might have rested. However the project at the
same time had brought the problem to the attention of one of the
local MPs, Roy Jenkins, who wrote to the then Home Secretary, receiving back a lengthy letter, promising to keep the matter under
review. Discussions were then proceeding between the CDP teams and
officials. A few weeks later came the General Election of February
1974. Roy Jenkins became Home Secretary; the decentralised information service began a pilot operation in Birmingham a few weeks
later.

Again the picture derived from the original CDP model with its
central forum of 'cool' rationality where policy questions would be
ultimately decided, breaks down on closer examination. No such
forum exists. Even other parts of the same department have their
own interests and reasons for not responding to a rational case.
But note that this is not an argument in favour of abandoning
rational evidence altogether, that the sole determinants are power
and interest. Clearly the simple idea that experimental action plus
research would be adequate to produce change is unfounded, but the
presentation of evidence is a powerful way of engaging otherwise reluctant groups in argument, an entry ticket to the forum but not a
trump card.

On this analysis, local projects have broken away from the original tight relationship with the centre as the main audience. Other
routes may be more effective, if the issue is contentious. And
there is no particular reason to go via a central mechanism where
the audience is other local groups. Indeed 'horizontal diffusion'
to groups at the same level may be a more effective way of spreading
ideas about community development, than to have them imposed through
the 'up, across and down' method.

In the face of this change, the conventional research practice of
compiling a massive final report looks increasingly out of place.
First there is the growing number of possible audiences, including a
greater accountability to the local project area, a group largely
ignored in most research projects, yet one on whom the resulting
publicity falls most heavily. And second there is the question of
timing. Important policy changes will not wait for final reports,
and there has to be more continuous sifting and presentation of
evidence.

Policy development rarely proceeds in predictable straight lines.
The particular coincidence of political forces, definitions of the

problem, research interest and resources present at the birth of a project, is unlikely to be found at its conclusion - or if it is, this must be more luck than design. In part the continual revision of objectives in CDP is an attempt to keep pace with the changing definitions of deprivation and inequality, but it has yet to develop a mechanism for the necessary second stage where its experience can be regularly fed into policy debate.

EXPERIMENTAL SOCIAL ADMINISTRATION?

Experimental social administration has taken a battering; many of its original assumptions have been shot away. Can anything be salvaged? Or must researchers either return to academic aloofness, shunning the disorganisation, the muckiness of practical reform as a possible context for research, or turn instead to partisan support of particular action? Clearly the original model was too simple to cope with the problem of conflicting interests, where there was no universal solution, but different possibilities each with its costs and benefits for different groups. Here there is no technical way of finding the most effective solution. It depends on standpoint and definition of the problem. Most effective for whom?

But nevertheless programmes will be evaluated, 'in the absence of formal, objective studies . . . by the most arbitrary, anecdotal, partisan and subjective means' (Evans and Schiller, 1970). In America

Congressional committees will hold hearings and parade before them a stream of witnesses who will testify on the one hand how marvelous the program is and how many needy mothers and children are being helped by it, and on the other, how mismanaged and frivolous the program is and what a shameful waste of the taxpayers' money (Evans and Schiller, 1970).

And in Britain, presumably the same process - though the means are less public.

Yet if we look again at the experience of CDP, there is an alternative role for research and evaluation trying to emerge; one that opens up possibilities by presenting the range of effects from any change and bringing forward the attitudes of otherwise unrepresented groups. This would contrast with an evaluation designed merely to pin a success or failure label on a single programme. Set against the grand claims for field-tested social policy, this may seem small return for the blood and sweat spent on action-research, but it could lead to more rational and more complex decision making, by making available more information on the costs and benefits of any change - though there is of course no guarantee that this information will be used.

CDP has progressed from social and community work, where there is some consensus about objectives and programmes, to issues such as housing, planning and job opportunities where there are obvious conflicts of interest. Clearly the same model of tested innovation is unlikely to apply in both situations. Where there is agreement about objectives, but the means are in dispute, then something close to the original model may be feasible. Some of the operations in the EPA project were of this kind, for example the testing of a reading kit, an acceptable answer to an acknowledged problem - though even here there are questions of side effects - on other parts of the curriculum, or on school organisation, that a simple study of improvement in reading quotients might miss. And these could have important implications for any wider implementation of the kit.

There is a second form of evaluation where programmes are under development - sometimes called 'formative evaluation', a stage before full field-testing, where there is continuous feedback of effects, so that improvements in design can be made. Frequently the first and second forms are run together, and an inadequately developed programme is put to the test. It has been argued that CDP is in this state, expected to present precise conclusions, before ideas have been fully developed in practice. But this is to ignore the turbulent conditions under which CDPs operate; the project is subject to the full range of pressures that apply to any programme; there is no laboratory where schemes can be developed before being tested in the real world. The idea of a 'formative' stage may be more applicable to areas such as medicine or education with their easily identifiable, captive population of 'subjects', children or patients.

Much 'action-research', however, clearly falls into an entirely different category of 'experimental social administration', if it can still claim that apparently 'scientific' title. The goals are extraordinarily vague, as John Greve pointed out for CDP - nothing less than the reassertion of basic democratic ideals, and the area of operation, 'community development', 'community education' or 'a total approach' to urban management, surrounded by a rhetoric of promise that could not conceivably be met. Yet pilot action and research in these areas, however frustrating for participants, is one way of placing the debate on a surer footing, exposing the rhetoric and indicating where promise may lie. Such an exploration must be unsatisfactory to those who expect precisely tested outcomes, or to researchers anxious for a stable situation to set up their evaluation. The dilemma is that almost by definition areas of social life where there is the leisure and stability to test out options in a systematic way, will tend to be those of specialist rather than general importance. Where the choice of policy is crucial, there major interests are in conflict; any testing of options must inevitably be a messy business.

NOTES

1 For example at the Anglo-American conference on the evaluation of social action programmes, Ditchley Park, October 1969.
2 In the process, they have at times apparently inherited form without understanding its purpose. Research is seen as a central part of innovation, but which part nobody is quite sure. In some of the later CDPs, the desire to preserve action-research harmony has meant that evaluation of action, originally a central role, has been pushed to one side, and become almost a taboo subject.
3 This approach was recommended in the discussion sparked off by

the Westinghouse study of Head Start, see R.J. Light and
P.V. Smith, Choosing a future: strategies for designing and
evaluating new programs, 'Harvard Educational Review', 1970:
1-28.

4   For the American experience, see Spiegel and Alicea (1970); for
recent British experience there is the Community Relations Commission's survey of black teenagers, and academic studies of
black groups which have met strong resistance.

BIBLIOGRAPHY

BATTEN, T.R. (1967), 'The Non-Directive Approach to Group and Community Work', Oxford University Press.

BYRNE, D.S. (1973), 'Problem Families, A Housing Lumpen-Proletariat', University of Durham Department of Sociology and Social Administration.

CANNING TOWN CDP (1974), 'Report on Industry and Employment in Canning Town', Canning Town CDP.

CARO, F.G. (1969), Approaches To Evaluation Research, A Review, 'Human Organisation', 1969: 28.

CASTLES, S. and KOSACK, G. (1973), 'Immigrant Workers and Class Structures in Western Europe', Institute of Race Relations and Oxford University Press.

CENTRAL ADVISORY COUNCIL FOR EDUCATION (1967), 'Children and their Primary Schools'.(The Plowden Report), HMSO, London.

CHERNS, A.B., SINCLAIR, R. and JENKINS, W.I. (eds) (1972), 'Social Science and Governmental Policies and Problems', Tavistock Publications, London.

CDP PROJECT (1974), 'Inter-Project Report, 1973', Centre for Environmental Studies, London.

COX, F., ROTHMAN, J. and ERLICH, J. (1970), 'Strategies of Community Organisation', Ithaca, Illinois.

DEAKIN, N. and COHEN, B. (1970), Dispersal and Choice: a Strategy for Ethnic Minorities in Britain, 'Environment and Planning', vol.2.

DEPARTMENT OF EDUCATION AND SCIENCE (1971a), 'The Continuing Needs of Immigrants', Education Survey 13, HMSO, London.

DEPARTMENT OF EDUCATION AND SCIENCE (1971b), 'Potential and Progress in a Second Culture', HMSO, London.

ECKSTEIN, H. and APTER, D. (1963), 'Comparative Politics', Free Press, New York.

EVANS, J.W. (1969), Evaluating Social Action Programmes, 'Social Science Quarterly', vol.50, no.3.

EVANS, J.W. and SCHILLER, J. (1970), How Preoccupation with Possible Regression Artifacts can lead to a Faulty Strategy for the Evaluation of Social Action Programs in J. Hellmuth (ed.), 'The Disadvantaged Child', vol.III, Brunner-Mazel, New York.

GOLDBERG, M. (1970), 'Helping the Aged', Allen & Unwin, London.

GREEN, G. (1974), Towards Community Power in S. Hatch and H. Glennerster, 'Positive Discrimination and Inequality', Fabian Research series, 314.
GREVE, J. (1973), 'Community Development in the Context of Urban Deprivation', paper prepared for the European Study Group on Community Development and Urban Deprivation, Oxford, unpublished.
GROSS, B.M. (1964), 'The Managing of Organisations', Free Press, New York.
HALSEY, A.H. (1970), Social Science and Government, 'Times Literary Supplement', 5 March.
HALSEY, A.H. (ed.) (1972), 'Educational Priority', HMSO, London.
HALSEY, A.H. (1974), Government against Poverty in School and Community in D. Wedderburn (ed.), 'Poverty, Inequality and Class Structure', Cambridge University Press.
HAWKES, NICHOLAS (1966), 'Immigrant Children in British Schools', Institute of Race Relations and Pall Mall Press, London.
HILL, M.J. and ISSACHAROFF, R.M. (1971), 'Community Action and Race Relations', Oxford University Press.
HILLERY, G. (1955), Definitions of Community, 'Rural Sociology', vol.20.
HOMSTEIN, H.A., BUNKER, B.B. et al. (1970), 'Social Intervention, a Behavioural Science Approach', Free Press, New York.
KIRBY, D.A. (1971), The Inter-War Council Dwelling, 'Town Planning Review', vol.42.
KRAUSZ, ERNEST (1971), 'Ethnic Minorities in Britain', Paladin.
LANE, D. (1972), The Urban Programme, 'Social Services Review', 2 September.
LEES, R. (1973), Experiencing an Experiment, 'Social Work Today', 13 December.
MACKENZIE, W.J.M. (1951), The Conventions of Local Government, 'Public Administration', vol.29.
MARCH, J. and SIMON, H. (1958), 'Organisations', Wiley, New York.
MARRIS, P. and REIN, M. (1967, new edition 1972), 'Dilemmas of Social Reform', Routledge & Kegan Paul, London.
MERTON, R. (1952), Bureaucratic Structure and Personality in 'Reader in Bureaucracy', Free Press, New York.
MIDWINTER, E. (1972), 'Priority Education', Penguin Education Special.
MILLS, C. WRIGHT (1959), 'The Sociological Imagination', Oxford University Press.
MOYNIHAN, D.P. (1969), 'Maximum Feasible Misunderstanding', Free Press, New York.
PATTERSON, S. (1969), 'Immigration and Race Relations in Britain, 1960-1967', Institute of Race Relations and Oxford University Press.
RAYNOR, J. and HARDEN, J. (eds) (1973), 'Equality and City Schools. Readings in Urban Education', vol.2, Routledge & Kegan Paul, London.
ROSE, E.J.B. et al. (1969), 'Colour and Citizenship, A Report on British Race Relations', Oxford University Press.
ROSSI, P. and WILLIAMS, W. (1972), 'Evaluating Social Programs', Seminar Press.
ROTHMAN, J. (1970), Models of Community Development Practice in F. Cox, J. Rothman and J. Erlich, 'Strategies of Community Organisation', Ithaca, Illinois.

SELECT COMMITTEE ON RACE RELATIONS AND IMMIGRATION SESSION (1972-3), 'Education', vol.1, Report (House of Commons Paper 405/1).
SHIPMAN, M.D. (1973), The Impact of a Curriculum Project, 'Journal of Curriculum Studies', vol.5, no.1.
SINFIELD, A. (1967), Unemployed in Shields, unpublished paper, University of Essex.
SMITH, G.A.N. and BARNES, J. (1970), Some Implications of Action-research Projects for Research, paper presented at 7th World Congress of Sociology at Varna.
SMITH, P. (1972), The Skills of Social Interaction in P. Dowell (ed.), 'New Horizons in Psychology' 2, Penguin Books.
SPIEGEL, H. and ALICEA, V. (1970), The Trade-off Strategy in Community Research in Zurcher and Bonjean (1970).
SUCHMAN, E.A. (1967), 'Evaluative Research', Russell Sage Foundation, New York.
TOWN, S.W. (1973), Action-Research and Social Policy, 'Sociological Review', 12(4).
TRUMAN, D.B. (1965), 'The Governmental Process', A. Knopf, New York.
WAHLKE, J.C., BUCHANAN, W., EVLAU, H. and FERGUSON, L.C. (1960), American State Legislators' Role Orientation Towards Pressure Groups, 'Journal of Politics', vol.22.
WEISS, C.H. (1972), 'Evaluation in Research', Prentice Hall, New York.
WEISS, R.S. and REIN, M. (1969), The Evaluation of Broad Aim Programmes: A Cautionary Case and a Moral, 'Annals of the American Academy of Political and Social Science', vol.385.
WILLIAMS, R.G.A. (1974), Consequences for the Community in A.E. Bennett (ed.), 'Community Hospitals: Progress in Development and Evaluation', Oxford Regional Hospital Board.
YATES, MICHAEL (1973), Getting Across in Gujerati, 'Teacher's World', 27 July.
ZALD, M. (1969), Organisations as Politics: Concepts for the Analysis of Community Organisation Agencies in R.M. Kramer and H. Specht (eds), 'Readings in Community Organisation Practice', Prentice Hall, Englewood Cliffs.
ZISK, B., EVLAU, H. and PREWITT, K. (1965), Councillors and the Group Struggle: A Typology of Role Orientation, 'Journal of Politics', vol.27.
ZURCHER, L.A. and BONJEAN, C.M. (eds) (1970), 'Planned Social Intervention: an Interdisciplinary Anthology', Chandler Publishing Co.